Johann Gottf

M000222483

Another Philosophy of History

and

Selected Political Writings

This book is due at the WALTER R. DAVIS LIBRARY on the last date stamped under "Date Due." If not on hold, it may be renewed by bringing it to the library.

DATE DUE	RETURNED	DATE DUE	RETURNED
JUL 0 8 2007			
	MAR 3 0 2008		
MAY 0 5 2013			
OCT 0 1 2013			
	NOV 2 3 2013		

Form No 513,
Rev. 1/84

B3051
.127
J6
2004
c.2

Johann Gottfried Herder

Another Philosophy of History

and

Selected Political Writings

Discarded by University of
North Carolina Library

TRANSLATED, WITH INTRODUCTION AND NOTES, BY

Ioannis D. Evrigenis and Daniel Pellerin

V 5. 25.04

Hackett Publishing Company
Indianapolis/Cambridge

THE LIBRARY
THE UNIVERSITY OF NORTH CAROLINA
AT CHAPEL HILL

Copyright © 2004 by Hackett Publishing Company, Inc.

All rights reserved

10 09 08 07 06 05 04   1 2 3 4 5 6 7

For further information, please address
Hackett Publishing Company, Inc.
P. O. Box 44937
Indianapolis, IN 46244–0937

www.hackettpublishing.com

Cover design by *Listenberger Design Associates*
Text design by *Abigail Coyle*
Composition by *William Hartman*
Printed at *Sheridan Books, Inc.*

Library of Congress Cataloging-in-Publication Data

Johann Gottfried Herder : another philosophy of history and selected political
    writings / edited and translated by Ioannis D. Evrigenis and Daniel Pellerin.
        p. cm.
    Includes bibliographical references.
    ISBN 0-87220-716-1 — ISBN 0-87220-715-3 (paper)
    1. Herder, Johann Gottfried, 1744–1803. 2. History—Philosophy.
3. Philosophy. I. Evrigenis, Ioannis D., 1971–. II. Pellerin, Daniel, 1972–.

B3051.Z7J6 2004
901—dc22

                                                            2003056881

The paper used in this publication meets the minimum requirements of American National Standard for Information Sciences—Permanence of Paper for
Printed Library Materials, ANSI Z39.48–1984.

♾

The happiness of one people cannot be imposed upon another, upon any other, by pressure or persuasion, as a burden. The roses for the wreath of liberty must be picked by one's own hand, and they must have grown up joyfully out of their own needs, out of their own desires and love. The so-called best form of government, which unfortunately has not been discovered yet, will certainly not suit all peoples at once, in the same manner; the yoke of an alien, badly introduced freedom would be a terrible nuisance for a foreign people.

—J. G. Herder, *Letters towards the Advancement of Humanity*, 121st Letter

Nowhere on earth does the rose of happiness blossom without thorns; but what bursts forth out of these thorns is everywhere and in various guises the transient, yet beautiful rose of man's joy in living.

—J. G. Herder, *Ideas on the Philosophy of the History of Mankind*, Book 8, Chapter 5.

TO THE MEMORY OF DEMETRIOS EVRIGENIS

RUTH UND JÜRGEN GEWIDMET

CONTENTS

Acknowledgments

We would like to acknowledge the help and support of Tracie Sophia Evrigenis, Wulf Koepke, Harvey C. Mansfield, Clare Pellerin, Nancy L. Rosenblum, Jessica Theis, and Deborah Wilkes. Ioannis D. Evrigenis would also like to acknowledge the support of the Alexander S. Onassis Public Benefit Foundation, Athens, Greece.

INTRODUCTION

Always this world, the small, the Great!
—Odysseas Elytis, *Axion Esti*

I. Herder's Life

Johann Gottfried Herder was born on 25 August 1744, in Mohrungen, East Prussia, the third of five children of Gottfried Herder, a girls' elementary school teacher and church warden, and his second wife, Anna Elisabeth. His parents were poor but loving, and Herder recalled his childhood with fondness. As Herder's father was a pietist, his children were brought up with the Bible and the Lutheran song book, both of which had a formative influence on the young Herder's intellectual development.[1] As a child, Herder preferred to take walks in the countryside with a book in hand rather than engage in the usual pastimes of his peers; he also liked music and singing. Herder's

1. Compare *Erinnerungen* 1:4–7. Gillies claims that as a result of his early upbringing on the Bible and the Lutheran prayer book Herder came to see literature and religion as inseparable (1945: 10). On Herder's pietism, see Meinecke: 298–99. On the effect of this early pietism on Herder during the period of the composition of *Another Philosophy of History*, see Meinecke: 317–19. Isaiah Berlin defines German pietism of that period as "that wing of German Lutheranism, which, inspired by the revolt against book learning and intellectualism generally that broke out in Germany towards the end of the 17th century, laid stress on the depth and sincerity of personal faith and direct union with God, achieved by scrupulous self-examination, passionate, intensely introspective religious feeling, and concentrated self-absorption and prayer, whereby the sinful, corrupt self was humbled and the soul left open to the blessing of divine, unmerited grace" (2000: 258). On the emergence of pietism, see Dillenberger and Welch: 123 and 125–26.

formal education, and specifically his training in Greek and Latin, began at the local school under a rector, Grimm, of whom Herder later said: "Strict though he was and grim though he looked, as his name signifies, he was the reason for my knowledge."[2] At sixteen, Herder moved into the household of a vicar named Sebastian Friedrich Trescho and became his amanuensis. Although he admired Trescho's intellectual abilities, Herder soon came to dislike the man and later described his apprenticeship as slavery. Nevertheless, Trescho had a good library, and Herder gained access to a collection of theological works as well as the Greek and Roman classics, travel guides, and other literature.[3] The breadth of this knowledge, which extends from Homer to Hamann and beyond and strikes his reader from the first, has its origins in this period.[4] It was during this time that he published his first work, *Gesang an den Cyrus*, an ode to Czar Peter III.

In the winter of 1761–1762, a Russian regiment returning from the Seven Years' War stopped at Mohrungen. A Swedish surgeon[5] serving with the Russians, who knew Herder's parents and frequented the house of Trescho, came to know the then seventeen-year-old Herder, and offered to take him to Königsberg, make him a surgeon, and do something about a condition in Herder's left eye that had been plaguing him since his childhood—all in exchange for Herder's translating a medical treatise of his into Latin. However, at Königsberg Herder fainted during the first operation he was taken to, and so his medical career came to an abrupt end. A chance encounter on the street with a former classmate from Mohrungen who was a preacher in training led him to take the matriculation examination at the Faculty of Theology, in which he eventually enrolled, on 10 August 1762. To support himself, he began to work, first as teacher in the elementary grades and then as a resident tutor at the Collegium Fredericianum, overseeing wealthy foreign students. Soon there-

2. *Erinnerungen* 1:8.

3. See *Erinnerungen* 1:19. Compare Meinecke (304): "Herder's reading as a young man was gigantic."

4. According to Irmscher (11), it was in Trescho's household that Herder first read "Klopstock, Lessing, Wieland, Hamann, and Rousseau" in addition to the ancients and other classics.

5. Haym gives his name as "Schwartzerloh," as does Clark, whereas Arnold, Koepke (1987), and Irmscher give it as "Schwarz-Erla." According to the *Erinnerungen*, Herder himself had forgotten the name, remembering only that the man was a Swede between the ages of thirty and forty at the time (1:25, n. **).

after he was assigned the secondary classes as well, which was unusual for someone of his age. This work provided him with free room and heating. He supplemented his income by giving private lessons and eventually with a stipend given by the Count von Dohna to students from Mohrungen.

At the University, Herder met Johann Georg Hamann, who was fourteen years his senior and whose works he was familiar with from the time of his apprenticeship with Trescho. Herder's relationship with Hamann, whom he "revered . . . as a man of genius, [and] looked upon . . . as the greatest of his teachers,"[6] would prove to be important both intellectually and personally. The two men became friends quickly and remained so until Hamann's death in 1788. On 21 August, Herder attended for the first time one of Kant's lectures on metaphysics. Kant, who at the time was a private lecturer, was impressed with Herder and allowed him to attend his lectures free of charge. As a result, during his two years at Königsberg, Herder heard Kant lecture on a wide variety of topics in metaphysics, moral philosophy, and geography. In Letter 79 of his *Briefe zu Beförderung der Humanität* (Letters towards the Advancement of Humanity), Herder describes Kant as follows:

> I have enjoyed the good fortune of knowing a philosopher, who was my teacher. In the bloom of his youth, he had the gaiety of a boy, which, I think, accompanied him to his grayest old age. His open brow, built for thinking, was a seat of indestructible cheerfulness and joy. Speech brimming with ideas flowed from his lips. Jokes and wit and good mood were at his disposal, and his lectures were not only extremely learned but also most entertaining. . . . He was indifferent to nothing worth knowing; no cabal, no sect, no advantage, no honorary title ever had the slightest appeal for him compared to the expansion and illumination of the truth. He encouraged and forced one in a pleasant way towards independent thinking. Despotism was foreign to his nature.[7]

Despite this later eulogy, the two men had fundamental differences of opinion, which emerged almost immediately.[8]

---

6. Berlin, 2000: 256.

7. Sixth Collection, 79th Letter, DKV 7:424.

8. The first open sign of their disagreement came in the form of Herder's *Versuch über das Sein* (*Essay on Being*, 1763; DKV 1:9–21), which was a critique of Kant's *Der einzig mögliche Beweisgrund zu einer Demonstration des Daseins Gottes*

In October 1764, through Hamann, Herder found a teaching job at the Cathedral School in Riga. Although under Russian rule since 1710, Riga at that time was relatively autonomous and home to many Germans. Herder left Königsberg for his new home on 22 November 1764. In early 1765, he was ordained a priest and began to preach in some of the churches around the city. In Riga, Herder also befriended Johann Friedrich Hartknoch, who published Herder's first major works: *Über die neuere deutsche Literatur: Fragmente* (On Recent German Literature: Fragments, 1766–1767) and *Kritische Wälder* (Critical Forests, 1769) anonymously, as well as several of his later ones. Despite a generally successful tenure and productive stay, Herder wrote to Kant in 1768 that he was anxious to take the first opportunity to leave Riga and see the world.[9]

On 5 June 1769, with financial support from Hartknoch and other friends, Herder set out from Riga for Copenhagen, where he sought out Klopstock, and thence to Helsingør, and coast to coast past Holland and England, to France, arriving eventually at Nantes on 16 July, where he stayed for four months, to practice his French and make use of the local library. It was there that he began writing his *Journal meiner Reise im Jahr 1769* (Journal of My Travels in the Year 1769, published posthumously). In November of that year, Herder traveled to Paris, where he stayed for just under two months. There, he visited the important art collections and libraries and met some of the leading thinkers of his age, such as Diderot and d'Alembert. Herder found Paris magnificent but not to his liking. He left Paris towards the end of December, passing through Brussels and Antwerp on his way to Amsterdam. On that last part of the voyage, not far from The Hague, the ship carrying Herder hit a sandbank and came very close to sinking. The passengers were rescued on the following morning, and Herder continued his journey from The Hague, to Leyden, and then to Amsterdam.

While in Paris, Herder received a letter from Friedrich August, Prince-Bishop of Lübeck, who wanted Herder to accompany his then sixteen-year-old son, Peter Friedrich Wilhelm, on a tour of Europe beginning in the summer of 1770. This opportunity must have been welcome to Herder, who until then had

---

(*The Only Possible Grounds of Proof for a Demonstration of God's Existence*, 1763). In later years, Kant reviewed Herder's *Ideas* unfavorably; two of Herder's last major works, *Metakritik* (1799) and *Kalligone* (1800), were critiques of Kant's thought.

9. Herder to Kant, November 1768 (*Briefe* 1:120).

depended heavily on Hartknoch and others for financial support, so he accepted the post. In the meantime, he traveled to Hamburg, where he spent two weeks with Lessing and then continued on to Kiel, where he met up with his charge. Together they proceeded to the prince's home, the court at Eutin, where they stayed until 17 July, when they began their tour. The general plan was to head for Strassburg and thence to Italy. After a series of stops, the prince and his entourage made their way to Darmstadt, where they stayed for longer than usual, because it was home to the prince's maternal relatives. It was during this stop that Herder befriended Johann Heinrich Merck, who in turn introduced him to Caroline Flachsland, who later became Herder's wife and the mother of his eight children.[10]

Only a month and a half into his assignment, Herder had already grown tired of the demands of protocol and the frustrations that came with being one of many attendants to a prince. This situation was aggravated by the hostility with which von Cappelmann, the prince's chief attendant, treated Herder, who was not even permitted to dine at the same table as his charge. During his stay at Eutin, before the beginning of his tour with the prince, he had received a letter from a certain Westfeld, minister of the Count Wilhelm von Schaumburg-Lippe, offering him employment in Bückeburg. The count, the former patron of Thomas Abbt, had been impressed by Herder's tribute to his lost protégé[11] and could think of no one more fit to replace him than Herder himself. Having already made a commitment to Prince Friedrich August, Herder avoided giving a definite response to this new offer. By the time the prince's entourage had reached Darmstadt, however, Herder had experienced, if only briefly, the unpleasant reality of his appointment and was in a different frame of mind. There, he received a second letter from Westfeld urging him to accept the count's offer and come to Bückeburg. To this he replied by setting what he considered to be extravagant terms, including permission to continue his travels before moving to Bückeburg. With the matter still unresolved and the romance with Caroline Flachsland in full bloom, Herder followed the rest

10. According to Caroline, at their final meeting, before the continuation of Herder's journey, they were "One heart, one soul; the separation could not divide us" (*Erinnerungen* 1:154).

11. *Über Thomas Abbts Schriften, der Torso zu einem Denkmal* (On Thomas Abbt's Writings, the Torso for a Monument, 1768).

of the entourage to Strassburg, where on 20 September he announced his intention to resign to the very disappointed prince. Soon thereafter, he received word from Bückeburg that the count had accepted his terms.

At that time, Herder decided to take advantage of the presence, at the Strassburg medical school, of Professor Lobstein, who was a famous surgeon likely to be able to treat his eye condition. Lobstein promised a cure in three weeks, and Herder acquiesced, hoping for an end not only to his discomfort, but also to the concomitant facial deformity, at a time when his appearance was important to him both as a priest as well as a suitor. The painful procedure began towards the end of October, but did not turn out to be the success that Lobstein had predicted. An infection caused complications, which led to several successive operations, resulting in a protracted and trying experience for Herder. It was during this time, however, that Herder made the most significant intellectual acquaintance of his life, that of Johann Wolfgang von Goethe, who at the time was an unknown law student.

In his autobiography, *Aus meinem Leben: Dichtung und Wahrheit* (From My Life: Poetry and Truth, 1811–1822), Goethe describes their meeting and subsequent relationship as "the most important event, one that was to have the weightiest consequences for me."[12] He recalls with fondness and gratitude the interest that Herder took in him, but adds that Herder was neither always pleasant nor easy to get along with. Goethe was enthusiastic about a wide variety of interests, but he soon discovered that Herder's remarks had a sobering effect. Nevertheless, Goethe, who describes himself as valuing "highly everything that contributed to [his] own cultivation," saw the benefit of Herder's company and soon taught himself the difference between "just blame" and "unjust invectives." As a result, "no day passed that had not been, in the most fruitful manner, instructive."[13] He credits Herder with having shown him a new way of looking at poetry, as well as with having introduced him to the poetry of the Hebrews, popular poetry and folk songs, Hamann's writings, and many other useful things besides.

Goethe, whose recollections of that time are a source of important information about Herder's eye condition and treatment, tells us that Herder showed remarkable perseverance and

12. Goethe 2:8.
13. Goethe 2:16.

strength of character in dealing with the pain and frustration resulting from the numerous failed operations—all this at a time when the seeds of his later works had already been planted: "What an agitation there must have been in such a mind, what a fermentation there must have been in such a nature, can neither be conceived nor described."[14] Indeed, Goethe relates that Herder decided to compete for the prize of the Royal Prussian Academy of Sciences in Berlin for the best essay on the origin of language. He presented a draft of his *Abhandlung über den Ursprung der Sprache* (Essay on the Origin of Language, 1772) to Goethe, who confesses that he was unable to make any significant suggestions to its author. Eventually, Herder's essay, which shocked its audience by attributing the origin of language to man's own powers and not to God, won the prize and was published the following year.[15]

Goethe returned the favor of Herder's intellectual guidance by assisting him in a number of ways during his stay in Strassburg. By May, Herder decided to abandon the treatment, and left Strassburg with money that Goethe had borrowed for him. He arrived in Bückeburg, at the court of Wilhelm, Count of Schaumburg-Lippe, where he assumed the offices of court preacher, president of the consistory, and general superintendent of schools. Herder found Bückeburg to be too small for his intellectual curiosities, and his position there an uneasy balance between the count, who found him too religious and conservative, and the local clergy, for whom he was too progressive. He remained in Bückeburg for five years, which were frustrating yet productive on all fronts. On 2 May 1773, he traveled to Darmstadt and married Caroline, with Goethe in attendance. The couple then returned to Bückeburg, and in the same year, Herder published a collection of essays entitled *Von deutscher Art und Kunst* (On the German Way and Art), which included essays by Goethe and Möser. In 1774, Caroline gave birth to their first son, Wilhelm Christian Gottfried, and Herder published *Auch eine Philosophie der Geschichte zur Bildung der Menschheit* (Another Philosophy of History for the Education of Mankind) anonymously, as well as the first volume of *Älteste Urkunde des Menschengeschlechts* (The

14. Goethe 2:13.

15. See DKV 1:695–810. For Herder's arguments against alternative explanations, such as Süssmilch's and Rousseau's, see especially parts 1 and 2. For a summary of Herder's own argument, see 732:12–21.

Oldest Document of the Human Species), which was completed with the publication of a second volume in 1776.

After a failed attempt to obtain a post at the University of Göttingen, in 1776 Herder accepted a position in Weimar very similar to the one he had held at Bückeburg. This was secured for him, at the suggestion of Wieland, by Goethe, who had been employed in the service of Karl August, the Duke of Sachsen-Weimar since November 1775. On 1 October 1776, the new general superintendent and chief court preacher and his family moved to Weimar, which became Herder's home for the rest of his life. They settled into a house behind the main church, and although Herder found many reasons to like Weimar at first, this favorable impression did not last long. Eventually he discovered that despite his high office he did not have any great influence over the duke. To make matters worse, his association with Goethe was no longer what it had been in Strassburg. The publication of *The Sorrows of Young Werther* had made Goethe famous, and despite the fact that he continued to respect Herder, their relationship experienced a series of fluctuations from which it never recovered fully.

In Weimar, Herder immersed himself in his work, both in his official capacities as well as in his writings. He published a series of theological writings, including *Briefe, das Studium der Theologie betreffend* (Letters Concerning the Study of Theology, 1780–1781), *Vom Geist der ebräischen Poesie* (On the Spirit of Hebrew Poetry, 1782–1783), and *Gott: Einige Gespräche* (God: Some Conversations, 1787), as well as a collection of folk songs (1778–1779). He also devoted considerable time and energy to writings on history, which resulted in his *Ideen zur Philosophie der Geschichte der Menschheit* (Ideas on the Philosophy of History of Mankind), published in four parts in 1784, 1785, 1787, 1791, the first two parts of which received unfavorable reviews from Kant. In 1788, in an effort to alleviate his financial difficulties, Herder decided to accompany one Friedrich Hugo von Dalberg on a journey to Italy. They set out on 6 August, but soon thereafter Dalberg's mistress joined them, and when the party reached Rome, Herder decided to continue alone. He spent the next nine months traveling around Italy, during which time he received an offer of employment from the University of Göttingen, but on advice from Goethe and Caroline, and assured by the duke and duchess of the improvement of his financial situation, he declined. He returned to Weimar on 9 July, just before the outbreak of the French Revolution.

Herder saw the French Revolution as "the most important world-historical event since the Reformation,"[16] a view that he began to develop in his *Briefe zu Beförderung der Humanität* (Letters towards the Advancement of Humanity, 1793), a series of meditations on world history, which he wrote instead of the fifth and final part of the *Ideen*. Therein, one finds Herder's views on a wide variety of historical and political matters, although the letters also reflect his struggle with censorship as well as his difficulty in understanding the Jacobins and his disappointment at the way in which the Revolution turned out. His views of the events of that period also caused a series of clashes with both Goethe and the duke, whose own opinions regarding the French Revolution were quite different from Herder's. Herder's relationship with Goethe deteriorated even further after Goethe became close with Schiller, whom Herder disliked. Although he gradually withdrew from most of his personal relationships, in 1798, he received a visit from Jean Paul, who stayed in Weimar until 1800 and with whom Herder became friends.

Herder spent the rest of his life immersed in his official duties and writings. He published *Kalligone* in 1800, parts of *Adrastea* between 1801 and 1803, and began working on *Der Cid* in 1802. In October 1801 he was awarded a title of nobility by the Elector Palatine Maximilian Joseph.[17] Herder died on 18 December 1803, after a series of illnesses and was buried in the State Church of Saints Peter and Paul in Weimar. After his death, Caroline began the first edition of his collected works, which was completed in 1820.

II. Influences

While Herder had always shown promise as a student, he knew that his parents' means could not support him through university, and commentators have stressed the significance of this awareness.[18] On the one hand, this was what led him into Trescho's

---

16. Arnold: 78.

17. The title, which changed the family name to "von Herder," was never recognized by Herder's employer, the Duke of Weimar. On the history of the title, as well as its consequences, see Clark: 416–17. The diploma is reproduced as document 97 of Part 2 of Gebhardt and Schauer (154–55).

18. See, for example, Kedourie: 43–44.

household, where he took advantage of the extensive library and thus became acquainted with a wide variety of literature and history; on the other hand, it was Herder's first major experience of the limits imposed on him by his lower-middle class social standing. Difficult as it can be to document this kind of influence, Herder's reactions to similar constraints throughout his life were very clear to those around him and have been recorded by him in his correspondence;[19] moreover, his disgust for such fetters figures prominently in his political theory.

Nor is Herder's perception of his prospects likely to have changed much after his fortunate encounter with his Swedish benefactor in Mohrungen and his consequent arrival at the University of Königsberg, since the situation of the local prominent intellectuals was no less indicative of the limitations that someone like Herder should expect. At the time of Herder's arrival, Hamann was moving from one job to the next, and Kant had to supplement his position at the university with private lectures in order to earn a living.[20] As Barnard notes, "[o]utside the church and the universities there was virtually no field of public activity in which men of humble origins like Herder could hope to make any headway."[21] Keenly aware of this, Herder prepared for a career in the church, and although university posts were few and hard to come by, there were other means of pursuing a career of sorts in education, most notably as a tutor to the sons of noblemen—a more private activity, but one which afforded a man of Herder's standing the opportunity to speak directly into the ears of the holders of power. As he would soon discover, however, this occupation came with its own set of frustrations.

Where Herder's intellectual debts during the Königsberg period are concerned, his acquaintance with Kant and Hamann is clearly deserving of special attention. The very different personalities, views, and theories of these two men make for a tempting juxtaposition, in particular between reason (Kant) and irrationalism (Hamann), and such juxtaposition surely does correspond to a tension that figures prominently throughout Herder's writings.

---

19. According to Goethe, Herder "constantly embittered his finest days, both for himself and others, because he knew not how to moderate, by strength of mind in later years, that ill-humour which had necessarily seized him in his youth" (2: 19).

20. See Berlin, 2000: 266–67; Koepke, 1987: 2.

21. Barnard, 1965: 139. Compare Clark: 7–9; Greenfeld: 293–302. On Hamann's humble origins, see Berlin, 2000: 258.

But perhaps this should not be overstated, for as Clark points out, the Kant to whom Herder was introduced was not yet the thinker who springs to our mind. Besides, although Herder attended Kant's lectures on metaphysics and moral philosophy, it was the lectures on geography that really caught his attention.[22]

Unlike Kant, Hamann was not connected to the university, so the circumstances under which he and Herder met are unclear.[23] Nevertheless his influence on the young student was great and multifaceted. Aided by Herder's pietism and love of books, the spiritually transformed Hamann made an impression on Herder with his "rejection of rationalist analyses, and his unabashed sensualism and empiricism, as well as his simple Christian faith;"[24] exposed him to a new world of literature and thought, not least by teaching him English using Shakespeare's *Hamlet* as a textbook;[25] and most importantly taught him "the need to preserve sensitiveness to specific historical and cultural phenomena, to avoid becoming deadened by the passion for classification and generalization demanded by networks of tidy concepts."[26] The reader of *Another Philosophy of History* will have no difficulty in identifying these elements in Herder's thought, but here, as with Kant, there is the danger of overstating Hamann's influence. Despite the fact that his relationship with Hamann was Herder's strongest and most enduring, the two men had significant differences of opinion. Hamann found Herder's account of the origin of language unconvincing,[27] and for all his admiration for the "Magus of the North," Herder's opposition to the *philosophes* was never as extreme as Hamann's.[28]

22. See *Erinnerungen* 1:62. According to Clark, it was Kant who introduced Herder to Montesquieu and Buffon (Clark: 45); Compare Haym 1:44–50; Barnard, 1965: xi; Koepke, 1987: 2; Irmscher: 12. Zammito (150) argues that at that time, "there was no one in German philosophy who was more skeptical than Kant, and . . . at no moment was Kant closer to naturalism, or at least to an irreducible empiricism".

23. See *Erinnerungen* 1:63–64. On how they may have met see Clark: 45–46.

24. Berlin, 2000: 191. On Hamann's spiritual transformation see Berlin, 2000: 265–66.

25. *Erinnerungen* 1:64.

26. Berlin, 2000: 178. Compare Berlin, 1980: 170.

27. See Koepke, 1987: 24.

28. Some accounts tend to exaggerate Hamann's effect on Herder in this respect. For interesting correctives see Clark: 47 and especially Beiser: 191–97. Unlike most commentators, who see Hamann as the greater influence, Beiser

To these direct influences, Meinecke adds the effects of Platonism and of Shakespeare.[29] Neoplatonism, ably represented by Leibniz and Shaftesbury, whom Herder refers to as the "Plato Europens,"[30] had become particularly popular in the German world, and the clarity and depth of its ideas influenced Herder from early on,[31] although here too influence does not necessarily imply agreement.[32] As a result of Hamann's English lessons, Shakespeare's works also captivated the young Herder and acquired an increasing significance in his historical thinking. Meinecke argues that these two forces ultimately fused into one, and so Herder came to see a "universal soul" in Shakespeare's works, as a result of which the plays presented a truer history of the world than textbooks ever could.[33]

Two indirect influences on Herder's thought are perhaps as important to its development as his interactions with Kant and Hamann. As the reader of *Another Philosophy of History* will no doubt notice, Herder is often guided by the works of Montesquieu and Rousseau.[34] Here too, the precise extent of agreement and disagreement is a matter of debate.[35] This much, however, is clear: on the one hand, despite his dislike for the generalizations of *The Spirit of the Laws*, Herder appreciates Montesquieu's Aristotelian attention to surrounding circumstances that make for particularity and difference;[36] on the other hand, given the affinity between their respective projects against cosmopolitanism,

---

declares, "in the end, it was the influence of Kant that proved victorious" (192). Compare Meinecke (301): "Herder was of a more sensitive disposition and more universal interests than Hamann, and so was in closer affinity with the Enlightenment than Hamann, who was radically opposed to it." Compare Berlin, 1980: 170.

29. Meinecke: 298–99, 303.

30. *Another Philosophy of History*, 22.

31. Meinecke: 302. Compare Douglas J. Den Uyl, foreword to Shaftesbury 1: vii; Berlin, 2000: 208.

32. Compare *Another Philosophy of History*, 22, on what Herder sees as Shaftesbury's desire to Hellenize everything.

33. Meinecke: 303. Compare Koepke 1987: 38, 48.

34. On Montesquieu see, *Another Philosophy of History*, 15, 17, 88, 90; on Rousseau, *Another Philosophy of History*, 11–12, 19, 20, 44, 69, 76, 103; *The Influence of Free Legislation*, 314.

35. Clark (47), for example, argues that Rousseau's influence on Herder has been as exaggerated as Hamann's.

36. Compare Clark: 45; Koepke, 1987: 55, 62; Meinecke: 299; *Another Philosophy of History*, 88.

luxury, and alienation, it is not surprising that Herder found inspiration in Rousseau's *Discourse on the Sciences and the Arts* and *Letter to M. d'Alembert.*[37] Herder sees Rousseau and Voltaire's teachings as "canceling each other out,"[38] and so, in mounting his own attack on Voltaire's philosophy of history, he follows in Rousseau's footsteps and makes use of some of his most forceful arguments against the unchecked advance of reason. Indeed, the reader who is familiar with the various Discourses, the *Social Contract*, and the constitutional recommendations for Poland and Corsica will hear echoes of Rousseau at every major juncture of Herder's philosophy of history. Rousseau and Herder, however, are linked in another, even more problematic way: they have both been accorded the dubious honor of having fathered nationalism.[39] To see how this came about and why, it is necessary to examine briefly Herder's main arguments in *Another Philosophy of History.*

III. *Another Philosophy of History*

Those who have come across Herder's name in works on politics and history may have noticed an interesting paradox: although he is hailed as the "father of the related notions of nationalism, historicism and the *Volksgeist*," one of the most formidable critics of the *philosophes* of the French Enlightenment,[40] and although his name is mentioned in every major work on the history of nationalism,[41] there is hardly any work that would introduce a newcomer to Herder as a political thinker. The secondary literature on Herder is replete with works that examine his role as aestheticist, diarist, literary critic, philosopher, psychologist, theologian, sociologist, historian, critic of the Enlightenment, as German, even as Faust, and yet there are very few works that focus on his

37. On the relationship between the two thinkers, see Wolff, and Barnard, 1988, esp. 285–321. Herder said of Rousseau "his great theme is exceedingly close to my own" (quoted in Barnard, 1988: 285).

38. *Another Philosophy of History*, 105.

39. See, e.g., Popper: 247–48. For an examination of the equivalent problem in Rousseau, see Plattner.

40. Berlin, 2000: 168. Compare Ergang: 248.

41. See, for example, Kohn, Gellner, Anderson, Greenfeld.

political thought.[42] Frederick M. Barnard, whose own writings are a notable exception to this trend, hesitates to call Herder a political thinker, finding his interests "too heterogeneous" for such a designation, and points to the absence, among Herder's published writings, of a "single major work that could be unequivocally classified as a political treatise."[43]

One might be tempted to dismiss the issue regarding the extent to which Herder is a political thinker as a minor curiosity within the history of ideas, yet it turns out to be of perhaps surprising importance in understanding not only Herder's thought but also modern politics. Among historians, Hans Kohn began a systematic study of the rise of nationalism in the early 1920s and had been aware of Herder's importance in the context of the history of that idea, but he was one of few.[44] By 1965, when Isaiah Berlin made his first case in print for the connection between Herder and the concept of *Nationalismus*,[45] nationalism had already risen to prominence in politics, largely because of the national element in the Nazi nomenclature and creed, but it was events during the latter half of the 20th century, such as the breakup of the Soviet Union and of Yugoslavia, that forced many historians and political scientists to turn their attention to nationalism. These, along with endless calls from ethnic groups around the globe for self-determination, have led to an explosion of interest in the study of community and ethnicity, of the nation and its relationship to the state, as well as of nationalism and its relationship to patriotism.

In such a context, Herder, who "seems to have coined the word *Nationalismus*,"[46] assumed considerable political significance. Students of nationalism were eager to follow the lead of Kohn and

42. Irmscher, in his general introduction (9), argues that Herder exercised a great influence on European literature, philosophy, and political thought of the 19th and 20th centuries. Beiser, who in his study of German political thought at the end of the 18th century devotes a chapter to Herder, calls him "One of the most important and influential political philosophers of the 1790s" (189).

43. Barnard, 1965: 3–4, 6–7. Compare Ergang: 82, 239, 247.

44. Carlton J. H. Hayes is another example; Hayes' student Robert R. Ergang has written on Herder and German Nationalism (see Ergang).

45. See Berlin, "Herder and the Enlightenment" (Berlin, 1965), later reprinted in *Vico and Herder* (Berlin, 1977), *The Proper Study of Mankind* (Berlin, 1997), and *Three Critics of the Enlightenment: Vico, Hamann, Herder* (Berlin, 2000).

46. Berlin, 2000: 206. At *Another Philosophy of History*, 39:34, Herder uses the term "*Nationalism*." According to the *Oxford English Dictionary*, the earliest recorded use of the term in English occurred in 1798.

Berlin and to study Herder's thought on the nation but discovered that they were unable to do so because his works on politics and history were unavailable. His main work, the *Ideen zur Philosophie der Geschichte der Menschheit* (Ideas on the Philosophy of History of Mankind, 1784–1791), a work of well over 600 pages, was translated into English in 1800 for the first and last time.[47] With the exception of a limited reprint of the first English edition in 1966,[48] it has not been republished in its entirety; the only widely accessible edition is one which reproduces only nine out of Herder's original twenty parts of the book.[49] Other likely candidates suffer from being too long or too short: Herder's *Briefe zu Beförderung der Humanität* (Letters towards the Advancement of Humanity, 1793), written in place of the fifth and final part of the *Ideen*, numbers some 700 pages, and his more pointed and polemical essays are too small to be published on their own.[50] As a result, those who could not read the German text had to rely on quotations and references found in the works of those who could, but this has made for a very fragmentary and distorted picture of Herder and his political thought.[51]

Herder's importance in the study of the history of nationalism, his allegedly apolitical philosophy, and the lack of English translations of his works make *Another Philosophy of History for the Education of Mankind: One among Many Contributions of the Century* a particularly perplexing piece of this puzzle.[52] Herder himself

47. Johann Gottfried Herder, *Outlines of a Philosophy of the History of Man*, trans. T. Churchill (London: Printed for J. Johnson, St. Paul's Church-Yard, by Luke Hansard, Great Turnstile, Lincoln's-Inn Fields, 1800); in this edition the text numbers 630 large pages.

48. The facsimile of the Churchill edition was printed by Bergman Publishers, in New York.

49. Johann Gottfried Herder, *Reflections on the Philosophy of the History of Mankind*, abridged, with an introduction by Frank E. Manuel (Chicago: The University of Chicago Press, 1968).

50. See, for example, the selected political writings in this volume.

51. Surprisingly, this is true even of Isaiah Berlin, who, in his famous essay "Herder and the Enlightenment" (Berlin, 1977), refers to the original text of the Suphan edition, but also quotes from Barnard's translations (Barnard, 1969), although these references have been eliminated from subsequent editions of the essay (compare, for example, *Vico and Herder* [Berlin, 1977] notes 1 and 2, on p. 176, to the equivalent pages in *The Proper Study of Mankind* [Berlin, 1997: 392–93] and *Three Critics of the Enlightenment* [Berlin, 2000: 201]).

52. This work was translated by Eva Herzfeld in 1968, as part of a PhD dissertation at Columbia University, but that translation was never published.

called this work, written between 1772 and 1773,[53] a "pamphlet," but at the same time declared with pride that it contains *his* philosophy of history.[54] Its overtly political nature is apparent from its very title page. Herder had instructed his publisher, Hartknoch, to leave out the author's name as well as the place of publication and publisher information. The reason for Herder's instructions would have been evident to a late-18th-century reader from the work's polemical title and subtitle, which signal the author's ironical response to the philosophies of history published by the *philosophes*,[55] and which are supplemented by an equally polemical quotation from Epictetus' *Encheiridion*. The text itself dissolves any lingering doubt about his politics and intentions, and given its remarks on Frederick the Great,[56] it is not surprising that Herder did not want to be associated with it publicly. This work has been hailed as "the great charter of historism,"[57] and despite the later and much broader *Ideen*,[58] has been pronounced Herder's "greatest work as a historical thinker and pioneer of historism," a work possessing "an almost visionary power," and "the most successful synthesis of historical thought [Herder] ever achieved."[59]

As Meinecke and others have noted, what makes Herder remarkable is the convergence, in his thought, of the influences examined above. Herder was not just in the right place at the right time; he managed to bring these seemingly irreconcilable forces together in a philosophy of history, which for this and other reasons is truly his own.[60] From its outset, this philosophy of history

53. Irmscher, who has edited the manuscript, dates the composition to 1772–1773 (DKV 4:818).

54. Herder to Hartknoch, early August 1773, *Briefe* 3:35.

55. Voltaire's *La philosophie de l'histoire* (The Philosophy of History, 1765), which was translated into German in 1768, by Johann Jakob Harder (1768), and Isaak Iselin's *Philosophische Muthmassungen über die Geschichte der Menschheit* (Philosophical Conjectures on the History of Mankind, 1764, reissued under the title *Über die Geschichte der Menschheit* in 1768).

56. See, e.g., *Another Philosophy of History*, 99.

57. Stadelmann: 28.

58. See Koepke, 1987: 32; Irmscher: 122–23.

59. Meinecke: 298, 340. Beiser argues that Herder's critique of the Enlightenment "reached its climax" in *Another Philosophy of History* (203). Compare Barnard, 2003: 141, n. 24.

60. See Herder's letter to Hartknoch, early August 1773: "One of my books, a very beautiful one at that, is finished. It is called *Another Philosophy of History for the Education of Mankind: One among Many Contributions of the Century*, 1773; thankfully

is an attack against the relentless pursuit of reason advocated by the *philosophes*, although without denying reason its place. Herder sees the simplest delights that reason looks down upon as those that move mankind the most (12);[61] the simple relations, such as the family, that speak to the human heart and that were formed at humanity's very founding, were so formed for all time, which is why family will survive the attacks of reason (14–15). In so proclaiming the victory of their way of thinking, Herder's contemporaries have constructed their own version of Oriental despotism, one that picks and chooses isolated moments from what has come before them in order to characterize entire epochs with the words belonging to but a few glimpses (15) and then interprets them through its own prism. They follow Montesquieu in dismissing Oriental despotism for its reliance on fear, and yet they fail to see that there are times when learning through reason is not possible (15); mankind's Oriental forefathers learned from example and authority just as the child learns from his parents.

Our founding as individuals, according to Herder, requires an act similar to that which Machiavelli sees as necessary for states: authority will lay the foundations upon which we may then stand and reason.[62] To follow the *philosophes* and attribute reasoning to reason stripped of any content is but to engage in a vicious circle and ignore some of the most powerful forces at work in the development of mankind (15–16).[63] This realization already sets in motion the parallel between the life of man and the development of mankind that unfolds throughout the rest of *Another Philosophy*

---

it has nothing in common with Voltaire and Harder other than the title. It is truly *my* philosophy of history" (*Briefe* 3:35).

61. References to Herder's texts will be to page numbers of the German text, as given in the margins of the translation.

62. *Discourses on Livy* III: i. Herder's agreement with Machiavelli extends to what they both identify as one of the main tools of this authority—religion. Compare *Discourses on Livy* I: xi, III: i. Herder's view of the role of religion here anticipates some of the arguments advanced by Weber in "The Social Psychology of World Religions" (Weber: 267–301). Compare also Rousseau, *On the Social Contract* 2: vii (*SC*: 68–72, *OC* 3:381–84).

63. As Herder points out in the *Essay on the Origin of Language*, the *philosophes* commit a fundamental error when they consider whether reason is innate in man: they seem to believe that a child is born with the ability to reason fully, which leads him to wonder "Why, does thinking reasonably right away signify thinking with fully developed reason?" (EOL: 112). To distinguish between the *potential* to reason fully and the *ability* to reason fully, he employs one of his favorite metaphors— seeds (*Samenkörner*): "what is to grow must be there as a germ" (EOL: 113).

of History and sets the stage for historicism. Seeing the necessity
for despotism as a founding force, however, does not mean that
Herder is willing to go to the opposite extreme and ignore its evil
side. The cement of this foundation has to be allowed to set
before it can be built upon, and yet it comes with the inevitable
consequence that its own immediate environment will be fixed
with it. Herder sees this as the reason why conquerors were able
to impose their rule on the Orient so easily and predicts that despotism will always find a foundation there (16).

Thus instructed, the infant grew up to become a schoolboy,
and the Oriental world gave way to Egypt, where agriculture
replaced the shepherd's life, and the first division of land took
place. The arts emerged, and man came under the authority of
the law. It was under such conditions that man began to receive
his first lessons in civility, which paved the way for his subsequent
regimentation. To adapt to the new learning environment, religion receded into the background, but was painted on the wall, so
as not to be forgotten. At the same time, family began to give way
to concern over social rank.

Having two epochs before him, Herder compares them and
argues that the Oriental would have found the Egyptian's life distasteful, as any ancestor would likely feel the same way about a suc-
cessor's way of life, given the opportunity to judge it. Thus he sets
the stage for the development of one of his central methodological
principles—that one epoch should not be judged by the standards
of another—which he aims at what he sees as the hubris of the *philosophes'* readings of history, which find fault with times past in
order to exalt their enlightened age. In so doing, they lose sight of
the workings of Providence, whose wondrous works are manifest
throughout history, a testament to the existence of a grand design;
but they also sin doubly against mankind by belittling entire ages,
and thereby providing a false education to subsequent generations.

His next stop, Greece, witnesses the rise of republican freedom,
of the first commerce, of interaction among peoples, and of new
arts. In Herder's analogy, Greece represents the youth of mankind,
and it is always our youth that we remember "with pleasure and
joy" (26), for its readiness to seize the day. Here, one finds "obedience coupled with freedom and wrapped in the name *fatherland*,"[64]
a change in the form of government that Herder ascribes to

64. Compare Rousseau, *Discourse on the Sciences and the Arts* II (D: 21–23; *OC*:
23–6).

Greece's climate and other favorable circumstances.[65] These made for what Herder sees as the Greek paradox, that is, separation into a multitude of city-states and colonies, and yet a common bond of all through language and culture. This paradox offers us a first glimpse into his understanding of the nation, which he sees as bound primarily by those two forces.[66] These fundamental changes also affected the nature of religion, which became more public, a domesticated caricature of the austere, Oriental version.

For all its illustrative powers, Herder's presentation of the life of mankind along the lines of the life of man has its own set of limitations, of which he is only too aware: "No one in the world feels *the weakness of general characterization* more than I" (32). Once again, his is a balancing act. The effort required by the understanding and appreciation of the diversity of particulars is enough to make one dizzy, and our natural tendency is to simplify, because our capacity to understand is limited.[67] In doing so, however, we have to be careful to avoid both oversimplification and losing sight of the fact that a caricature is just that. Instead, we often condense an entire ocean of something distant and foreign into a single particle and believe that we have thus caught its essence. This, however, makes for dangerous comparisons, because it is on the basis of these oversimplifications that we then sing our praises and believe that we have become the epitome of everything that was ever good or noteworthy. Are we aggregations of the best that the Orientals, Egyptians, Greeks, and Romans had to offer? Let us not fool ourselves—the existence of any potential for heroism in a scoundrel does not make him a hero.

Herder's solution to the problem of the inherent limits of reason in providing us with a sufficient understanding of our historical surroundings is to supplement it with feeling. He urges his reader to feel his way into everything.[68] Like the Greeks, peoples

---

65. Compare Aristotle *Politics* 1325b–1330a; Montesquieu, *The Spirit of the Laws* III: xiv–xviii.

66. In so placing Greece, Herder believes that he is also solving the great question of his time, namely, How original were the Greeks? In the context of his understanding of history, they could not have come about without what came before, but they were neither Oriental nor Egyptian, because *they could not have been*. They did import various elements from other times and peoples, but in so doing, they made them Greek (*Another Philosophy of History*, 29–30).

67. Compare EOL: 110.

68. Elsewhere Herder declares: "*Ich fühle mich! Ich bin!* [I feel (myself)! I am!]" (Suphan 8:96). According to both Meinecke (297) and Berlin (2000: 196–97),

of all eras have exhibited traits borrowed from other times and places, but this is only part of the way in which mankind moves forward in time. It is part of what Providence intends, and it can never be the whole story. One also needs to pay attention to the particulars that mix with these inherited and borrowed elements to make for the specific circumstances that render each setting, moment, and people unique. Part and parcel of his emphasis on our limited capacity to see things for what they are is the realization that every entity, whether individual or nation, is insufficient in some way. Therefore, one who expects to find the whole world in one spot will fail to appreciate that spot for what it is. The good always coexists with the bad, no matter how much we may want to beautify our own age and scorn others. This is precisely what Herder sees in the *philosophes*, who claim to be historians but are really poets; they are not describing the truth, but painting their own images, the way they want them to look. This tendency is also illustrated well in questions like that of the Berne Patriotic Society: "Which people was the happiest in history?" Herder finds the question absurd, because human happiness is particular to the circumstances, so comparison of the kind sought by the Society is futile; it only contributes to their continued delusions of grandeur.

Herder's claim that every nation has its own center of gravity, and therefore the means for its happiness within itself, is also central to his larger purpose in that it paves the way for his defense of a communal way of life, against the universalizing tendencies of the Enlightenment. This center of gravity, too, is due to Providence, which has ordered things so that the arousal of a few dispositions is sufficient to satisfy our limited scope. If, then, those who proclaim his century the culmination of human *progress* are also implying that it is the time of the greatest happiness for every individual, they seem to be wrong, because Herder cannot find any evidence for this. As he has pointed out from the beginning, they have done mankind a disservice, since to come up with this "progress" they have torn up everything that was good in the past, in Penelopean fashion. Instead, one should focus on the particular but also not lose sight of the universal within which it is situated. The stream flows, but whether it becomes a river, a sea, or an

---

Herder invented the concept of "*Einfühlung*", which he saw as the first step towards understanding, and which had a formative influence on the *Sturm und Drang* movement.

ocean, every drop in it is still a drop and will always be made of water. Everyone builds on what came before, and it is simply meaningless to say that the young man is happier than the contented child, the calm old man, or the vigorously striving man.

This is *his* philosophy of history, then, and for all its limitations it is better than those that look like "ants' games," confusing everything in order to explain a minute episode. *His* philosophy of history offers an appreciation of the whole, in which one is given enough cause to believe even if one may not see everything. By themselves, the seeds of Herder's defense of the local community can provide sufficient grounds for the kinds of accusations that Herder has often drawn for allegedly having failed to foresee the nasty consequences of these "narrow inclinations." His examination of these inclinations in *Another Philosophy of History*, however, shows that these accusations are in large measure unfair. Having defended them, Herder immediately recognizes that when the inclinations and circles of happiness of two nations collide, the result is "*prejudice, loutishness,* narrow *nationalism*" (39). Instead, he calls on parents to take over the education of their children and raise them according to their community's "center of happiness," rather than abandoning them to the centrifugal universal education advanced by the *philosophes*, which will teach everyone to speak French and make all the same.[69]

The world reached its manhood in Rome, where it turned from the play of the arts to the serious business of ruling the earth "with sovereign might." Yet for all its greatness and spread, Rome met its end, too. Providence once again intervened, and with the help of excess, vice, and license it caused the Roman spirit to weaken and eventually to die down.[70] Herder finds the shift that took place at this juncture so monumental that he speaks of the life of mankind, whose stages he has been describing up to this point, coming to an end (43). While the Oriental, Egyptian, and Greek moments fed their successors through their achievements in life,[71] drained of such energies the Roman world achieved the same effect in its death. Like the farmer who burns his field to

---

69. Compare *Another Philosophy of History*, 39, 41, 52, 75, 82, 94, 102.

70. With respect to the decline of Rome, Herder is following a well-established line of explanation that has its origins in Roman historiography, as for example in Sallust, but was advanced most famously by Augustine, in his *City of God against the Pagans* (see, e.g., II.xviii).

71. What Herder refers to as the "spirit of life," or "driving forces," or even "vital fluids."

prepare it for the planting of the next seed, Rome razed the world and thereby prepared it for the new, stronger plants of the north—the Germanic tribes.

Initially, the Northern peoples succeeded because of their contempt for the arts and sciences, which had wrought havoc upon mankind.[72] This allowed for a period of fermentation, in which the various elements of the first stages of the development of mankind mixed with those that were brought over from the north, and during which "despotism was kept at bay for so long" (44). Providence then interfered with what Herder sees as the central force behind the subsequent development of mankind, Christianity.[73] For Herder, the conditions and timing of the rise of Christianity are further evidence for the existence of a grand design: an unlikely religion from an unlikely place, tried and tested by the might of Julian and his empire, and yet in the end thriving because of the very fact that that same empire had prepared the ground for a universal religion by bringing peoples together in a way that had never been seen before (46–47).

In pointing to the workings of Providence through man and nature, Herder is expanding on one of the main themes of his prize-winning essay on the origin of language. There, he had argued that while the potential for language was put in man by God, it was man himself who developed it into a complete tool for communication.[74] Here, he is making a broader and more explicit argument for a deism that sees God as acting through man and nature to advance the cause of mankind: "Religion is meant to accomplish nothing but *purposes for human beings, through human beings*" (48)—the Christian religion in particular, through its universal character and its unique adaptability to any constitution (49).

Turning to the Middle Ages, Herder notes that there are those who have extolled the period as the height of adventure and chivalry, and those who have condemned them as years of darkness.

72. Herder is following Rousseau's *Discourse on the Sciences and the Arts* here.

73. Despite his earlier agreement with Rousseau regarding the arts and sciences, Herder is here taking a different view of the effects of Christianity than that advanced by Rousseau in *On the Social Contract* 4, viii (*SC*: 142–51; *OC* 3:460–69). To demonstrate his impartiality toward his subject, Herder quickly points out that in privileging Christianity in this manner he is losing sight neither of the various impure elements that went into the leaven that gave rise to it, nor of the ways in which it has been abused by its own proponents in subsequent ages (46–48).

74. Compare EOL, Section 2.

All he is willing to do is acknowledge their uniqueness—"A singular condition of the world"—nothing more, nothing less. Beyond the fact that it renews his attack on the histories of the *philosophes*, his insistence on this point marks an important methodological consideration, which lies at the heart of his method but also at the center of his critique of *other* philosophies of history. Herder argues that the partial historian betrays his art on two grounds: first, he does not paint an accurate picture of the world; but second, and in some ways most important, in thinking that he is justified in being partial, he is deceiving himself and thereby doing a disservice to the education of his readers, even if unwittingly. The reason for this is simple: no one can *know* what another time and place was like, and to pretend to is to deceive oneself, or others, or both (50–51).

Herder finds an example of this "utopian" historiography in the Enlightenment's treatment of the Middle Ages in particular, as well as its view of the course of human freedom more generally. Looking around, he sees no reason to join in the *philosophes'* celebration for the alleged increase in human freedom in the Age of Enlightenment; enslavement to reason is enslavement nonetheless. Moreover, past, so-called "unfree" times have their own achievements to show, and it is only by seeing each epoch as a tool, a driving force in the service of progression, that one can begin to make sense of its proper place (51–52). As at the beginning of *Another Philosophy of History*, here too Herder responds to Voltaire that it is not light and tranquility, but rather emotion that nourishes human beings, even though it may be fleeting, inconsequential, and even dangerous: "Nothing could be further from my mind than to defend the endless mass-migrations and devastations, the vassals' wars and feuds, the armies of monks, the pilgrimages and crusades: I only wish to explain them, [to show] how *spirit* breathes in everything, after all!" (53). At the same time, however, his generosity in forgiving the faults of past times opens his own theory to the same criticism that he directs at the *philosophes*. If nothing can be classified as an atrocity simply because it cannot be understood except in the context in which it took place, then one begins to see that this opens the door to revisionism and the rewriting of the past in a different, but equally potent and frightful, way, and this is precisely one of the elements of Herder's thought that were eventually abused, not least by those who sought to build a history for their nation from scratch. The best consolation that Herder has to offer in this respect is that the bad

will be followed by some good, making for balance in the course
of mankind's progression. To think, with the philosophies of the
age, that there can be *only* good is to be blind to the facts of history but also to the very origins of this "purist" philosophy, which
itself emerged from the filth it so despises.[75]

Finally, after the fall of the yeast came an epoch of light more
agreeable to the *raisonneurs*, the Renaissance. Herder objects to
the beautification of this transition and notes that the shift from
darkness into the light was not the product of reason (after all,
how could it have been, if reason had ceased to exist?), but of fate;
factors beyond man's control, much like those stressed by Aristotle and Montesquieu, were crucial.[76] Herder reminds those who
are not convinced that there have been countless Luthers who
have stood and shouted, but only one who started the Reformation (58). To those who might nevertheless persist in wondering
whether all this could have happened without the violence and
the bloodshed, his response is still "No." Yet he reminds his
reader of the fundamental principle at work here: all these
momentous events have their beginnings in small seeds. Just as
the plant in time bursts from the seed and assumes its full potential, so it is with the fundamental discoveries and revolutionary
ideas that have been pushing mankind forward in its progression.

As Herder has pointed out, however, everything good has its
bad side, and so it is with these inventions, which he sees, in a
Rousseauean spirit, as responsible for the disappearance of the
ancient virtues. Courage has given way to superficiality, and this is
nowhere more apparent than in modern armies, in which soldiers
are no longer citizens but, rather, civil servants. The same is also
true of philosophy, which used to be about real life but has
become a trade and thus also "light" and "mechanical." Having
become diluted in this way, philosophy then turns back and re-
enters all areas of life, but only to pollute them and weaken them.
Activities cease to have meaning in their own right, and everything is done in the name of philosophy, but what good is its light

75. Compare *Letters towards the Advancement of Humanity*, 24: "Even the evils
that the human species encounters, my friends, even they are good, and at times
still necessary. Rain, wind, and tempests make the field fertile; the snow provides a
blanket for the seeds; and if here and there hail smashes the stems, the harvest
elsewhere—and perhaps, before long, here as well—will be all the richer and
more beautiful for it" (DKV 7.806). On whether or not Herder's position here is
relativist, see Barnard, 2003: 136–37.

76. Compare *Politics*, Book 7; *The Spirit of the Laws* 3: xiv–xviii.

if it comes at the expense of our will to live? This universal perme-
ation of philosophy extends to the way we perceive our very selves,
demanding from us a love of mankind, but this too comes at the
expense of local ties. Like Rousseau, Herder points to the cost of
following the *philosophes* down this path and claiming to love peoples at the end of the earth but really loving no one.[77] Everyone
learns one universal language—French—and thus prepared begins
a course in the "education of mankind" along uniform lines, but
this education robs children of their childhood and makes old men
of the young. So-called "progress" in religion and ethics has led
his contemporaries to proclaim themselves the champions of virtue, allegedly possessing more than any other people at any other
moment in time, and yet Herder wonders, Where is this virtue?

It should come as no surprise that one thus transformed by this
kind of "education" will be unable to perceive the workings of
Providence in the course of events that Herder has been survey-
ing, and this is the loss that he laments most. Little harm would
have come from the ideas of the *philosophes* had they kept them to
themselves, but by spreading them as they have, they have made
the rest of the world impotent along with themselves. Before rulers took over education from the institutions that were properly
charged with it, concentrated it in their courts for their amusement, and turned it into frivolity and meaningless art, it used to
come in a thousand different guises, each narrowly national and
thereby appropriate to its people. Herder suspects that having
pointed this out, he will be attacked for praising the past and
being overly critical of the present, but he declares himself ready
to concede all that is good in his age.[78] The first and foremost of
its benefits is to be found in its place at the top of the tree of
humanity, from whence it can look down and see the ages that led
to its formation. But once again, every good comes with some
bad, and having acknowledged the benefit of his century's vantage
point he adds that its spreading of light around the world goes
hand in hand with means that are less than noble. Just as the
leaven of the peoples of the north included impure elements, we
have to be aware of the fact that the so-called "enlightenment" of

77. Compare Rousseau, "Geneva Manuscript" 1: ii (*SC:* 158; *OC* 3:287); *Émile*
(*OC* 4:249).

78. That we lack the characteristics of the past is neither surprising, since no
two moments are the same, nor a fault, except by our trying to make it seem like a
virtue (*Another Philosophy of History*, 79).

the world is prepared by liquor and luxury, and its newfound freedom can only be sustained by the existence of slaves, even though
we console ourselves that not being European and Christian, they
are also not human.

Is there any way, then, in which mankind can claim to be
marching towards its perfection? Herder finds no reason to think
so: man will always be man in a fundamental sense, a "hieroglyph
of good and evil" (81), with a myriad different manifestations
through space and time, but man nonetheless. The "wise man"
who sees progress must have failed to consider God's plan, even
though it should have been clearer to him, at the top of his tree,
than it has ever been. Had he paid attention, he would have
noticed that what he considered a whole world was but a moment
in a vast sequence. And yet Herder understands why this is the
case, since each moment in itself *is* indeed a world unto itself, no
matter how small a part of the whole it may be. This is consistent
with his view that everything in this grand design is simultaneously means and end: a tool in the hands of Providence, but
also a universe all of its own. Some may be more important than
others, but none is useless.

Having called attention to this grand design, Herder invites his
reader to reconsider the historical moments that he surveyed at
the beginning of *Another Philosophy of History*, in the hope that he
will come to see them in a whole new light, in their proper context, and therefore appreciate them for what they really were.
This sequence is "God's march across the nations," and Montesquieu's simplistic classifications of regimes cannot do justice to its
complexity. Herder's method here follows his argument that one
cannot assess peoples properly until after excessive adoration for
them has ceased; bias leads one to "caress" one's favorite nation,
but this is akin to opening Pandora's box.

Herder's despair, towards the end of *Another Philosophy of History*, about the upheaval that his age has witnessed in customs, traditions, and order, as well as his lament for the loss of mankind's
vital fluids cannot help but remind one of his examination of
Rome. Like Rousseau, who prefers the honesty of the naked
wrestlers to the extravagantly clothed pretenders of his time,[79]
Herder would pick Machiavelli over Frederick's *Anti-Machiavelli*
gladly, and he wonders whether it may not be that the next phase
will emerge only through the demise of his own. His chief lesson,

79. Compare *Discourse on the Sciences and the Arts* 1 (D: 7; *OC* 3:8).

however, to which he returns at the end of *Another Philosophy of History*, is that we must strike a balance between the particular, which in itself is a whole world, and the universal, in the context of which our overwhelming worlds are but fleeting moments. Only thus can we appreciate our significance, as well as that of others, in Providence's grand design.

IV. Nationalism

As the emphasis on the relationship between the particular and the universal in *Another Philosophy of History* shows, for Herder the nation is situated firmly within the wider context of humanity.[80] It is a natural, organic social group, whose common identity can be found in its language and customs and not in other characteristics such as race.[81] Herder's choice to concentrate on these particular attributes, coupled with his explicit recognition of the dangers inherent in "narrow nationalism," reveals that for him the nation

80. Meinecke (333) argues that in facing this relationship Herder is addressing one of the key questions that the Enlightenment was unable to deal with in any depth. This emphasis of the place of the particular within the universal in Herder's thought also reveals the Platonism that Meinecke speaks of, and is indeed one of the elements picked up by Herder's successors, who came to see nations and peoples as particular manifestations of God on earth (See, e.g., Schleiermacher quoted in Ergang: 250).

81. Compare *Letters towards the Advancement of Humanity*, letter 116: "Above all one ought to be as *impartial* as the genius of mankind itself; one ought to have no favorite tribe, no favorite people [*Favoritvolk*] on earth. . . . Even less ought one to be disdainful of any people and insult those who have never insulted us. . . . How gladly we rely on disdainful judgments about other peoples to justify our dark deeds and wild inclinations! . . . Thus . . . the entire history of mankind was destroyed [when] the most insolent arrogance and the cruelest usurpation were granted privileges in the name of the greater glory of god. So let no people on earth be handed the scepter over another on account of its '*inborn superiority*,' let alone the sword or the slave-master's whip. . . . A negro would consider the white man an abomination, a born cockroach, by the same right by which a white man would consider him a beast, a black animal" (DKV 7:698–99). See also Barnard, 2003: 38. Herder's unwillingness to consider race in these terms was one of the reasons behind Kant's dissatisfaction with the *Ideas*. For an example of the role of race within other theories of history of the period, see Voltaire; compare Barnard, 2003: 64–65. According to Berlin (2000: 191–2), Herder sees the nation as natural and finds the notion of a solitary human being—such as is found at the theoretical beginnings of social contract theories, as well as in Kant—to be unintelligible.

is not the political entity that it has become since. As long as nations focus on their own center of gravity, there will be no conflict with other nations and peoples. Herder argues that this is within the reach of every community. Given the limited ability of the human mind to perceive that which surrounds it, an education based on the elements that comprise the center of happiness of a particular nation will form a centripetal force that will be sufficient to counteract the centrifugal tendencies of the universal, uniform education recommended by the *philosophes*.[82] But is it necessary that such an attachment to a particular community will sooner or later reveal a nasty side?

Despite the fact that in *Another Philosophy of History* and elsewhere Herder explicitly rejects chauvinism and any form of aggression in the service of the nation, he has been accused of having laid the foundations for subsequent theories of aggressive nationalism.[83] It has to be admitted that, adaptable though they may be to a Christian humanist point of view, Herder's observations regarding nations and peoples might also open the door to a more aggressively nationalist outlook; indeed, with the benefit of hindsight, one may even be able to see how the seeds of distinction inherent in the very concept of a *Volk* or a *Kulturnation* might have triggered some of the outrages that have become synonymous with nationalism, and this should come as no surprise given the weight that he himself accords to seeds as tools in the hands of Providence, in his philosophy of history. Herder, however, never meant for his vision of *Humanität* to be seen as distinct from or lesser than that of local community. In the words of Wulf Koepke, he "saw dangers and was always trying to find a middle ground between two extremes"; as a result, "[i]t is easy to see only one side of his struggles."[84] His nationalism was never political, and his personal politics simply had no room for aggression, violence, and disrespect.[85]

Perhaps it is in the nature of the matter that emphasis on particularity and group identity will necessarily lead to polarization.

82. See *Another Philosophy of History*, 39, 41, 52, 75, 82, 94, 102.

83. See, e.g., Popper: 247–48.

84. Koepke, 1987: 119.

85. See Berlin, 2000: 180–81; compare Koepke, 1989: 1658; Barnard, 2003: 64. According to Beiser (212), "There is no trace of German chauvinism in Herder." For a useful discussion of the extent to which Herder's nationalism is political see Barnard, 2003: Chapter 2.

Still, Herder's own intentions had to be set aside as the concepts of *Volk* and *Nation* were transformed, at the hands of such successors as Fichte, into a rallying point for nascent German nationalism.[86] For Fichte, Herder's seemingly innocuous criterion of language became the measure on the basis of which the Germans formed a cohesive and meaningful group, but also that by which they were pronounced the *Favoritvolk*, destined to lead mankind.[87] Building on a different idea that figures prominently in *Another Philosophy of History*, Hegel proceeded to speak not of the *progression* of mankind, but rather of its *progress*, of which the Prussian bureaucratic state was the culmination.[88] One might also be tempted to seek a connection between the rise of German nationalism and Herder's plea to study one's folklore. A German choosing to heed Herder's call would discover a long tradition encapsulated in the popular prophecy that Frederick Barbarossa and his soldiers would awaken from their slumber and reunite the German peoples.[89] Connections of this kind may be more or less tenable and persuasive, but in making them one needs to be mindful of the plasticity of the ideas in question and the eagerness of political doctrines to seek legitimizing roots. In so doing, they often pick and choose from complex theories, and this is what happened in Herder's case, because in order to extract from his political philosophy any element that would legitimize German nationalism and eventually National Socialism, one had to ignore other elements that are methodologically and substantively integral to Herder's theory. It is interesting, then, to note in this respect that on the anniversary of his death, in 1903, he was claimed both by leftist internationalists and right-wing nationalists.[90] Eventually, however, the latter prevailed, and with the rise of National Socialism in the early part of the 20th century,

86. See Kohn: 241–42.

87. Fichte: 3–4.

88. Compare Hegel's *The Philosophy of History.*

89. Legend had it that Frederick Barbarossa and his soldiers were asleep inside the Kyffhäuser Mountains, and that the Royal Prussian eagle would come to drive away the crows living in the area, thereby awakening the kaiser, who would reclaim his kingdom. This legend, parts of which are also found among the tales collected by the Brothers Grimm, was revived in the 19th century and brought to prominence in the early 20th century. Most famously it is found in Heinrich Heine's *Deutschland: ein Wintermärchen* (Germany: A Winter's Tale), 1844. Compare Bellmann, 37–39.

90. See Koepke, 1994: 130.

Herder's ideas regarding the nation were manipulated and selec-
tively promoted as the ideological and philosophical precursors of
German nationalist ideology.[91] This misappropriation notwithstanding, the reader who will look past the fragmented and piece-
meal, often second-hand, renditions of Herder's thought and
listen to Herder himself will discover that, as he argues, the good
and the bad go hand in hand and his own influence extends far
beyond the nation and nationalism.

The works that follow offer a glimpse into other important
aspects of Herder's political thought. His praise for the republi-
canism of Greece and his criticism of Frederick's enlightened despotism[92] are elements of his general preference for a republican
form of government in which the state is a means rather than an
end: "Nature creates nations, not states,"[93] and the best states are
those that incorporate the people in order to serve them. Nor is
his vision of such a government naive: Herder anticipates Mill's
"Considerations on Representative Government" by recognizing
that some of the technical aspects of government will have to be
addressed by experts, but goes even further than Mill in arguing
that this need not entail the exclusion of ordinary people from
power.[94] As *Another Philosophy of History* shows, for Herder government is legitimate only when acting in the service of the people, and his writings and sermons attest to the fact that he was
well aware of their needs. Although education figures most prominently among them, his thinking about politics shows keen
insight regarding a wide array of social and political issues, such as
the devastating effects of unemployment and alienation.[95]

91. See Otto. In his *Reflections on the Revolution in France*, Edmund Burke
addressed the parallel problem of the relationship between Rousseau's political
theory and its reception thus: "[W]ere Rousseau alive and in one of his lucid inter-
vals, he would be shocked at the practical frenzy of his scholars, who in their paradoxes are servile imitators, and even in their incredulity discover an implicit faith"
(Burke: 150).

92. See *Another Philosophy of History*, 99 ff.; *Do We Still Have the Fatherland of
the Ancients?*

93. Compare Berlin, 2000: 181; Passmore: 347.

94. So strong was Herder's opposition to any dichotomies on the basis of power
that he took issue with Kant, with whom he is in fundamental agreement on the
issue of autonomy, overall. To Kant's assertion that "Man is *an animal that . . . has
need of a master,*" he replied that he who has need of a master is an animal. Compare
Kant: 33; Suphan 8:383–84; *Governments as Inherited Regimes*, 368–69.

95. See, e.g., Suphan 30:234.

Herder's originality and influence on subsequent thought have been underappreciated. He contributed to the rise of the passionate and powerful expression of the *Sturm und Drang* and had a profound impact on Goethe, one of the world's great poets. His philosophy of history set the stage for subsequent historical thinking, and its influence on Hegel, Marx, and Nietzsche is only the most noticeable evidence of its broad effect.[96] His observations about the role of folk customs in a people's way of life have been considered fundamental to the rise of anthropology as a modern discipline. As for his influence on politics, Herder's thought continued, in the tradition of Rousseau, to establish some of the more powerful arguments for what we have come to call communitarianism, precisely because it advances the cause of communities within the context of a peaceful and respectful mankind. To the extent that we have become more sensitive to and appreciative of particularity, we owe something to Herder.

96. Compare Hegel's *The Philosophy of History* and Marx's *The German Ideology* and "Introduction" to *A Contribution to the Critique of Hegel's Philosophy of Right*. One can see examples of Herder's influence even in Nietzsche's theory of history, despite their fundamental disagreement on a number of key issues (compare Nietzsche, *On the Advantage and Disadvantage of History for Life*). Compare also Taylor: 567–69.

CHRONOLOGY

(Unless otherwise identified, italicized titles are Herder's)

1744   Herder born on 25 August in Mohrungen, Prussia.

1748   Montesquieu's *The Spirit of the Laws* published.

1750   Rousseau's *Discourse on the Sciences and the Arts* published.

1751   Publication of Diderot's *Encyclopédie* begins in Paris.

1756   Seven Years' War begins.

1758   Rousseau's *Letter to M. d'Alembert* published.

1761   Herder becomes Trescho's assistant and amanuensis.

1762   Rousseau's *On the Social Contract* and *Émile* published; Herder leaves Mohrungen for Königsberg; meets Kant and Hamann.

1764   Herder leaves Königsberg for Riga.

1766   *Fragments on Recent German Literature.*

1768   *On Thomas Abbt's Writings.*

1769   Herder travels from Riga to Scandinavia, England, and France, where he meets Diderot and d'Alembert; experiences shipwreck; writes *Journal of My Travels in the Year 1769.*

1770   Begins travel as tutor to the son of the Prince-Bishop of Lübeck; Herder quits in Strassburg; meets Caroline Flachsland; meets Goethe; writes the *Essay on the Origin of Language.*

1771   Wins Berlin Academy's prize for his *Essay on the Origin of Language.*

1773   Marries Caroline Flachsland.

1774   *Another Philosophy of History for the Education of Mankind; Oldest Document of the Human Race;* wins Berlin Academy's prize for his essay "The Causes of the Deterioration in Taste Among the Various Peoples Where It Had Blossomed."

1775   Outbreak of the American Revolutionary War.

1776   Declaration of Independence; Herder moves to Weimar.

1778   *Sculpture; Folk Songs; On the Influence of Poetry on the Customs of Peoples.*

1779   *The Influence of Free Legislation on the Sciences and Arts.*

1780   Wins Berlin Academy's prize for *The Influence of Free Legislation on the Sciences and Arts; Letters regarding the Study of Theology.*

1781   Kant's *Critique of Pure Reason* published; Herder wins Munich Academy's prize for *On the Influence of Poetry on the Customs of Peoples.*

1782   *On the Spirit of Hebrew Poetry.*

1784   First part of *Ideas on the Philosophy of History of Mankind* published.

1785   Second part of *Ideas* published.

1786   Frederick II of Prussia dies.

1787   Third part of the *Ideas* published; *God: Some Conversations.*

1788   Kant's *Critique of Practical Reason* published; Hamann dies; Herder travels to Italy.

1789   Outbreak of the French Revolution; Herder returns to Weimar.

1790   Kant's *Critique of Judgment* published.

1791   Fourth part of *Ideas* published.

1792   Establishment of the French Republic.

1793   Execution of Louis XVI; beginning of Jacobin dictatorship; *Letters towards the Advancement of Humanity.*

1794   End of Jacobin dictatorship.

1798	Jean Paul visits Herder in Weimar.
1799	Napoleon Bonaparte's coup on 18 Brumaire.
1800	*Kalligone.*
1801	First part of *Adrastea* published; Herder receives title of nobility from the Elector Palatine Maximilian Joseph.
1802	First part of *Der Cid* and second part of *Adrastea* published.
1803	Third part of *Adrastea* published. Herder dies on 18 December.
1804	Kant dies.
1820	Caroline Herder publishes the *Erinnerungen.*
1877	Suphan begins the publication of his edition of Herder's collected works, which was completed in 1913.

A Note on the Texts
and the Translation

"[T]ranslations have in them this property: that
they may much disgrace, if not well done; but if
well, not much commend the doer."
—Thomas Hobbes[1]

"A translator for our day faces a situation whose
delicacy few readers will appreciate, and he
should not expect much gratitude for his
labors. For wary as he must be of spoiling the
beautiful arrangement of flowers and vines by
cutting into what lies before him, this is exactly
what he must do if [his translation] is to
become readable for us. But then again, he
must do no more than what will allow the
beautiful live plant to stand before us without
any diminution in its stature, as if it had just
blossomed before our very eyes."
—Johann Gottfried Herder[2]

Herder attached great significance to the irreducible peculiarities
of all peoples, and especially to the languages by which their
unique cultures and histories are expressed, preserved, and trans-
mitted through time. Perhaps it is only appropriate, then, that
his own German should illustrate so vividly the challenges facing
anyone who would translate one historically, culturally, and

1. Hobbes: xxi.

2. From Herder's preface to his own translation of Johann Valentin Andrea's
poetry (Suphan 16:593).

grammatically conditioned idiom into another. Add the more personal peculiarities of Herder's often tangled prose, the ample "solecisms" (Hamann) and stylistic idiosyncrasies with which he strains the patience of even his most sympathetic readers, and one may well question the judgment of anyone choosing to undertake his translation.

In this vein, we might begin by admitting to some of our failures. Take *Bildung:* no doubt this term is often adequately rendered as "education" or "learning"; but there are problems with this remedy even beyond the resulting overlap with *Erziehung.* For *Bildung* implies much more than schooling or acquired learning: to call someone *gebildet* in German is a high and unambiguous accolade in a way that labeling someone "educated" is often not, at least in much of the English-speaking world. *Bildung* expresses the aspiration and formation to an imposing ideal, a comprehensive shaping and refinement not only of the mind but also of the character and perhaps of the very soul. Wilhelm von Humboldt's "highest and most harmonious development of [man's] powers to a complete and consistent whole," so famously reprised in J. S. Mill's *On Liberty*,[3] is no mere affectation shared by two dreamy reformers, but rather the project and commitment by which the Germans have long defined and distinguished themselves from cultures more light-hearted and endearing. The unabashed confidence in *Bildung*—its vestiges seldom worn too lightly—provides much of the bedrock on which the German perspective on the world rests, even today. But Herder, so often cast as a prophet of nationalist narrowness, will mock such self-satisfaction without mercy—all the while insisting on waging his battles on the hallowed ground of *Bildung* itself.

Herder's overarching objective, in *Another Philosophy of History*[4] especially, is to expose the childishness of believing in "beautiful" progress along "a nice *straight line*" defined by the chimerical ideals of the philosophers.[5] For Herder, the maturation of mankind cannot amount to any such "*perfection* in the narrow sense of the schoolhouse,"[6] but only to a gradual formation by often erratic

3. Mill, Part III, 64.

4. For the more detailed citations of Herder's texts, please see the bibliography at the end of this note.

5. *Another Philosophy of History*, 81:10–14.

6. *Another Philosophy of History*, 78:13–15.

steps: *Bildung*, to be sure, but without the vaunted sense of the linear rarefaction and redemption of the human species on earth. Thus Herder uses *Fortgang* (progression) and its permutations to distance himself from the prophets of progress (*Fortschritt*)—all the while employing (and often enough, deploying) a term whose literal meaning is all but indistinguishable from the one favored by those whom he sets out to embarrass,[7] and then *stressing that literal reading*.[8] In such a literal light, then, pro-*gress(ion)* (like Fort-*gang* or Fort-*schritt*) appears to Herder as a process of "walking-forth" (Latin: *gradi* = to walk): a succession of countless steps along a winding, sometimes crooked path that will lead forward eventually, but never in a direct or predictable way.[9] (Unable to convey all the rich subtleties and ambiguities of these distinctions in translation, we have marked instances of *bilden* or *Bildung* with a single asterisk throughout the text, and of *Fortgang* and its variations with two asterisks).

Another set of challenges surrounds the English word "reason," which covers rather more ground than any of Herder's terms for which we shall be using it. Yet, fortunately, this turns out to be less problematic than one might expect. Our rendering of *raissonieren* and *Raisonnement* as "to reason" and "reasoning," respectively, might strike one as too neutral: after all, this is a term borrowed from the French and introduced, early on in *Another Philosophy of History* (13:28), in the context of "the hastiest reasoning . . . à la Voltaire." But German simply lacks native equivalents of these terms, and Herder uses them in a wide range of contexts throughout *Another Philosophy Of History;* hence his shades of meaning are better conveyed by the particular context than by more tendentious translation. Where Herder means to be unequivocally disparaging, he uses *vernünfteln* (a mocking

7. Though Herder tends to reserve *Fortschritt* for characterizing views he opposes, that is not always the case. At *Another Philosophy of History,* 77:23–24 he uses it at the height of his polemic, to be sure; but *Another Philosophy of History,* 34:9 is quite neutral and *Do We Still Have the Fatherland of the Ancients,* 336:19 not uncongenial to his argument. (See below for full titles and citations.)

8. This habit of using terms in what might be called an *over-literal* fashion is characteristic of Herder's writing and lays many traps for the unwary: quite frequently, Herder's reinterpretations of established terms not only defy conventional usage but also turn it on its head.

9. This theme could hardly be more central to Herder's project and we do not need to belabor it here. It receives what may be Herder's most sustained discussion at *Another Philosophy of History,* 40–42.

diminutive derived from *Vernunft*), which we have translated accordingly, for as Herder writes, "everyone *plays the game of reason* [*vernünftelt*] only according to his fancies."[10]

While the distinction between *Vernunft* and *Verstand* is lost in the English "reason," the line between the two is rarely drawn very clearly in German, either. *Vernunft* (derived from *vernehmen*, to hear) does tend to be reserved for loftier and more sweeping uses than *Verstand*. Turned ironic, it is the root for the unpleasant *vernünfteln* above, and it is introduced in the context of "dry and cold reason" at *Another Philosophy of History*, 15:23; but it is also the root of *vernünftig* (reasonable), which Herder uses without irony at *Do We Still Have a Fatherland?*, 49:20 ("an honest, reasonable religion is the foundation of thrones and states") and at *Governments as Inherited Regimes*, 366:16.[11] In his essay on the fatherland of the ancients (*Do We Still Have a Fatherland of the Ancients?*), Herder uses *Vernunft* to speak without qualification of the "course of reason" (330:6) and praises *Vernunft* in one breath with vigor and truth when discussing the German language (p. 337:12). In his essay on the origins of governments (*Governments as Inherited Regimes*), Herder acknowledges the potential of common, natural *Vernunft* and justice (363:29,35 and 367:24), and at *Another Philosophy of History*, 100:19 he proclaims that *Vernunft* (along with religion and virtue) "must inevitably *gain*, sooner or later, by the ridiculous attacks of [its] opponents!" Thus *Vernunft*, though often the rallying cry of the shallow, still remains a term of hope. *Verstand*, on the other hand (derived from *verstehen*, to comprehend), tends to be focused more on individual mental capacity, which is why we will be translating it as "(healthy) intelligence" at *Another Philosophy of History*, 44:9 ff. But Herder also warns of the "excessive homage" that *Verstand* invites just as well as *Vernunft* (*Another Philosophy of History*, 57:11 ff.), while on the other hand identifying it as similarly indispensable for the construction of "higher edifices" upon the basic foundations of a society (*Governments as Inherited Regimes*, 362: 24). In sum, we cannot discern any very clear divide between the two, and we have supplied the German terms whenever they come up.

One could deplore at great length the more general and familiar troubles of translating such German words as *Geist*,

10. Compare *Another Philosophy of History*, 16:2–3 and 22:23.

11. See below for full titles and citations.

Geschlecht, bürgerlich, Sitten, Recht, Kraft, Sinnlichkeit, or *Volk*—but such is the translator's lot. Suffice it to say that in rendering these troublesome terms, we have often found it necessary to use a variety of translations, depending on the context. Finally, the attentive reader may notice that we have at times rendered *Mensch* and *Menschheit* as "man" and "mankind" respectively. We do so without hesitation: *Mensch* may seem to incline less towards the male; but the hold of the masculine is not so easily escaped, for it is *der Mensch* in German just as well. Our "men" and permutations of "mankind" do most emphatically include women—as they have in fact done, ideological distortions notwithstanding, for as long as there have been rules governing the proper usage of these terms.

From a sufficiently pedantic point of view, then, it may appear that genuinely adequate translations are simply impossible, for no one could hope to preserve all of a text's shades of nuance, its unique texture and wealth of subtle associations. But Herder was no pedant, and it is too often overlooked that his reflections on what distinguishes and separates peoples were always accompanied by an abiding desire and tireless effort to "open doors" and make the treasures of one culture accessible to another. Herder sought, above all else, to *move* things along in a remarkably wide array of cultural and intellectual fields, as a tireless facilitator and mediator in the exchange of ideas. The highest compliment from Herder's own perspective may well be just the one paid to him by Benno von Wiese, who declared Herder "perhaps the single greatest inspirer and mover of minds in the history of German ideas." (That this may be overly effusive matters rather less than the orientation of the praise).

What is more, Herder was himself a noted translator who enthusiastically encouraged anyone acting on "the bold and philanthropic thought" of not only presenting an author *to* a new time or language, but also making him a resource *for* that time.[12] Proclaiming the need for quality translations, Herder denounced word-for-word translation as necessarily inadequate and instead envisioned "the translator as a 'creative genius' who could become

12. Suphan 16:592

the 'morning star' of a new epoch of German literature."[13] We may not want to go so far: but enthralled as many remain to the dream of strictly literal and simply reliable translation, it bears stressing that as far as we are concerned, there are no magic formulae in this art. As in politics, the translator always faces different choices—sometimes a number of good ones—and nothing can absolve him of the responsibility to decide between them, to take his stand, and to answer for his judgment. Much as we have struggled, then, to remain true to Herder at all times, this could not trump the demands of correct grammar and established idiom in the host language, or those of producing a reasonably engaging text. To replicate Herder's twists and turns in all their jarring authenticity, to bend the English to the breaking point in accommodating all his stylistic caprices, would be to do a bitter disservice to a man who indignantly refused, in wrestling with Shakespeare, for example, to "do violence to the German."[14] No one would agree more than Herder that a champion of free men does not deserve a slavish translator.

Any selection from the works of someone who has been misrepresented as unconscionably as Herder must invite suspicion. In facing the thankless task of making our choices from so rich an oeuvre, our primary consideration has been that of letting Herder's most immediately political writings speak for themselves while at the same time preserving a sense of the range of his thought. We have decided to give such prominence to Herder's *Another Philosophy of History* not only because it offers an especially concise, self-contained formulation of Herder's philosophy, but also because he appears to have identified himself with it particularly. Thus, in a letter to his publisher in early August 1773,[15] Herder announced the completion of his work with evident pride:

13. Among Herder's own translations, his passionate efforts at reproducing the unique tone of folk songs may be particularly noteworthy; but he also produced his own version of the *Song of Songs*, for example, and became, through his work on Shakespeare especially, "the godfather of some of the greatest translations ever achieved." Schlegel, whose celebrated translations of Shakespeare are still considered defining classics of German literature, gratefully and explicitly acknowledged Herder's preliminary labors. (Cf. Menze: 152, 153, 158, 161.)

14. Menze: 154.

15. *Briefe* 3:35.

"[The book] is finished, and what a fine one it is. I have called it *Another Philosophy of History, etc.*, but apart from the title, I am glad to say that it has nothing in common with Voltaire and Harder. This is truly *my* philosophy of history. . . . It is full of fire and burning coals [heaped] upon the heads of our age as I know it."

Turning to *Another Philosophy of History*, then, the reader may be struck and taken aback by the undeniable marks of careless writing and poor editing, by Herder's often peculiar syntax and his incomplete sentences, and especially by the egregious overuse of emphases and exclamations. We, too, have found these exasperating at best and at times indefensible. Herder had great difficulties, however, in getting his manuscript printed properly, and one should bear in mind that the greater grammatical richness of German makes it more forgiving of sloppy, affected, or otherwise unavailing writing. As for the emphases, Herder did not intend them to be quite as glaring as our italics make them appear: visually, the calmer effect of Hartknoch's or Suphan's pages (in which the emphases are spaced differently rather than italicized) is surely closer to what Herder had in mind. And third, what appear to be the most illogical emphases in the German text (at *Another Philosophy of History*, 64:34 and 89:32, for example) are in fact usually overlooked cases of one layer of emphasis canceling another.[16] We hope that the awkwardness and occasional tedium of Herder's faithfully preserved signature will prove helpful, at least, to those readers interested in tackling the German alongside.

Without wishing to dampen Herder's enthusiasm, we have taken the liberty of substituting the occasional full stop where Herder would otherwise be swamping entire pages in exclamations. Brackets in the text will identify words and phrases that we found necessary for clarification but that are either implied or often simply omitted in the German.

As the source for all our German texts, we have used the authoritative current edition of Herder's works published by Deutscher Klassiker Verlag (DKV) beginning in 1985. (The page numbers of the German texts as they appear in these volumes are identified

16. Compare *Another Philosophy of History*, 64:34: ". . . *individual beings who are to be* something *in the world*"

in the margins throughout our translations. For easier reference, we will also cite by line numbers; DKV pages have approximately 35 lines each. Herder's own footnotes will be distinguished by daggers.) On occasion, we will also refer to the classic Suphan edition of Herder's works, citing by volume and page number, as well as to Herder's collected letters in the Weimar edition. The German titles of our selections, their respective volumes and page numbers, and the abbreviations used in our own references to these works are as follows:

Another Philosophy of History for the Education of Mankind: "Auch eine Philosophie der Geschichte zur Bildung der Menschheit." In vol. 4, *Schriften zu Philosophie, Literatur, Kunst und Altertum: 1774–1787*, ed. Jürgen Brummack and Martin Bollacher (DKV 1994), 9–107. [Suphan 5: 475–593]

Of the Changes in the Tastes of the Nations through the Ages: "Von der Veränderung des Geschmacks der Nationen durch die Folge der Zeitalter (ein Fragment)." In vol. 1, *Frühe Schriften: 1764–1772*, ed. Ulrich Gaier (DKV 1985), p. 157, line 4–p. 160, line 19. [Not included in Suphan.]

Do We Still Have a Fatherland?: "Haben wir noch ein Vaterland?" In vol. 1, *Frühe Schriften: 1764–1772*, ed. Ulrich Gaier (DKV 1985), p. 48, line 11–p. 53, line 6. [Suphan 1: 21–26]

Do We Still Have the Fatherland of the Ancients?: "Haben wir noch das Vaterland der Alten?" In vol. 7, *Briefe zu Beförderung der Humanität*, ed. Hans Dietrich Irmscher (DKV 1991), p. 329 line 6–p. 338 line 5. [Suphan 27: 311–19]

On the Characters of Nations and Ages. In vol. 7, *Briefe zu Beförderung der Humanität*, ed. Hans Dietrich Irmscher (DKV 1991), p. 493, line 25–p. 495. [Suphan 28: 56–59]

Governments as Inherited Regimes: "Die Regierungen sind festgestellte Ordnungen unter den Menschen, meistens aus ererbter Tradition." In vol. 6, *Ideen zur Philosophie der Geschichte der Menschheit*, ed. Martin Bollacher (DKV 1989), p. 362 line 6–p. 372 line 3. [Suphan 13: 375–87]

The Influence of Free Legislation on the Sciences and Arts: "Vom Einfluß freier Gesetzgebungen auf Wissenschaften und Künste." In vol. 9/2, *Journal meiner Reise im Jahr 1769, Pädagogische Schriften*, ed. Rainer Wisbert with Klaus Pradel (DKV 1997), p. 307, line 14–p. 321, line 8. [Suphan 9: 324–37]

SUGGESTIONS FOR FURTHER READING

Herder's Works in English

The following editions include translations of entire works: *The Spirit of Hebrew Poetry*, trans. James Marsh (Burlington: E. Smith, 1833), which was reprinted in 1971 by Aleph Press; *God: Some Conversations*, trans. Frederick H. Burkhardt (New York: Veritas Press, 1940), reprinted in 1963 by Bobbs-Merrill; *Philosophical Writings*, ed. and trans. Michael N. Forster (Cambridge, U.K.: Cambridge University Press, 2002), which includes the "Essay on the Origin of Language" and "Another Philosophy of History"; *Sculpture: Some Observations on Shape and Form from Pygmalion's Creative Dream*, ed. and trans. Jason Gaiger (Chicago: The University of Chicago Press, 2002). The *Ideas* has been published as *Outlines of a Philosophy of the History of Man*, trans. T. Churchill (London: Luke Hansard for J. Johnson, 1800), reprinted in 1966 by Bergman Publishers.

Books 7, 12, 13, 14, 15, 17, 19, and 20 of the Churchill translation of the *Ideas* were published as *Reflections on the Philosophy of History of Mankind*, abridged and with an introduction by Frank E. Manuel (Chicago: The University of Chicago Press, 1968). Some parts of the *Ideas*, supplemented by excerpts from other works, are available in *Herder on Social and Political Culture*, ed. and trans. Frederick M. Barnard (Cambridge: Cambridge University Press, 1969), as well as in *On World History: An Anthology*, ed. Hans Adler and Ernest A. Menze (Armonk, New York: M. E. Sharpe, 1997). A large part of Herder's prize-winning *Essay on the Origin of Language* is available in *On the Origin of Language*, trans. John H. Moran and Alexander Gode (Chicago: The University of Chicago Press, 1986), which also includes Rousseau's essay on the same topic.

Introductions and Biographies

Rudolf Haym's *Herder: Nach seinem Leben und seinen Werken* ([1880, 1885] 2 vols., Berlin: Aufbau Verlag, 1958) is the most important intellectual biography of Herder, on which almost all subsequent accounts are based. In English, the most helpful equivalent is Robert Clark's *Herder: His Life and Thought* (Berkeley: University of California Press, 1955).

The most helpful general introduction to Herder is Wulf Koepke's *Johann Gottfried Herder* (Twayne's World Author Series: German Literature, Boston: Twayne Publishers, 1987). Also useful are Alexander Gillies' *Herder* (Oxford: Basil Blackwell, 1945), Günter Arnorld's *Johann Gottfried Herder* (Leipzig: VEB Bibliographisches Institut, 1988), and Hans Dietrich Irmscher's *Johann Gottfried Herder* (Stuttgart: Philipp Reclam, 2001).

Herder's Thought

The most influential discussion here is Isaiah Berlin's "Herder and the Enlightenment," which has been reissued recently in *Three Critics of the Enlightenment: Vico, Hamann, Herder*, ed. Henry Hardy (Princeton: Princeton University Press, 2000). On Herder's role in the development of historicism see Friedrich Meinecke's *Historism: The Rise of a New Historical Outlook*, trans. J. E. Anderson, with a foreword by Sir Isaiah Berlin (London: Routledge & Kegan Paul, 1972). On Herder's political thought see Frederick M. Barnard's *Herder's Social and Political Thought: From Enlightenment to Nationalism* (Oxford: The Clarendon Press, 1965), as well as his *Herder on Nationality, Humanity, and History* (Montreal: McGill-Queen's University Press, 2003), Robert Ergang's *Herder and the Foundations of German Nationalism* (New York: Columbia University Press, 1931), and the chapter on Herder in Frederick Beiser's *Enlightenment, Revolution, and Romanticism: The Genesis of Modern German Political Thought, 1790–1800* (Cambridge, Massachusetts: Harvard University Press, 1992). For an interesting discussion of the relationship between the progression of mankind and progress or perfectibility in Herder and beyond, see John Passmore's *The Perfectibility of Man*, 3rd ed. (Indianapolis: Liberty Fund, 2000). On Herder and Kant, see John H. Zammito's *Kant, Herder, and the Birth of Anthropology* (Chicago: The University of Chicago Press, 2002).

General Resources

Editions of Herder's works and secondary sources on Herder and his thought for the period 1977–1992 are listed in Doris Kuhles' *Herder Bibliographie 1977–1992* (Stuttgart: Verlag J. B. Metzler, 1994). Bibliographies for subsequent years, as well as recent studies on Herder, and other related announcements are available in the International Herder Society's *Herder Yearbook*.

BIBLIOGRAPHY

DKV   Herder, Johann Gottfried. *Werke in zehn Bänden*, 10 vols. in 11, ed. Günter Arnold et al. Frankfurt am Main: Deutscher Klassiker Verlag, 1985–2000.

Suphan   Herder, Johann Gottfried. *Herders sämmtliche Werke*, 33 vols., ed. Bernhard Suphan. Berlin: Weidmannsche Buchhandlung, 1877–1913.

Briefe   Herder, Johann Gottfried. *Briefe*, 11 vols., ed. Wilhelm Dobbek and Günter Arnold, under the supervision of Karl-Heinz Hahn. Weimar: Hermann Böhlaus Nachfolger for the Stiftung Weimarer Klassik, 1977–2001.

Erinnerungen   Herder, Maria Carolina von and Johann Georg Müller, eds. *Erinnerungen aus dem Leben Joh. Gottfrieds von Herder*, 2 vols. in 1. Stuttgart and Tübingen: J. G. Gotta, 1820.

EOL   Herder, Johann Gottfried. "Essay on the Origin of Language," in *On the Origin of Language*, ed. and trans. John H. Moran and Alexander Gode. Chicago: The University of Chicago Press, 1986.

D   Rousseau, Jean-Jacques. *The Discourses and Other Early Political Writings*, ed. and trans. Victor Gourevitch. Cambridge: Cambridge University Press, 1997.

OC   Rousseau, Jean-Jacques. *Œuvres complètes*, 5 vols., ed. Bernard Gagnebin and Marcel Raymond. Paris: Gallimard, 1959–1995.

SC   Rousseau, Jean-Jacques. *The Social Contract and Other Later Political Writings*, ed. and trans. Victor Gourevitch. Cambridge: Cambridge University Press, 1997.

Anderson, Benedict. *Imagined Communities: Reflections on the Origin and Spread of Nationalism*. London: Verso, 1983.

Arnold, Günter. *Johann Gottfried Herder*. Leipzig: VEB Bibliographisches Institut, 1988.

Barnard, Frederick M. *Herder on Nationality, Humanity, and History*. Montreal: McGill-Queen's University Press, 2003.

———. *Self-Direction and Political Legitimacy: Rousseau and Herder*. Oxford: The Clarendon Press, 1988.

———, ed. *Herder on Social and Political Culture*. Cambridge: Cambridge University Press, 1969.

———. *Herder's Social and Political Thought: From Enlightenment to Nationalism*. Oxford: The Clarendon Press, 1965.

Beiser, Frederick C. *Enlightenment, Revolution, and Romanticism: The Genesis of Modern German Political Thought, 1790–1800*. Cambridge, Massachusetts: Harvard University Press, 1992.

Bellmann, Werner. *Heinrich Heine, Deutschland Ein Wintermärchen*. Erläuterungen und Dokumente. Stuttgart: Philipp Reclam, 1980.

Berlin, Isaiah. *Against the Current: Essays in the History of Ideas*. New York: The Viking Press, 1980.

———. "Herder and the Enlightenment." In *Aspects of the Eighteenth Century*, ed. Earl R. Wasserman (Baltimore, Maryland: Johns Hopkins University Press, 1965), 47–104.

———. *The Proper Study of Mankind: An Anthology of Essays*, ed. Henry Hardy and Roger Hausheer. London: Chatto and Windus, 1997.

———. *The Roots of Romanticism*, ed. Henry Hardy. Princeton: Princeton University Press, 1999.

———. *Three Critics of the Enlightenment: Vico, Hamann, Herder*, ed. Henry Hardy. Princeton: Princeton University Press, 2000.

———. *Vico and Herder: Two Studies in the History of Ideas*. New York: Vintage Books, 1977.

Burke, Edmund. *Reflections on the Revolution in France*, ed. J. G. A. Pocock. Indianapolis: Hackett Publishing Company, 1987.

Clark, , Robert T., Jr. *Herder: His Life and Thought*. Berkeley: University of California Press, 1955.

Diderot, Denis, et. al. *Prospectus for "Encyclopédie, ou Dictionnaire raisonné des sciences, des arts et des métiers, etc."* 1751. Reprint, Paris: Imprimerie Nationale, 1950.

Dillenberger, John and Claude Welch. *Protestant Christianity Interpreted through Its Development*. New York: Charles Scribner's Sons, 1954.

Ergang, Robert Reinhold. *Herder and the Foundations of German Nationalism*. New York: Columbia University Press, 1931.

Fichte, Johann Gottlieb. *Addresses to the German Nation*, trans. R. F. Jones and G. H. Turnbull. Westport, Connecticut: Greenwood Press, 1979.

Gebhardt, Peter von and Hans Schauer. *Johann Gottfried Herder: seine Vorfahren und seine Nachkommen*. Leipzig: Zentralstelle für Deutsche Personen- und Familiengeschichte, 1930.

Gellner, Ernest. *Nations and Nationalism*. Ithaca: Cornell University Press, 1983.

Gillies, Alexander. *Herder*. Oxford: Basil Blackwell, 1945.

Goethe, Johann Wolfgang von. *The Autobiography of Johann Wolfgang von Goethe*, 2 vols., trans. John Oxenford, with an introduction by Karl J. Weintraub. Chicago: The University of Chicago Press, 1974.

Greenfeld, Liah. *Nationalism: Five Roads to Modernity*. Cambridge, Massachusetts: Harvard University Press, 1992.

Haym, Rudolf. *Herder: Nach seinem Leben und seinen Werken* [1880, 1885], 2 vols. Berlin: Aufbau Verlag, 1958.

Hegel, Georg Wilhelm Friedrich. *The Philosophy of History*, trans. J. Sibree, with an introduction by C. J. Friedrich. New York: Dover Publications, 1956.

Hobbes, Thomas. "To the Readers." In Thucydides, *The Peloponnesian War*, trans. Thomas Hobbes, ed. David Grene. Chicago: The University of Chicago Press, 1989.

Iggers, Georg G. *The German Conception of History: The National Tradition of Historical Thought from Herder to the Present*, revised ed. Middletown, Connecticut: Wesleyan University Press, 1983.

Irmscher, Hans Dietrich. *Johann Gottfried Herder*. Stuttgart: Philipp Reclam, 2001.

Kant, Immanuel. "Idea for a Universal History with a Cosmopolitan Intent." In *Perpetual Peace and Other Essays*, ed. Ted Humphrey. Indianapolis: Hackett Publishing Company, 1983.

Kedourie, Elie. *Nationalism*. London: Hutchinson, 1960.

Koepke, Wulf. "Herder als Deutscher? Zur Herder-Rezeption im 20. Jahrhundert vor 1933." In *Herder im "Dritten Reich*," ed. Jost Schneider. Bielefeld: Aisthesis Verlag, 1994: 127–43.

———. *Johann Gottfried Herder*. Twayne's World Author Series: German Literature. Boston: Twayne Publishers, 1987.

———. "Johann Gottfried Herder's Concept of 'Nation,'" in *Transactions of the Seventh International Congress on the Enlightenment*. Studies on Voltaire and the Eighteenth Century, 265. Oxford: The Alden Press for the Voltaire Foundation at the Taylor Institution, 1989: 1656–9.

Kohn, Hans. *The Idea of Nationalism: A Study in Its Origins and Background*. 1944. Reprint, New York: The Macmillan Company, 1967.

Kuhles, Doris. *Herder Bibliographie 1977–1992*. Stuttgart: Verlag J.B. Metzler, 1994.

Marx, Karl. "The German Ideology." In *The Marx-Engels Reader*, 2nd ed., ed. Robert C. Tucker. New York: W.W. Norton, 1978.

Meinecke, Friedrich. *Historism: The Rise of a New Historical Outlook*, trans. J. E. Anderson, with a foreword by Sir Isaiah Berlin. London: Routledge & Kegan Paul, 1972.

Menze, Ernest A. "On Herder as a Translator and on Translating Herder," in *Herder: Language, History, and the Enlightenment*, ed. Wulf Koepke. Columbia, South Carolina: Camden House, 1990.

Mill, John Stuart. *On Liberty and Other Essays*, ed. John Gray. New York: Oxford University Press, 1991.

Montesquieu, Charles-Louis de Secondat, Baron de La Brède et de. *The Spirit of the Laws*, ed. Anne Cohler et al. Cambridge: Cambridge University Press, 1989.

Nietzsche, Friedrich. *On the Advantage and Disadvantage of History for Life*, trans. Peter Preuss. Indianapolis: Hackett Publishing Company, 1980.

Otto, Regine. "Herder-Editionen 1933–1945." In *Herder im "Dritten Reich*," ed. Jost Schneider. Bielefeld: Aisthesis Verlag, 1994: 19–36.

Passmore, John. *The Perfectibility of Man*, 3rd ed. Indianapolis: Liberty Fund, 2000.

Plattner, Mark F. "Rousseau and the Origins of Nationalism." In *The Legacy of Rousseau*, ed. Clifford Orwin and Nathan Tarcov. Chicago: The University of Chicago Press, 1997: 183–99.

Popper, Karl R. *The Open Society and Its Enemies*. Princeton: Princeton University Press, 1950.

Shaftesbury, Anthony Ashley Cooper, Earl of. *Characteristicks of Men, Manners, Opinions, Times*, 3 vols. Indianapolis: Liberty Fund, 2001.

Stadelmann, Rudolf. *Der historische Sinn bei Herder*. Halle/Saale: Max Niemeyer Verlag, 1928.

Stiftung Weimarer Klassik. *Johann Gottfried Herder: Ahndung künftiger Bestimmung*. Stuttgart: Verlag J. B. Metzler, 1994.

Taylor, Charles. *Hegel*. Cambridge: Cambridge University Press, 1975.

Voltaire, François-Marie Arouet de. *The Philosophy of History*, with a preface by Thomas Kiernan. New York: Philosophical Library, 1965.

Weber, Max. "The Social Psychology of World Religions." In *From Max Weber: Essays in Sociology*, ed. H.H. Gerth and C. Wright Mills. New York: Oxford University Press, 1946: 267–301.

Wolff, Hans M. "Der junge Herder und die Entwicklungsidee Rousseaus." *PMLA* 57:3 (September 1942): 753–819.

Zammito, John H. *Kant, Herder, and the Birth of Anthropology*. Chicago: The University of Chicago Press, 2002.

Auch

eine Philosophie
der Geschichte

zur

Bildung der Menschheit.

Beytrag
zu vielen Beyträgen des Jahrhunderts.

Ταρασσει της ανθρωπης ε τα πραγματα, αλλα τα περι των

πραγματων δογματα ——

1774.

Title page of the first edition of Johann Gottfried Herder's *Auch eine Philosophie der Geschichte zur Bildung der Menschheit* (Riga: Hartknoch, 1774), reproduced by permission of the Houghton Library, Harvard University.

Another Philosophy of History for the Education of Mankind

One among Many Contributions of the Century (1774)

DKV *Werke*, vol. 4, pp. 9–107 (Cf. Suphan vol. 5, pp. 475–593)

> "It is not things but opinions about things that disturb men."
> —Epictetus, *Encheiridion*, chapter 5.1: 1–2

First Section

The more investigation brings to light[1] about the most ancient history of the world, its migrations, languages, customs, inventions, and traditions,[2] the more likely becomes, with every new discovery, *the single origin of the whole species*. One gets closer and closer to the *fortunate climate* where *one human couple* began spinning the thread—under the mildest influences of the *creating Providence*, with the *aid* of a most facilitating *fate* all around—that was later drawn so far and wide with such confusions; where, therefore, all original *coincidences*, too, can be taken for the provisions of a maternal Providence to develop a delicate double seed of the whole species, with all the deliberateness and caution of which we must always hold the creator of so noble a type, with his view of millennia and eternity, to be capable.

---

1. Or more literally, "the more [things] enlighten themselves" (*je weiter es sich aufklärt*): a mocking play on the powers of enlightenment.

†2. [As we know from the] latest historical inquiries and travels in Asia.

It is natural that these first developments were as simple, delicate, and *miraculous* as *anything* we see in the *creations of nature*. The seed falls into the ground and dies:[3] the embryo is formed* in concealment, as it would hardly be approved a priori from the philosopher's perspective, and emerges fully formed.* The history of the earliest developments of the human species, as described to us by the oldest book, might thus sound so *short* and *apocryphal* that we may be embarrassed to appear with it before the philosophical spirit of our age,[4] which despises nothing more than that which is *miraculous* or *concealed*. Precisely for this reason it is *true*. Let only one thing be noted: does not a *longer life*, a *nature calmer and more coherent in its effects*, in short, a *heroic period of the patriarchal age*, seem necessary—even from this illustrious age's mole's-eye perspective—in order for the progenitors of all descendants to imagine and be molded* for all time according to the first *forms of the human species*, whichever they may be? We are merely passing by now, through the world—shadows on earth! All the good and bad that we bring along (and we bring along little, because it is only here [on earth] that we receive anything), we are usually destined to take away with us again. Our years, biographies, idols, endeavors, impressions—the sum of our impact on earth is but the feeble dream of a watch in the night—*chatter! Let them pass away*, etc.[5] When we find such a *great store* of *developed powers* and *abilities* before us today, and such an *accelerated pace* in our *[vital] fluids* and *motions*, our *life-age*[6] and *thought-plans*; when one thing chases after another like one water bubble racing to destroy another; when *relations* are so often *unbalanced* between *power* and *prudence*, *competence* and *cleverness*, *disposition* and a *good heart*—all of which invariably characterizes an age of decay—then it seems a *deliberate* and *judicious wisdom* for the *great mass of childish forces* to be *moderated* and *secured* by a *short, feeble duration of the play of life*.

11/12

3. Compare John 12:24. (All references are to the King James Version of the Bible.)

4. Here as in the title, Herder uses *Jahrhundert* not in the strict sense of century but also in the sense of age or period, much as *siècle* is used in French.

5. A condensation of Psalm 90:4, 5, 9 in Luther's translation, the retranslation of which might read: "For a thousand years in your sight are like yesterday when it is past, or like a watch in the night. You let them pass away like a stream; they are like a dream. . . . Thus all our days pass away by your wrath; we spend our years like chatter."

6. *Lebensalter*, i.e., one of the phases in man's biological life, not a cultural stage.

*For our use of asterisks, please refer to A Note on Texts and Translation.

Likewise, was not that *first, quiet, eternal tree's and patriarch's life* necessary in order to *root* and *ground* humanity in its first inclinations, customs, and institutions?

What were these inclinations? What should they have been? The most natural, strongest, simple ones! The eternal foundation for the education* of mankind in all ages [has been]: *wisdom* instead of science, *piety* instead of wisdom, the love of *parents, spouses, children* instead of pleasantries and debauchery. *Life well-ordered, the rule by divine right of a dynasty*—the model for all civil order and its institutions—in all this mankind takes *the simplest,* but also the *most profound delight.* How should all this be developed and passed on, let alone brought forth[7] in the first place   *12/13* except through the *quiet, eternal power of example* and *a range of [concrete] examples* with their authority about them? By the measure of our own lives, every invention would have been lost a hundred times, springing forth and escaping as in a trance. Who among the immature should have received it? And who, relapsing too soon into immaturity, should have forced it upon others? Thus the first bonds of mankind were dissolved at the very outset. The thin, short threads of yore—how could they have ever become the strong bonds without which, even after millennia of formation,* the human species continues to be dissolved *through sheer weakness?* No! I shudder with joy as I stand before the holy cedar of an original progenitor of the world! Surrounding it are a hundred young, blooming trees already, a beautiful forest of posterity and perpetuation! But look, the old cedar[8] continues to bloom, and its expansive roots are sustaining the whole young forest with their sap and their strength. Wherever the first progenitor may have *gotten* his knowledge, inclinations, and customs *from,* whatever they may be and however paltry—all around him, *a world of present and future generations* has already been formed* and fixed, in accordance with these inclinations and customs, by nothing more than the *quiet, forceful, eternal contemplation of his divine example!* Two millennia were only two generations.

Meanwhile, even apart from these heroic beginnings of the human species' formation,* going by the mere *ruins of world history*

---

7. *erbildet, angebildet, fortgebildet.*

8. Compare Ps. 92:12, 14.

and by the hastiest reasoning[9] about it à la Voltaire: what *conditions* could be imagined to lure, to form* and fix *the first affections of the human heart* than those that we actually find already to have been applied in the *traditions of our most ancient history?* The *shepherd's life in the world's fairest climate,* where an obliging nature anticipates or helps to meet all basic needs; *the calm yet nomadic way of life of the fatherly patriarch's hut* with everything that it yields and withholds from the eye; the *range of human needs, activities, and pleasures at the time,* together with everything that *guided* these *activities* and *pleasures* according to myth or history—imagine all this in its natural, living light! What a choice *Garden of God* for the raising of the first, most delicate *human crop!* Behold this man full of *strength* and the *feeling of God,* whose feelings run as *deeply* and *calmly* as the sap in this tree here, or the instinct that is distributed in a thousand ways among the creatures there, running through each of them as forcefully as such a concentrated, quiet, healthy drive of nature possibly could! The whole surrounding world full of God's blessing: one big, brave family. Every day, the father of us all[10] faced this world, bound to it with his needs and desires, striving against it with his labor, caution, and a gentle protection. Under such a sky, in this element of vital energy, *what kinds of ideas, what a heart was he bound to form!** Great and cheerful, altogether quiet and brave like nature itself! A *long life, delight in himself* in the most indivisible way, *distinction of days* by *rest and exhaustion, learning and retaining*—behold, that was the patriarch *by himself,* alone. But *by himself, alone?* [When] the blessing of God that ran through all of nature was nowhere deeper than in the *image of mankind as it felt its way forth*** and *was formed** accordingly?* In the *wife* created *for him;* in the *son* [begotten] in *his own likeness,* after his image;[11] in the *race of gods* that would fill[12] the earth around and after him—[in all this] God's blessing was then [*the patriarch's own*] blessing; *his* those whom he ruled; *his* those whom he raised; *his* all the children and

9. Here and elsewhere, Herder writes *Raisonnement* for reasoning (*raisonnieren* for "to reason," *raisonneur* for "reasoner," etc.), often, but not always, to mock certain intellectual fashions and their French origins.

10. *Allvater.* Often a word for God (compare p. 82:6), especially in the context of Nordic mythology (compare p. 84:6). But here Herder is using the term, more literally, for the first progenitor of mankind. We are marking the distinction by translating "father of *us* all" here but "father of all" elsewhere.

11. Compare Gen. 5:3.

12. Compare Gen. 1:28, 9:1.

grandchildren surrounding him, unto the *third and fourth genera-tion*,[13] all of whom he led with religion and justice, order and hap-piness. Such was the unforced ideal of the *patriarch's world* toward which everything in nature tended: no purpose of life beside him, no thought of a moment's comfort or exertion—God, what a con-dition for the formation* of nature according to the simplest, most necessary, most pleasant inclinations!

Human being, man, woman, father, mother, son, heir, priest of god, ruler and master of the house—to be formed* for all millennia! Aside from the Thousand-Year Reign[14] and the fantasies of the poets, the *realm* and *tent of the patriarch* will forever remain *the golden age of mankind in its infancy.*   14/15

Induction will easily demonstrate that this world of inclinations contained *conditions* that we often *imagine*, by one of our age's deceits, to have been far *stranger and more terrible* than they actu-ally were. We have construed for ourselves an *Oriental Despotism* by singling out the most extreme and violent occurrences from what are usually decaying empires, which resort to it only in their final throes and thus reveal their very fear of death! And as, in our European terms (and perhaps emotions), one cannot speak of anything more terrible than despotism, so we console our-selves by alienating it from itself and *putting it in a context* where it could *not* have been *the terrible thing* that we dream up *on account of our own condition.*[15] It may be that in the patriarch's tent *esteem, example, authority* alone ruled and that, as the artificial language of our politics would have it, *fear* was the driving force of this regime.[16] O man, do not allow yourself to be deceived by the *words of the expert philosopher,*[17] but look first what kind of

13. Compare Exod. 20:5, 34:7.

14. Compare Rev. 20:4.

†15. Boulanger, *Inquiries into the Origin of Oriental Despotism;* Voltaire, *The Phi-losophy of History, Treatise on Tolerance*, etc.; Helvétius, *On the Mind*, 3rd discourse, etc., etc.

16. Compare Montesquieu, *The Spirit of the Laws*, I, iii.

†17. Montesquieu's hoards of followers and imitators, slavish herd. [Compare Horace, *Epistulae* I, 19, 19, also cited by Shaftesbury, in *Characteristicks of Men, Manners, Opinions, Times* III: "Miscellaneous Reflections" II, ii [95]. Herder cites this work below, on p. 22.]

esteem, what kind of *fear* is at issue here. Is there not in every human life an age when we learn nothing by dry and cold reason,[18] but everything by *inclination* and *formation,** by authority? When we have neither ear, nor sense, nor soul for pondering and reasoning about the good, the true and beautiful, but *everything* for the so-called *prejudices* and *impressions of education?* Behold how *powerful*, how *profound*, how *useful* and *timeless* these so-called prejudices are if only we conceive them without mnemonic devices[19] and without demonstrations of natural law! The *cornerstones* of everything that is to be built upon them later, or rather already fully-formed *seeds* out of which everything subsequent and weaker *develops*, be it given as glorious a name as it may (for everyone plays the game of reason[20] only according to his fancies): [they are] the strongest, eternal, almost divine *traits* that either fill our whole life with *bliss* or else *ruin* it; when they desert us, we are left utterly forsaken. And behold, what is indispensable for every *individual human being in his infancy* must surely be no less so for the *whole human species in its infancy*. What, in its most delicate seed, you call *despotism*, and what was really merely the *paternal authority* to rule over house and hut—look what things it accomplished that you, with all your *cold philosophy of the age*, would surely have to leave undone today! How, without demonstrating anything, it *forged into eternal forms* that which was *right* and *good*, or was *deemed* to be such at least; how together with the splendor *of the deity and love of the father*, and with the sweet *husk*[21] *of early habituation* and *all that was lively in the childlike ideas* of *[the patriarch's] world*, together with all the *first delights of mankind*, one memory was conjured up that was like nothing, nothing else in the world. How necessary! How good! How useful to the entire species! There *foundations* were laid that could not have been laid in any other way—or not so easily and deeply. Yet *lie* they do! Centuries have *built* upon them, the storms of the ages have *flooded* them like the base of the pyramids with seas of sand, without *being able to rock* them. [There] they lie yet! And happily so, as *everything rests upon them.*

18. *Vernunft*. On the distinction between *Vernunft* and *Verstand*, see A Note on the Texts and the Translation.

19. Lit.: "without *barbara celarent*," a mnemonic device used in teaching logic.

20. *vernünfteln*, a mocking diminutive of "reasoning."

21. *Schlaube*. This will be a recurring theme: at its most elementary, the surface (or husk) of a matter as opposed to the inner meaning (or kernel).

Orient, you ground of God chosen just for this![22] The *delicate
sensitivity* of these regions, with the quick, soaring imagination
that so readily clothes everything in divine splendor; *reverence* for
everything that is might, esteem, wisdom, strength, God's foot-
step, and right along with this, a childlike *submission* that is combined—naturally for [the Orientals], incomprehensibly for us
Europeans—with the feeling of reverence; the defenseless, scattered, tranquility-loving, *herd-like condition* of the shepherd's life
that *wants to live itself out* gently and without exertion on a plain
of God. Of course all of this, *aided* more or less *by circumstances*,
later also provided ample support for the *despotism of the conquer-   16/17
ors*—such ample support that perhaps there will always be despotism in the Orient, and that no despotism has ever been
overthrown in the Orient by *foreign, external* forces. With *nothing
standing opposed to it*, and *expanding without measure*, [despotism]
could only *fall apart under its own weight*. Certainly, this despotism
also often produced the most terrible effects; the most terrible of
all, as the philosopher will say, being that *no Oriental*, as such, can
yet have any deep concept *of a humane, better constitution*. But
granting and leaving aside what came later, was it not, in the
beginning, precisely the Oriental with his *delicate child's sense* who,
under the *gentle government of the father*, was the *happiest* and *most
obedient pupil*? Everything was tasted [first] as mother's milk and
father's wine! Everything was stored in children's hearts and
sealed there with the stamp of *divine authority!* The human spirit
received the first forms of wisdom and virtue with a *simplicity*,
strength, and *majesty* that—to put it bluntly—has no equal, no
equal at all in our philosophical, cold, European world. And just
because we are so incapable of *understanding* this anymore, of *feeling* it, let alone *taking delight* in it—we *mock*, we *deny*, and we *mis-
construe!* The best proof!

No doubt this is also where *religion* belongs, or rather, *religion*
was "the *element* within which *all of this lived and moved*." Even disregarding all *divine impression* in the *creation* and earliest *care* for
the human species (as necessary to the *whole* as the care of parents
is to every *single* child after his birth); disregarding, too, how naturally an elder, father, king took his place as *God's representative*

---

22. Herder's *Morgenland* refers to the East (Orient), where the sun rises in the
morning. The same logic makes the West (Occident) the land of the evening. The
Morgenland is also where mankind spent its "childhood," the morning of the species. Compare p. 85:14.

and how, just as naturally, *obedience to the paternal will, clinging* to *old habits*, and *reverent submission* to the *nod of superiors*, distinguished by the memory of ancient times,[23] was combined with a kind of *childlike religious feeling*—did it really have to be none but *swindlers* and *scoundrels*, as we are so sure to imagine according to the spirit and the sentiment of our time,[24] who *imposed* and, in their rage, *abused* these kinds of ideas, having guilefully *fabricated* them? It may be that this kind of religious feeling, as an element of our actions, would be utterly disgraceful and pernicious for *our philosophical part of the world*, for our educated* time, for *our* free-thinking constitution, both internally and externally (what is more, alas, I think that this constitution is *entirely impossible* for our part of the world!); let it be granted that the messengers of God, if they were to appear now, would [indeed] be swindlers and scoundrels: [but] do you not see that things are entirely different with the spirit of that other time, with that land and that level of the human species? Naturally, the most ancient philosophy and forms of government in all countries would originally have had to be *theology!* A man *marvels* at everything before he *sees:* only through *astonishment* does he arrive at the *luminous idea* of the true and the beautiful, only by *submission* and *obedience* at the first possession of the good—and it is surely just so with the *human species.* Have you ever taught a child a language by the *philosopher's grammar* or taught him to walk by some abstract *theory of motion?* Was it ever necessary to explain a duty, whether the easiest or hardest, to him by a *demonstration* of *moral philosophy?* Was it permissible, or even possible? Thank God for the fact that it is *not permissible* or *possible!* This delicate nature lacks *knowledge* and is therefore eager for everything; *gullible*, and thus *receptive* to all *impressions; trusting-obedient*, and thus inclined to be led towards everything good—grasping everything with imagination, amazement, admiration, but precisely thus also *acquiring* everything *all the more firmly* and *wonderfully.* "*Faith, love*, and *hope*[25] in his delicate heart are the only seeds of *understanding, inclination*, and *happiness*"— Are you rebuking God's Creation? Or can you not see in every one of your so-called faults *a vehicle, a singular vehicle for all that is*

†23. Montesquieu, *Spirit of the Laws*, books 24–25. [Literally, Herder does not distinguish ancient, medieval, and modern times—as we shall, in order to avoid confusion—but between the old(er), middle, and new(er) ages.]

†24. Voltaire, *Philosophy of History*, Helvétius, Boulanger, etc.

25. 1 Cor. 13:13; compare p. 107.

good? How foolish [it would be] for you to tarnish this ignorance and admiration, this imagination and reverence, this enthusiasm and child-sense with the *blackest devilry of your age*, with *fraud* and *stupidity, superstition* and *slavery*—to fabricate for yourself an army of *priest-devils* and *tyrant-ghosts* that exist only in your soul! A thousand times more foolish [still] for you magnanimously to bestow upon a child your *philosophical deism*, your *aesthetic virtue* and *honor*, your *universal love of all peoples*[26] full of tolerant *subjugation, blood-sucking*, and *enlightenment* according to the high taste of your time! Upon a *child?* O, it is you who is the worst, most foolish child! You would rob [a child] of his *better* inclinations, of the *bliss* and *foundations* of his nature; you would turn him—if your absurd plan were to succeed—into the most monstrous thing in the world: into an *old man of three years*.

18/19

Our age has used *aqua fortis*[27] to etch the name "Philosophy!" on its forehead, and this seems to be having its effect deep inside the skull. So I have had to respond to *this* sidelong *philosophical critique of the most ancient times*—with which, as is well known, all *philosophies of history* and *histories of philosophy* are brimming today—with a sidelong glance of my own, albeit a reluctant and disgusted one, and without feeling obliged to concern myself with the *consequences of one* or *the other*. Go ahead, my reader, and feel, even now, the *pure Oriental nature* that has been preserved for so long behind the millennia; revive it for yourself by [studying] the *history of the most ancient times*, and you will "encounter *inclinations* that could only have been formed* and set *upon the human species* in *that land*, in *that* manner, for the *great purposes* of *Providence*." What a painting, if only I could present it to you *as it* was!

Providence carried along the thread of development—from the *Euphrates, Oxus*, and *Ganges* down *to the Nile* and on toward the *Phoenician coasts*—great strides!

26. In the "Geneva Manuscript," Rousseau writes of "supposed cosmopolites," who "boast of loving everyone in order to have the right to love no one" (*OC* 3:287). Compare *Émile* I: "Distrust those cosmopolites who search far and wide in their books to discover duties they disdain to fulfill around them. Such a *philosophe* loves the Tartars so as to be spared the trouble of having to love his neighbors" (*OC* 4:249).

27. *Scheidewasser*, nitric acid used by engravers to etch copper plates.

It is seldom without reverence that I leave behind ancient Egypt and the consideration of what it had become *in the history of the human species!* The land where part of the *boyhood* of mankind was formed* in its inclinations and knowledge, just as its childhood was in the Orient! The metamorphosis here was as easy and inconspicuous as the genesis had been there.

Egypt was without *pastures or shepherd's life:* the patriarchal spirit of the first hut was therefore lost. Yet, *formed* out of the mud of the Nile* and *fertilized* by it, there was, almost as readily, the most superb *agriculture*. Thus the shepherd's world with its customs, inclinations, and knowledge became a province of *farmers*. The nomadic life came to an end; fixed abodes, *property in land* came about. Lands had to be parceled out, each to be given his own, each protected in that which was his. [Now] everyone could be found where he had his property—thus *public security, the administration of justice, order, law enforcement* came into being, which would never have been possible in the Orient's nomadic condition. There was a *new world*. Now arose an *industry* such as had been unknown to the happy, idle hut-dweller, the pilgrim and stranger on earth. *Arts* were invented for which the former neither had use nor desired to have use for them. Given the Egyptian spirit of *precision* and *agricultural diligence*, these arts could not but attain a high degree of *mechanical perfection*. The sense of *strict diligence*, of *security and order*, pervaded everything. Everyone was *familiar with the law*, bound to it with need and pleasure. Thus *man was placed under the bondage of the law:* the inclinations that had once been merely paternal, child-like, shepherd-like, patriarchal now became *civil, village-like, city-like*. The child had outgrown his dresses and ribbons:[28] the boy now sat on the school bench[29] and learned *order, diligence, customs of civility*.[30]

An exact comparison of the Oriental and the Egyptian spirit should show that my analogy with the life-ages of man is no mere child's play. Clearly, everything the two ages had in common was deprived of its *heavenly tint* and tainted with *soil* and *fertilizer*. Egypt's *insights* were no longer *paternal oracles of the deity*, but already *laws, political rules of security;* and what remained of the

28. *Flügelkleid*, a dress for children that has wide sleeves ("wings") or ribbons.

29. Compare Rousseau, *Discourse on the Sciences and the Arts* I: "Consider Egypt, that first school of the Universe" (D 9; *OC* 3:10).

30. *Bürgersitten*.

former was merely a *holy image*[31] painted on the blackboard so
that it would not perish, so that boys should stand before it, ponder, and learn wisdom. Egypt's *inclinations* were no longer as delicate and child-like as those of the Orient: the sense of family
weakened and became instead *concern* for the same, *social rank,
artistic talent*[32] that was handed down, *along with one's station,* like a
house or field. The idle tent ruled by the man had become a *hut of
labor,* wherein the woman, too, was *now* a *person,* wherein the
patriarch now sat *as an artist,*[33] *eking out a living.* God's open pastures were filled with herds, *the fields with villages and cities:* the
child that ate milk and honey became a boy who *was rewarded with
cake* for his duties. A new kind of virtue—which we might call
Egyptian diligence, civil loyalty, but which was not an Oriental sentiment—weaved throughout everything. How distasteful, even
now, are *agriculture, city life,* the *slavery* of the *artisan's shop* to the
Oriental! How few are the beginnings he has made in all this even
after millennia: he lives and roams as a free animal of the field. To
the Egyptian, on the other hand, how loathsome and repulsive
was the shepherd and all that clung to him! Likewise, when the
more refined Greek later elevated himself above the Egyptian *and
his vices,* this meant nothing more than when a boy is repulsed by
an infant in his diapers, or when a youth loathes the boy's school-
prison. Yet, in sum, all three belong *together, following one upon the
other.* The Egyptian would not have been *Egyptian* without his
Oriental childhood instruction, the Greek no *Greek* without his
Egyptian schoolboy's diligence—their very loathing demonstrates
*development, progression,*** steps on the ladder!*

They are astonishing, the easier ways of Providence: she, who
lured and educated the child with religion, brought up the boy
through nothing but *needs* and the *dear duty of school.* Egypt *had no
pastures*—thus its inhabitants *surely* had to *learn* agriculture. How
much easier she made this hard learning by the *fertilizing Nile!*
Egypt had *no wood:* one had to learn to build with stone. There
were *plenty of quarries,* and the *Nile* made it *convenient* to carry the
stones away. How high was the art raised! How much [Provi-
dence] developed other arts! *The Nile burst its banks:* one needed
land surveys, drains, dams, canals, cities, villages—how many were

21/22

31. A literal German translation of *hiero-glyph.*

32. I.e., the skills of an artisan or craftsman, not strictly those of an artist as we
might commonly understand the term.

33. Or an artisan.

the ways in which one was *attached* to the *earth!* Yet how varied are
the institutions developed on this *earth!* On a map, [the earth]
appears to me as nothing but a *board full of images,*[34] where everyone has found [his own] meaning: *each country* and its *products* so
original, each its own *human species!* The human mind has learnt
much [in the world], and perhaps there is no region on earth
where this learning was so evidently *culture of the soil* as here; even
China reflects its example—one must judge and guess.

Here, again, it would be foolishness to tear a *single Egyptian
virtue* away from the land, the time, and the boyhood of the
human spirit and to measure it by the *standard of another time!* If,
as it has been shown, the Greek could be so very wrong about the
Egyptian, and the Oriental could loathe the Egyptian, then I
reckon that it should be our first concern to see him in none but
his own place—or else we would see, from the European perspective especially, [his face distorted into] the most hideous grimace.
This development took its course from the Orient and childhood, so it is natural that *religion, fear, authority, despotism* had to
be the *vehicles of education:** for even with a boy of seven one cannot *play the game of reason* as with a grown or an old man. It is
likewise natural that this vehicle of education,* for our taste a
tough husk [to chew on], would often have caused *the kinds of troubles* and so many of the *diseases* that are called *boy-quarrels* and
canton-wars.[35] Pour out as much gall as you like over Egyptian
superstition and *clericalism*[36]—like that kindly Plato Europens,[37]
for example, who is only too eager to model everything after the
Greek original. All quite true, all quite well, if Egyptianism were
meant *for your country* and *your time!* Of course the boy's coat is
too short for the giant, and the youth with his bride by his side
finds the school-prison distasteful! But look, your gown is, in
turn, too long for the next person! Can you not see, if you are at
all familiar with the Egyptian spirit, how your *bourgeois cleverness,
philosophical deism, easy frivolousness, cosmopolitanism, tolerance,
pleasantries, law of peoples,* and whatever other names you give to

22/23

34. I.e., full of hieroglyphs (compare p. 21:1–3).

35. I.e., conflicts between close neighbors or, more specifically, between such
minor subdivisions of countries as the Swiss cantons.

36. *Pfaffentum,* a derogatory term that does not have a proper English coun-
terpart; somewhat less negative than *Pfäfferei,* which Herder uses in his fifteenth
Letter towards the Advancement of Humanity, for example (DKV 7:86:15).

†37. Shaftesbury, *Characteristicks of Men, Manners, Opinions, Times* III, "Miscellaneous Reflections."

this stuff, would, once again, have made a miserable old man of the boy? He needed to be confined; a certain privation of knowledge, inclinations, and virtues was necessary in order to develop what was in him and what, in the sequence of world events, could then only be developed in *that country, that place!* Thus these disadvantages were [in fact] *advantages* for him, or [at least] *unavoidable ills*, like the cultivation with foreign ideas for the child, or quarreling and school-discipline for the boy. Why would you want to pull him away from his place, from his proper life-age—why kill the poor boy? How vast is the library of such books!

Some of the time, the Egyptians are made *too old*, and there is no limit to the *wisdom* that is garnered from their hieroglyphs, the beginnings of their art, their administrative constitution![38] Other times, they are thoroughly despised in comparison with the Greeks[39]—just because they were Egyptians and not Greeks, just as the admirers of the Greeks were themselves often despised when they returned from their favorite country. What an evident injustice!

The best historian of the art of antiquity, *Winckelmann*, clearly judged the Egyptians' artworks solely according to Greek standards, doing very well as far as *condemnation* was concerned, but describing so little of their *own nature and kind* that a blatantly one-sided and cross-eyed quality comes to light in almost every one of his sentences in this major treatment. The same goes for *Webb*, when he contrasts their *literature* with *that of the Greeks*, and for so many others who wrote about the *customs and form of government of the Egyptians* in the European spirit, no less. As it is usually the Egyptians' lot to be approached from Greece, and thus with an exclusively Greek eye, how could they fare any worse? My dear Greek: the purpose of these statues could hardly have less in common (as you might have been able to discern from everything) with the models of fine art *according to your ideal*—so full of allure, action, movement, of which the Egyptian knew nothing, or which his very purposes cut off for him! They were meant to be *mummies! Memorials to deceased parents* or *ancestors*, accurate in every *facial expression or dimension*, following hundreds of *determinate rules* by which the boy was bound—thus naturally

23/24

†38. Kircher, d'Origny, Blackwell, etc.

†39. Wood, Webb, Winckelmann, Newton, Voltaire: sometimes they do the one, sometimes the other, depending on place and time. [Herder is referring to Newton's *The Chronology of Ancient Kingdoms Amended* (1728).]

without allure, without action, without movement, *thus in this sepulchral position* with their hands and feet full of stillness and death. Eternal marble mummies—behold, that is what they were meant to be, *and what they are in fact*, on account of the *utterly mechanical quality* of their art, by the *ideal of their intention!* There your pretty dream of censure is lost! When you enlarge the boy into a giant by a tenfold magnifying glass and turn your light on him, you cannot *clarify*[40] anything about him anymore. All the *boyishness* is gone, and yet he is anything but a giant!

Closely related as the *Phoenicians* were to the Egyptians, they became almost their *opposites by education;** the latter, in later times at least, *haters of the sea* and of *foreigners*, concerned only with developing domestically "*all contrivances and arts of their country*," the former retreating beyond the mountains and the deserts to the coast in order to found a new *world on the sea*. And on what sea? On an *island-sound*, a *gulf between lands*, which seemed to have been designed, with its coasts, islands, and peninsulas, precisely to facilitate a nation's *travel by water and exploration*. How famed you are, Mediterranean archipelago, in the history of the human spirit! *The first commercial state, founded entirely on trade*, which expanded the world *beyond Asia*[41] for the first time, *planting peoples* and *binding them together*—what a great *new step* for *development!* Now of course the Oriental shepherd's life had to become well-nigh *incomparable* to this emerging state. Life's family-feeling, religion, and quiet delight in the land faded: the *form of government* took a giant stride towards *republican freedom*, of which neither the Oriental nor the Egyptian had any proper idea. A trading coast had soon to give rise, against all knowledge and intention, as it were, to *aristocracies* of cities, houses,[42] and families—all in all, what a change *in the form of human society!* As the hatred of foreigners and imperviousness towards other peoples faded—even if the Phoenician did *not* visit other nations *out of a love of mankind*—a kind of *friendship among peoples, understanding between peoples, and law of peoples* emerged, such as would quite naturally have been inconceivable to a land-

24/25

---

40. *erklären*, which shares a common root with *aufklären*, to enlighten.

41. I.e., Asia Minor.

42. I.e., extended families, clans, or lineages.

locked tribe or some little Colchian people.[43] The *world* became wider, the *human races*, more *connected* and *closer*. Along with commerce, a host of arts were developed and, more particularly, an entirely new *artistic drive* towards *advantage, comfort, abundance,*[44] and *magnificence!* Suddenly the diligence of men descended from the heavy *industry of the pyramids* and the *diligence of the plow* to a *"charming little game of smaller activities."* From useless, *simple obelisks*, architecture turned to *complex ships*, every bit *useful*. The silent, resting pyramid became the *moving, talking mast*. After the Egyptians' sculptures and their big and intimidating works, one began to play so advantageously with *glass*, with pieces of decorated *metal, purple fabric*, and *canvas*, with Lebanese *utensils, jewelry, pottery, ornamentations;* one played it right into the hands of foreign nations—what a different world of *activity*, of *purpose, benefit, inclination, application of the soul!* Naturally, the heavy, mysterious hieroglyphs now had to turn into "a *light, abbreviated, serviceable arithmetic* and *alphabet*. Now the ship- and coast-dweller, the expatriated *roamer across seas* and *amidst peoples*, had to appear an entirely different creature to the tent- and hut-dweller. The Oriental must have needed to accuse him of weakening *that which is human*, the Egyptian, of *weakening patriotism;* the one, that he had abandoned *love* and *life*, the other, that he had *forsaken loyalty and diligence;* the one, that he knew nothing of the *holy sentiment of religion*, the other, that he had *put on display* in his marketplaces the *secrets of science*, if only in scraps." All true. It is only that something very different developed at the same time (though something that I am by no means willing to *compare* with the former, since I do not wish to *compare* anything at all!): *Phoenician liveliness* and intelligence, a new kind of *comfort* and *commodious living*, the transition to Greek *taste*, and a kind of *study of peoples*,[45] the transition to Greek *freedom*. Despite all the contrasts in their ways of thinking, then, the

25/26

43. Colchis, on the eastern coast of the Black Sea, is surrounded by the mountains of the Caucasus.

44. Abundance or material plenty (*Üppigkeit*) is sometimes used neutrally by Herder, but more often with a decidedly negative slant. At p. 52:37, for example, he warns that abundance "can never be the happiness and destiny of all men"; at p. 66:30 he envisions a man made sick by it; and at p. 81:25 he suggests that it is as wearying as indolence. Where Herder's indictment of *Üppigkeit* is strongest, for example at pp. 44:7, 60:18, 71:6–7, 74:24–25, and *Governments as Inherited Regimes* 366:4 ff., we will also be translating it as luxury, opulence, or excess.

45. *Völkerkunde*.

Egyptians and *Phoenicians* were *twins* of the same Oriental mother, who together, later, educated* *Greece* and thereby *the world*. They were therefore both *instruments of transmission*** in the hands of destiny, and if I may stick to the allegory, the Phoenician was the more adult *boy*, who *ran about* and peddled the remains of ancient wisdom and ingenuity *for a quick coin* in *the markets and the streets*. How much the education* of Europe owes to the swindling, avaricious Phoenician! And now on to the beautiful Greek *youth*.

It is above all the *time of our youth* that we remember with pleasure and joy: when our powers and limbs were formed* for the *bloom of life;* when our capacities were developed for the most agreeable *chatter* and *friendship;* when all our inclinations were first attuned to *freedom* and *love, pleasure* and *joy,* all sounding their sweet notes for the first time then. We consider these years *the golden age* and an *Elysium of our memory* (for who remembers his own undeveloped childhood?), years that *strike the eye* most brilliantly and that—just as the *blossom* first *breaks open—bear within their bosom* all our future efforts and hopes. Just so, in the history of mankind, *Greece* will always be the place where she[46] lived during *the most beautiful* part of her *youth* and her *bridal bloom*. The boy has outgrown the hut and school and stands before us: a noble *youth* with beautiful, anointed *limbs, the favorite of all the Graces* and *the lover of all the Muses, champion at Olympia* and in all other games, *spirit and body* united in *one blossoming bloom!*

26/27   The *oracles of childhood* and the *teaching-models of the toilsome school* had now almost been forgotten; but out of them the youth developed for himself everything he needed along the way to *youth-wisdom* and *virtue,* of *song* and *joy, pleasure* and *life*. He despised the *crude arts of labor* as much as [all] merely barbarian magnificence or the excessively simple *life of the shepherd;* but above all, he brought about the *blossoming* of *a new, beautiful nature*. Through him, *craftsmanship* became *fine art,* agricultural servitude [became] the free *professional association of citizens,* the strict Egyptian's heavy fullness of meaning became *light, beautiful Greek dalliance* of every kind. What a new, *beautiful* class of *inclinations* and *abilities* appeared now, such as had been unknown to the earlier age

46. Mankind.

that provided its germ. Must not the *form of government* have made a swinging descent from the Oriental *despotism of the father* to the Egyptian *landed estates* and the Phoenician semi-*aristocracies*, until *the beautiful idea of a republic in the Greek sense*—"obedience coupled with freedom and wrapped in the name *fatherland*"—could have emerged?[47] The blossom broke forth by the name of *"Greek liberty"*: exquisite phenomenon of nature! *Customs*, from the sense of the Oriental *father* and the Egyptian *day laborer*, must have been tempered by the Phoenician *travel-intelligence*. And behold, the new, beautiful blossom broke forth [as] *"Greek lightness, mildness, and patriotism."* Love had to dissolve the harem's veil in several stages before becoming the *beautiful play* of the Greek *Venus*, of *Amor* and the *Graces*.[48] Thus [also] *mythology, poetry, philosophy, fine arts:* developments out of ancient seeds whose *season and place* had come to *blossom* and to disseminate their *fragrance* throughout the world. Greece became the cradle of *humaneness*, of *friendship between peoples*, of *fine legislation*, of all that is *most agreeable*, in *religion, customs, prose, poetry, common practices*, and *arts*. All this: the *joy of youth*, grace, play and love!

It has been shown, for the most part, what the circumstances were that contributed to this singular achievement of the human species, and I shall merely place these circumstances *within the wider context of the general combination of ages and peoples.* Behold this lovely Greek *climate* and, within it, this *well-formed* human species* with its free brow and refined senses—a real *crossroads* of *culture*, where everything flowed together *from two ends* and was so easily and nobly transformed! The beautiful bride[49] was served by two boys, one on the left and one on the right; all she did was to *create a beautiful ideal. Precisely the blend* of the Phoenician and the Egyptian *ways of thinking*, the one purging the other of its national narrowness[50] and idiosyncrasy, formed the Greek head for the *ideal*, for *freedom*. Then [there were] the *strange occasions* of their *division* and *unification* from the earliest of times onward, their *separation* into peoples, *republics, colonies;* and yet their *spirit of community* [persisted], *the feeling of one nation, one fatherland, one language!* [There were] the particular *opportunities* for forming*

27/28

47. Compare Rousseau, *Discourse on the Sciences and the Arts* II (D: 21–3; *OC* 3:8).
48. I.e., Aphrodite, Eros, and the Charites.
49. Greece.
50. The narrowness is only implied here, but it is made explicit at pp. 39:34, 47:8, 68:33.

this *common spirit*, from the expedition of the *Argonauts* and the *campaign against Troy* to the victories *against the Persians* and the defeat by *the Macedonians*—when Greece died! Their *establishment of common games and competitions* for even the minutest places and peoples, always with minor *differences* and *variations*—all this, and ten times more, gave Greece *a unity and diversity* that here, too, made for the *most beautiful whole. Hostility* and *assistance, striving* and *moderating:* the powers of the human spirit were most beautifully *balanced and unbalanced.* The harmony of the Greek lyre!

Yet who could deny that, just thereby, unspeakably much of the old, earlier *strength* and *nourishment* had to be lost? As the Egyptian hieroglyphs were stripped of their *heavy cover,* it is always possible that *something deep, meaningful, natural,* which had been the *character* of this nation, would have evaporated as it crossed the sea. The Greek retained nothing but *a beautiful image, a plaything, a feast for the eyes*—call it what you will in comparison to the Egyptian heaviness. Enough: *he wanted only this!* The religion of the Orient was deprived of its *holy veil,* and naturally, since everything was *put on display* in the *theater* and the *market* and the *dancing-square,* it soon became *"a fable,* nicely drawn out, gossiped about, composed and composed anew—a *dream of youths* and a *myth of maids!"* The Oriental wisdom, removed from behind the screen of mysteries, [became] *pretty chatter, a teaching-construct,* and *the squabbling of the Greek schools* and *markets.* Egyptian art was bared of its heavy craftsman's garments and thereby also lost its over-precise *mechanical* [*quality*] and its *artistic sternness,* for which the Greeks did not aim. The colossus lowered himself and became a *statue,* the *giant temple* a *stage:* Egyptian *order* and *security* subsided all by themselves within the multiplicity of Greece. That old priest[51] could say in more than one regard: "O you eternal children who do not know anything and yet chatter so much, who have nothing and yet display everything so nicely"; and the old *Oriental* would speak even more vehemently from his patriarch's hut—giving them credit, not for religion, humanity, and virtue, but instead for nothing but *flirtation with all of this,* etc. Let it be so. *After all,* the human vessel is *in no way capable of perfection:* it must always *depart* as it *moves on.* The Greeks moved on: Egyptian *industry* and *law enforcement* could not help them, because they had no *Egypt* and no *Nile* behind them, nor could *Phoenician* commercial intelligence, because they had no *Lebanon* and no *India.*

28/29

51. See Plato, *Timaeus* 22b–23b.

The time had passed for *Oriental* education—enough! It became what it was: *Greece!* The original and model of all beauty, grace, and simplicity! The bloom of youth of the human species—O would that it had lasted for ever!

I believe that the position in which I am placing Greece also contributes to the disentangling of "the endless disagreements about the *originality of the Greeks* as opposed to their *imitation of foreign nations.*" Here, as everywhere else, one would have been *united* [in agreement] long ago if only one had understood another better. That Greece *received seeds of culture, language, arts, and sciences from elsewhere* strikes me as undeniable and is easily demonstrated in their *sculpture, architecture, mythology, literature.* Yet further reflection on these ideas leaves it just as certain, I believe, that the Greeks received all this *as if they never had* [*received it*], that they *endowed* it with an entirely *new nature*, that in every way the "*beautiful*" in the truest sense of the word was most certainly their work. Nothing Oriental, Phoenician, or Egyptian retained *its nature:* it became *Greek*, and, in some respects, they who *dressed* and *redressed* everything according to their way were almost *too fully* original. From the greatest *invention* and the most important *history* on, down to *words and signs*, everything is full of this: step-by-step, it is the same for all the nations—let him who wants to build further systems or argue about names do so [on his own]! 29/30

Then came the *manhood of human strength* and *striving*—the *Romans.* Virgil *contrasted* them *with the Greeks*, leaving to the latter *fine art* and the *exercises of youth:* "Remember, Roman, to rule with sovereign sway over the peoples"[52]—thus also roughly contrasting their features with the *men of the North*,[53] who perhaps exceeded them in *barbarian hardness, strength on the attack*, and raw *courage*— but "remember to *rule with sovereign sway* over the peoples"! *Roman courage* idealized: *Roman virtue, Romanness! Roman pride!* [There was] the *magnanimous disposition* of the soul that looked past lusts, effeminacy, and even the more refined pleasures and *acted [instead] for the fatherland.* [There was] *the composed hero's courage* never to be reckless and plunge into danger, but *to pause, to think, to*

---

52. Lit.: "*tu regere imperio populos (Romane, memento)*" (Virgil, *Aeneid* VI.851).

53. I.e., the Germanic peoples whom the Empire failed to subdue.

prepare, and *to act*. There was the unperturbed stride that was not deterred by any obstacle, that was greatest in misfortune and did not despair. There was, finally, the great, *perpetually pursued plan* to be satisfied with nothing less than their eagle's dominion over all the world.[54] He who can grasp all these characteristics by coining an authoritative word, comprising within it at the same time their *manly justice, intelligence*, the *completeness of their designs, decisions, executions*, and of *all the dealings of their world-edifice*—let him name his word! Enough: here stood the man who partook of the adoles- cent and needed him, but who, for himself, desired only to per- form *miracles of courage* and *manliness—with head, heart, and arms!*

30/31

What *heights* the Roman people commanded, what a *giant tem- ple* they built at those heights! Their *state and war-edifice*, whose *plan* and *means* of *execution* [stand as] a colossus for all the world! Could a mere boys' prank be played in Rome without blood flow- ing in three continents? And the *great, dignified* men of this Empire: *where* and how was their influence not felt? How the parts of this great machine served it almost unconsciously and with such easy powers! How all its instruments were *exalted* and *fortified: Senate* and *art of war—law and discipline—Roman purpose* and the *power* to carry it out—I shudder! What with the Greeks had been *play, the rehearsals of youth*, now became a *serious, fixed institution*. The Greek examples on their small stage, their narrow earth, their small republic: what *showpieces for the world* they became when they were staged at *that* height and with such *power!*

However one may take the matter: *"the fortune of the old world was ripe."* The trunk of the tree, having grown to its greater height, strove to take the peoples and nations under its shadow, [to turn them] into branches. It was never the Romans' *main concern* to *compete* with Greeks, Phoenicians, Egyptians, and Orientals; but by *putting everything that had preceded them to manly use*, what a *Roman world* they created! The *name* [of Rome] *bound peoples and parts of the world together* that had never so much as heard of each

54. Compare *Ideas* 14, 6: "Foreign peoples were judged according to customs with which they were unfamiliar, presented with vices and punishments that they had never even heard of. And was not the ultimate outcome of this entire legisla- tion, which was really only appropriate to the constitution of Rome, such a diminishment and debasement of the conquered peoples' characters, after a thousand oppressions, that instead of their original features, nothing remained in the end but the Roman eagle who, after pecking out their eyes and devouring their entrails, covered the sad corpses of the provinces with its feeble wings?" (DKV 6:624).

other before. *Roman provinces!* In all of them, *Romans* trod: Roman *legions, laws,* ideals of *propriety, virtues* and *vices.* The *walls* that separated *nation from nation* were *broken down,* the first step taken *to destroy the national character of them all, to throw* everyone into *one mold* called *"the Roman people."* Of course the first *step* was not by itself the whole *work:* each nation retained its *rights, freedoms, customs,* and *religion;* indeed, the Romans flattered them by letting them bring images of their gods to Rome itself. But the wall lay [in pieces]. *Centuries of Roman rule*—visible in all parts of the world where they had been—*accomplished very much:* a *storm* that penetrated the innermost *recesses of the national way of thinking* of every people. With time the *bonds* became *more and more firm,* and in the end the whole *Roman Empire* was supposed to be only the *city of Rome,* as it were—all subjects *citizens*—until Rome itself sank.

So far we are in no way talking of advantage or disadvantage, only of *effect.* When all the peoples under the Roman yoke ceased, one might say, to be the people they were; when one *statecraft, art of war,* one *law of peoples* was introduced, of which there was no previous example; when the machine *stood,* just as when the machine *fell apart* and *covered* all the nations of the Roman world in wreckage—does anything in the history of the ages offer a *more spectacular view?* All nations *building from or upon* those ruins! An entirely new world of languages, customs, inclinations, and peoples—a new time has begun. A view as of the wide, open sea of new nations—but let us remain on the shore for now and take a look at the peoples whose histories we have run through.

I. No one in the world feels *the weakness of general characterization* more than I. One paints *an entire* people, age, part of the earth—*whom* has one painted? One captures successive peoples and times in an *eternal alternation,* like waves of the sea—*whom* has one painted? *Whom* has the describing word depicted? In the end, one summarizes them in Nothing, as a *general word,* when everyone perhaps thinks and feels what he will—flawed *means of description!* How one can be *misunderstood!*

Whoever has noticed what an *inexpressible thing* the *peculiarity* of one human being is; how difficult it is to be able to *put the distinguishing distinctively,* how he feels and lives, how *different* and *peculiar* all things become for *him* after *his* eye sees them, *his* soul measures, *his* heart senses—what *depth* there is to the character of

31/32

32/33   even *one nation* that even though one may have perceived and
marveled at it often enough, yet *flees the word* so persistently, and
that put into words, rarely becomes recognizable to *anyone*, so
that he may understand and empathize—such an observer will
marvel and become dizzy all the more before what one calls the
"spirit of the inclinations" in such distant peoples, times, and
countries. For him[55] it is as if one had to capture the mighty ocean
of entire peoples, ages, and countries in *a single glance, feeling,
word!* Dull half-image and *shadow* of the word! The whole living
painting of manners of life, habits, needs, peculiarities of lands
and skies would have to *follow later* or to have *preceded*; one would
first have to *sympathize* with a nation to feel a *single* of its *inclinations* and *actions*, to feel them *all together*, to *find* one word, to *think*
all in its richness: or else one reads . . . *a word*.

   We all believe, even now, to have the *paternal* and *domestic* and
humane drives of the Oriental, to be as capable of *loyalty* and *artistic diligence* as the Egyptians were. *Phoenician liveliness, Greek love of
freedom, Roman strength of soul:* who does not feel predisposed to
all of this but for *time, opportunity?* And behold, my reader, that is
just where we are! The most cowardly scoundrel no doubt retains
a faint *disposition and potential* for the most magnanimous heroism—but between this and "the entire feeling of being, the existence within such a character": chasm! If you lacked nothing, then,
but *time* and *opportunity* to turn your predisposition to be an Oriental, a Greek, a Roman into *skills* and *sound drives:* chasm! We are
talking of nothing but drives and skills. To empathize with the
entire nature of a soul, which *rules* through everything, which
molds all other inclinations and forces of the soul *after its own
model, coloring* even the most indifferent actions, do not answer
with words, but enter into the age itself, follow the compass, enter
into all history, feel your way into everything—only then will you
be on your way to understanding the word; only then will the
thought fade whether all this, taken separately or taken together,
is really you! You as everything taken together? *The quintessence of
all ages and peoples?* That already shows the foolishness!

         Character of the nations! Nothing but the *facts* of their *constitu-*
33/34   *tion* and *history* must decide. Did not a patriarch also have, or
could he not have had, inclinations *besides* those that you attribute
to him? To both of which I say only: *indeed!* Indeed he had others,

55. Translation based on the variations suggested in the editorial notes to the
DKV text, at 4:869.

secondary traits that follow self-evidently from what I have or have not said, that I, and perhaps others contemplating his story with me, already acknowledge in the word. And [I acknowledge] even more readily that he *could* have turned out very differently—in a *different* place, in *that* age, with the *progress* of education,* under *different circumstances.* Could not *Leonidas, Caesar,* and *Abraham* have been *gentlemen of our century?*—could have been: but were not. Ask *history* about this: *that is what we are talking about.*

So I am likewise preparing myself for petty objections out of the *great detail* of peoples and ages. That no people ever remained or could have remained what it was *for long,* and that *each one,* like any *art* and *science* and what not in the world, had *its period of growth,* of *blossoming,* and of *decline;* that each and every such change lasted only the *minimum of time* that the wheel of human fortune was able to grant; that finally, in the world, *no two moments are ever the same,* and that, accordingly, the Egyptians, Romans, and Greeks were also not the same at *all times.* I tremble when I think what wise objections some wise folks, and those versed in history to boot, may raise about this! Greece consisted of *many lands:*[56] *Athenians* and *Boeotians, Spartans* and *Corinthians* were anything but the same! Was not *agriculture* practiced in *Asia,* too? Did not the *Egyptians* once trade just as well as the *Phoenicians?* Were not the *Macedonians* conquerors just like the *Romans? Aristotle* just as speculative a thinker as *Leibniz?* Did not our Nordic peoples surpass the Romans *in courage?* Were all *Egyptians, Greeks, Romans*—are all rats and mice—the same? No! But they are still rats and mice!

How annoying it gets to address an audience when one has to be prepared for ever *the same* and even *worse* objections, and presented in *what tone,* by the *screaming* part (the part that thinks more nobly remains silent!); and when one must expect, at the *34/35* same time, that the *great mass* of sheep that cannot distinguish right from left will readily follow suit! Can there be any *general image* without *mutual subordination* and *integration,* or any *broad perspective* without *elevation?* When you keep your face close to the picture, fumbling with this splinter or groping at that speck of color, you will never see the *entire image*—you will see anything but an *image!* And when your head is full of a group with which

56. Herder writes "countries" (compare also *The Influence of Free Legislation,* 307:25), but he is well aware of the imprecision of this term (compare *Do We Still Have the Fatherland of the Ancients?,* 331:21).

you have become infatuated, would your sight be able to *grasp* the *whole* of such *alternating ages*, to *impose order* on them, to *pursue* them *gently?* To isolate only the *main causes* underlying each scene, to *follow* the *currents* quietly, and then—to name them? But if you are not able to do any of this—if history flickers and flares before your eyes, a welter of scenes, peoples, and ages—then read first and learn to see! I know by the way, like you, that every *general image*, every *general concept*, is nothing but *abstraction*—the Creator alone is the one who *conceives* the full *unity* of *any one* and of *all* nations, in all their *great diversity*, without thereby losing sight of their *unity*.

II. Away, then, from these petty objections that miss all purpose and perspective! Placed within the design of the great and necessary whole, how miserable do "certain *fashionable judgments of our century appear, made from merely general scholastic concepts, about the merits, virtues, happiness of such distant, such varied nations!*"

Human nature is no deity *self-sufficient* in goodness: she needs to *learn* everything, to be *formed** by *progressions,*** to *stride* ever onward in a *gradual struggle.* Naturally, she is therefore developed* *most*, or even *exclusively*, on *those sides* giving the most *occasion* for virtue, for struggle, for progression**—and in a certain sense all human perfection is therefore *national, secular,* and, examined most closely, *individual.* One does not develop anything but that *for which time, climate, need, world, fortune* gives occasion: *separated* from the rest, inclinations and abilities slumbering in the heart can never become *skills.* Therefore a nation may, alongside the most eminent virtues, have *deficiencies on another* side, making *exceptions* and displaying *contradictions* and *uncertainties* that are astonishing—but that will surprise only someone who brings along his *idealistic shadow-image* of virtue from the compendium of his own century and who has philosophy enough to want to find the entire earth in one of its spots! For anyone wanting to recognize the human heart from *within the circumstances of his own life*, such *exceptions* and *contradictions* are perfectly *human—proportions* of *forces* and *inclinations* for *a particular purpose* that could never be *attained* without them—thus no *exceptions* at all, but the *rule.*

Be it, my friend, that the childish *Oriental religion*, the *attachment* to the most tender *sentiment* of human life, contributes *weaknesses*, on the other side, that you condemn on the pattern of other ages. A patriarch cannot be a Roman *hero*, a Greek *runner*, or a *merchant* from the coast; still less, that to which the ideal of your lectern or your whims would raise him in order to *praise him falsely* or *denounce him bitterly.* Be it that he would appear, by later standards, *fearful, scared of death, weak, ignorant, lazy, superstitious* to you, and with gall in your eye, *detestable:* he is what God, climate, time, and stage of world development could make* him—a *patriarch!* As against all the losses of later ages, he thus retains an *innocence, fear of God, humanity* that will forever make him *a god* to every later age! The *Egyptian, crawling, slavish,* an *animal of the soil, superstitious* and *sullen, harsh* against *strangers,* a *thoughtless creature of habit*—as against the light-handed *Greek, turning all towards beauty* on the one hand and a *friend of mankind* according to the *high taste of our century* on the other, who carries all wisdom in his head and all the world in his breast! But then also the Egyptian's *undaunted spirit,* his *loyalty* and *forceful calm*—can you compare this to Greek *pederasty* and the *adolescent wooing* of everything *beautiful* and *pleasurable?* And again, compare the Greek *lightness* and *dalliance* to religion, the lack of certainty in *love* to *discipline* and *respectability*—taking whose ideal you will. But could those *perfections* have been developed on such a *scale* and to such a *degree* without these *deficiencies? Providence* herself, you see, did not require this but only wanted to fulfill her purpose by *change, leading things along* through the *awakening of new forces* and the *demise of others. Philosopher* in the northern *valley of the earth,* holding the *cradle of your century* in your hands, do you know better than she? 36/37

Decrees of praise and censure that we pour out on all the world, from the *discovery of a favorite ancient people* with which we have become infatuated—by what right do you exist? Those *Romans* could be as no other nation; they could do what *none has done since:* they were *Romans.* At the *top of the world,* and all around them *valley;* at the top from youth on, *educated** to the *Roman spirit,* they *acted* in accordance with it—no wonder! And no wonder that a *small pastoral and agricultural people* in one valley of the earth was no *iron animal*[57] that could act thus! And no wonder, again, that they, in turn, possessed *virtues* that the noblest Roman lacked, and that the noblest Roman at his height could in extremis decide, in cold blood, on *cruelties* that the shepherd in the *little valley* did not have *on his soul.* At the pinnacle of that gigantic

57. An allusion to Dan. 7:7 (also 7:19), conventionally interpreted as an anticipation of the Roman Empire: "After this I saw in the night visions, and behold a fourth beast, dreadful and terrible, and strong exceedingly; and it had great iron teeth: it devoured and brake in pieces, and stamped the residue with the feet of it: and it was diverse from all the beasts that were before it; and it had ten horns."

machine, alas, sacrifice was often *trifle*, often *emergency*, often (poor mankind, what conditions you are capable of!) *beneficence*. The very machine that made *extensive vice* possible was also the one that *lifted* the *virtues* so *high* and spread *effectiveness* so *widely*: is mankind in its present state at all capable of pure *perfection?* The peak borders on the valley. Around the noble *Spartans* live the *Helots*, treated inhumanly. The *triumphant Roman general*, robed in *the red of the gods*,[58] is invisibly *painted with blood* as well: *rapine*, *sacrilege*, and *violent lusts* surround his chariot; *oppression* leads the way: *misery* and *poverty* follow close behind. Thus *want* and *virtue*, in this sense, too, always dwell together in one human hut.

37/38

Beautiful *art of poetry* conjuring up a *favorite people* of the earth in superhuman splendor—and the art of poetry is also *useful*, since man is ennobled even by beautiful *prejudices*. But when the poet is a *historian*, a *philosopher*, as most pretend to be, *modeling all centuries* after *the one cast* of their own age, which is often a very small and weak one! *Humes! Voltaires! Robertsons!* Classic ghosts of the twilight! What are you by the *light of the truth?*

A *learned society* of our day,[59] no doubt with the loftiest of intentions, has proposed the question, "Which people, in history, might have been the happiest?"[60] If I properly understand the question, and if it is not altogether *beyond* the scope of a human answer, I can think of nothing to say except that at a certain time and under certain circumstances every people must have experienced such a moment or else it *never* was [*a people*]. Then again, human nature is no vessel for an *absolute, independent, immutable happiness*, as defined by the philosopher; rather, she everywhere draws *as much happiness towards herself as she can:* a supple clay that will *conform* to the most different situations, needs, and depressions. Even the image of happiness changes with every condition and location (for what is it ever but the *sum* of "*the satisfaction of desire, the fulfillment of purpose*, and the *gentle overcoming of needs*," all of which are shaped by *land, time*, and *place?*). Basically, then, all *comparison* becomes *futile*. As soon as the inner *meaning* of

58. I.e., wearing royal purple.

†59. These gentlemen must have had frightfully high ideals, since, to my knowledge, none of their philosophical challenges have ever been met.

60. Herder is alluding to an essay competition on this question, among others, that was called in 1762 by the "Patriotic Society" in Bern, in response to which he had submitted an essay. The jurors appear to have been dissatisfied with the quality of the submissions, and the competition was reopened the following year— hence Herder's jibe (DKV 4:871).

happiness, the *inclination* has changed; as soon as external *opportunities* and *needs develop* and *solidify* the *other* meaning—who could compare the *different* satisfaction of *different* meanings in *different* worlds? Who could compare the shepherd and father of the Orient, the ploughman and the artisan, the seaman, runner, conqueror of the world? It is not the *laurel wreath* that matters, *38/39* nor the *sight of the blessed flock*, neither the *merchant vessels* nor the *conquered armies' standards*—but the *soul* that *needed* this, *strove* for it, finally *attained* it and *wanted* to attain nothing else. Every nation has its *center* of happiness *within itself*, as every ball has its center of gravity![61]

Here, too, the good mother has provided well. Placing *manifold* dispositions in the heart, she made any one of them so little *urgent* in itself that even when only *a few* are satisfied, the soul soon creates *a concert* from these awakened tones, not feeling the ones not awakened except insofar as they *support* the ringing songs *silently* and in the dark. She placed *manifold* dispositions in the heart and assembled *some of them* in a circle around us, at our disposal: then she *moderated* the human *gaze* so that after a short period of habituation this circle became man's *horizon*. Not to *look beyond:* hardly even to *suspect* what lies beyond! Everything that remains *akin* to my nature, that can be *assimilated* into it, I envy, pursue, appropriate; *beyond this,* kindly nature has armed me with *insensitivity, coldness,* and *blindness.* She may even turn to *contempt* and *disgust*—yet she has no purpose but to push me back *upon myself,* to give me sufficiency at *the center* that sustains me. The Greek appropriated as much from the Egyptian, and the Roman from the Greek, as he needed for himself: once he is *satiated,* the remains *fall to the floor,* and he pursues them no further! Or when in this development of particular national inclinations to a particular national happiness the *distance from people to people* has already expanded too far—see how much the Egyptian *hates* the shepherd, the vagrant! How he *despises* the carefree Greek! Likewise any two nations whose inclinations and circles of happiness *collide*—one calls it *prejudice, loutishness,* narrow *nationalism!*[62] Prejudice is *good* in its time: it makes men *happy.* It pushes peoples

---

61. Compare lines 23 and 36 below, also pp. 41:20, 52:24, 75:1–2, 82:29–33, 94:5–8, 102:31–32.

62. Lit.: *Nationalism.* Compare *Letters towards the Advancement of Humanity,* letter 115: "It is a well-known, saddening pronouncement that the human species is never less lovable than in the effects that *nations* have upon one another" (DKV 7:688).

together at their *center*, making them stand firmer upon their *roots*, more flourishing *in their way*, more virile, and also happier in their *inclinations* and *purposes*. The most ignorant, prejudiced nation is in this sense often the first: the age of dreamy wanderings and hopeful journeys abroad is already *sickness*, flatulence, *bloatedness, premonition of* death!

III. And should the *general, philosophical, philanthropic tone of our century* so generously and readily bestow "our own ideal" of *virtue* and *happiness* on every remote nation, every ancient age of the world? Is it the only judge, to be *assessing, condemning*, or *prettifying* their mores all by itself? Is not the good *dispersed* throughout the earth? Because one shape of mankind and one corner of the earth could not contain it, it was distributed among a thousand shapes—an eternal Proteus![63]—strolling through all the parts and ages of the world. Moreover, as he strolls and strolls on, it is not the greater *virtue* or *happiness of the individual* after which he strives, for mankind always remains only mankind—and yet a *plan of striving onward* becomes visible. My great subject!

Whoever has so far undertaken to trace the *progression*** of the centuries* usually brought along a favorite idea on his journey: progression** towards *greater virtue* and *happiness of individual human beings*. Towards this end, then, one has *exaggerated* or *fabricated* facts, *diminished* or *passed over* contrary facts *in silence*; entire pages have been *covered*, words *taken* for words, *enlightenment* for *happiness*, several and more refined *ideas* for *virtue*; and thus one has produced novels "about the *generally progressing improvement*** of the world*"—that nobody believed in, at least not the true student of *history* and of the *human heart*.

Others who *saw the tediousness of this dream* and did not know any better saw *vices* and *virtues change* like climates, saw perfections *come into being* and *perish* like a spring of leaves, saw human mores and inclinations flying and turning like *pages* of *fortune—No plan! No progression!*** Eternal revolution—weaving* and *tearing up! Penelopean labors![64]* They fell into a *maelstrom*—skepticism towards all virtue, happiness, and destiny of man—into which they wove all history, religion, and ethics: the latest fashion of the

63. Herder's choice of *wandeln*, to stroll, plays on an alternate meaning, "to change," that refers this to Proteus, the Greek god of shape-changing.

64. Penelope promised her suitors that she would pick one of them to replace Odysseus, who was thought dead, as soon as she finished weaving a web. To postpone the decision, she would undo by night what she had woven by day (see Homer, *Odyssey* II.85–109).

newest *philosophers*, particularly the *French*, is a tone of doubt![65]
Doubt in a hundred *shapes*, all under the dazzling title *"From the
History of the World"*! Contradictions and waves of the sea: one
fails, or what one *rescues* of *morality* and *philosophy from the shipwreck* is hardly worth the mention.

But should there not be evident progression** and *development*
in a higher sense than one has been imagining? Do you see this
stream flowing along: how it sprang from a little source, growing, ceasing there, commencing here, always winding along and
burrowing wider and deeper—yet always remaining *water?*
Stream! Drop always only a drop until it plunges into the sea—
what if things were so with the human race? Or behold that
growing *tree!* That human being striving upward! He has to pass
through life's different *ages*, all evidently in *progression;*** one
striving after another, continuously; between each of them are
apparent *resting* places, *revolutions! Changes!* And yet each has the
center of its happiness *within itself!* The young man is not *happier*
than the innocent, contented child, nor the calm old man,
unhappier than the vigorously striving man: the pendulum swings
always *with the same force*, whether it reaches the widest and
strives with *all the more speed* or whether it sways the slowest,
approaching calm. All the while an eternal striving! No one is
alone in his age; he builds on *what has come before*, which turns
into and wants to be nothing but the foundation of the
future[66]—thus speaks the *analogy in nature*, the talking *image of*   41/42
God in *all works!* Evidently it is so with the *human race!* The
Egyptian could not exist without the Oriental; the Greek built
upon them, the Roman lifted himself atop the back of the entire
world—true *progression,*** *progressing development*, even if none in
particular were to benefit from it! It enters into the great! It
becomes something of which *the history of empty hulls* boasts so
much and of which it shows so little: the *stage* for a *guiding intention on earth!* Even if we should not immediately discern the final
design, a stage for the deity, even if only through the *openings*
and the *wreckage* of *individual scenes*.

†65. The good, honest *Montaigne* began; the dialectician *Bayle*, a thinker whose
contradictions—in the articles of his form of expression, the *Dictionary*—neither
Crousaz nor *Leibniz* could resolve, continued to influence the age. And then the
more recent philosophers, doubters of all with their own most daring propositions, *Voltaire, Hume*, even *Diderot and his followers*—it is the great century of
doubt and wave-making.

66. Compare notes to p. 91:32, 35.

At least this view is wider than that philosophy which *mixes up top and bottom*, which only ever clarifies particular *confusions* here and there, turning everything into a *game of ants*, into a striving of individual *inclinations and forces* without *purpose*, into a chaos where one despairs of virtue, purpose, and deity! If I could succeed in *binding* together the most disparate scenes without *entangling* them, to show how they are *mutually related*, *growing out* of one another, *losing themselves* in each other, all only moments in the particular, mere *means towards a purpose* through progression**—what a *view!* What a noble *application of human history!* What *encouragement* to *hope*, to *action*, to *belief*, even where one sees *nothing* or does *not* see *everything*.

Second Section

The *Roman world-constitution*, too, met its end; and the *greater* the edifice and the *higher* it stood, the greater the plunge when it *fell*: half the world lay in *ruins!* Peoples and continents had lived under the tree, and now, when the voice of the holy watcher called "Hew it down!"[1]—how great was the *void!* Like a break in the thread of world events! Nothing less than a *new world* was needed *to heal the tear.*

This [new world] was *the North*. And whatever origins and systems one may devise regarding the condition of *these peoples*, the simplest [account] seems the truest: left alone, they were what one might call "*patriarchies such as there could be in the North.*" As *such a climate* made an Oriental *shepherd's life* impossible, since *more burdensome needs bore down* on the human spirit here than where nature provided almost by itself for man, so it was just these *burdensome needs* and the Northern air that *hardened* men more than they could have been hardened in the warm, aromatic greenhouse of the East and the South. Naturally, their condition remained *rougher*, their small societies *more isolated* and *wilder:* but human bonds retained their *strength*, the human *drives* and energy their fullness. Here could arise the land that *Tacitus* describes.[2] And when this Northern sea of peoples became agitated, waves crashed upon waves,

42/43

1. Compare Dan. 4:13–14.
2. Tacitus, *Germania*.

peoples upon other peoples! The wall and dam around Rome burst: [the Romans] themselves had pointed out the breaches and had lured [the intruders] to make repairs. Finally, when everything *broke,* how the South was flooded by the North! And after all the turmoil and atrocities, what a *new Northern-Southern world!*

Whoever observes the condition of the Roman lands in their last centuries (and they were then the *educated* universe!*) will marvel at and admire Providence's way of *preparing* such a *strange replacement of human forces.* Everything was *exhausted, unnerved, shattered:* abandoned by men, inhabited by unnerved men, going under in excess, vice, disorder, license, and savage martial pride. The fine *Roman laws* and *insights* could not *replace forces* that had disappeared, *restore* nerves that no longer felt the spirit of life, revive *driving forces* that had been depleted; thus *death!*—an emaciated *corpse* lying in a pool of blood—when in the North a *new man* was born. Under a fresh sky, in the wasteland and the wild where nobody expected it, a spring of strong, nutritious plants was ripening that, once transplanted to the finer, Southern lands—now miserable, deserted fields—would take on a new nature and bring a great harvest for the fate of the world! *Goths, Vandals, Burgundians, Angles, Huns, Herules, Franks* and *Bulgarians, Slavs* and *Lombards* came, settled down—and the whole new *43/44* world, from the Mediterranean to the Black Sea, from the Atlantic to the North Sea, is *their work, their race, their constitution!*

Not only what *human forces* but what *laws* and *institutions* did they thus bring onto the *stage of the education* of the world!* Of course they despised arts and sciences, luxury and refinement— which had wrought havoc on mankind.[3] But as they brought *nature* instead of the arts, *healthy Northern intelligence*[4] instead of the sciences, *strong* and *good,* albeit *savage customs* instead of refined ones, and as everything *fermented together*—what a spectacle! How their laws breathed *manly courage, sense of honor, confidence in intelligence, honesty,* and *piety!* How their *institution of feudalism* undermined the welter of populous, opulent cities, building up the land, employing hands and human beings, making *healthy* and therefore *happy* people. Their later *ideal, beyond [mere] needs,* tended towards *chastity* and *honor,* [and] ennobled the best part of the human inclinations. Though a *novel,* it was an *exalted novel:* a true *new blossoming* of the human soul.

3. Compare Rousseau, *Discourse on the Sciences and the Arts.*
4. *Verstand* (both here and just below).

One needs to consider, among other things, what a *period of recuperation* and *exercise* these centuries of fermentation meant for mankind through the crumbling of *everything* into *small attachments, divisions,* and *orders of mutual subordination,* and the emergence of so *many, many* different parts! One thing always *rubbed up* against another then, and everything was kept in *suspense* and *vigor.* A time of *fermentation:* but it was precisely this that kept despotism at bay for so long (truly the maw by which mankind is devoured in the name of "tranquility and obedience"—meaning, in reality, *death* and uniform *demolition!*).[5] Now, is it better, is it *healthier* and *really more efficient* for mankind to produce lots of lifeless cogs for a huge, wooden, thoughtless machine? Or, rather, to *awaken* and *stir forces?* Even if it be [done] through so-called *imperfect* constitutions, *disorder, barbarian points of honor,* the *savage addiction to quarreling,* and the like; if it serves the purpose, [it is] always better than *to be dead while living,* and *decaying.*[6]

44/45   Meanwhile, Providence thought fit to prepare and add one more new ingredient to this new *fermentation of Northern-Southern fluids—the Christian religion.* Surely I do not first have to ask forgiveness, in our Christian century, if I will speak of [Christianity] as one of *the world's driving forces*—[even if] I will be considering it only as a *ferment, leaven,* to be used for good or bad, and for whatever else one wishes.

But my point is liable to *misunderstanding* from *two sides* and deserves some explanation.

The *religion of the ancient world,* which had come to *Greece* and *Italy* from the *Orient* via *Egypt,* had become in all regards a *desiccated, feeble thing,* truly a *mere shadow*[7] of what it had been and was supposed to be. If one only contemplates the *later mythology of the Greeks* and the Romans' *puppet*[8] of a *political religion of the people,* no more needs to be said. Yet now there was hardly "*any other*

---

5. This passage may explain why Herder paints such an unflattering picture of *Ruhe* (quiet, calm, or even order) at pp. 51:27, 52:37, and 72:24–25. It is the cynical suppression of men in the name of public calm and order that Herder objects to, not quiet itself, as the dramatic change in tone at 105:28–30 confirms.

6. The German *modern* (to decay) also has the same meaning as in English. Herder, however, does not distinguish ancient, medieval, and modern in this text, but rather the old(er), middle, and new(er) ages.

7. Lit.: *caput mortuum,* "skull (of the dead)": a term from alchemy referring to a worthless residue.

8. This refers to the physical representations of the many gods welcomed into Rome (compare p. 31:34–35).

principle of virtue" in the world! The Roman *sacrifice for the father-land*[9] had sunk from its pinnacle and lay in the morass of decadence and martial cruelty. The Greek *honor of youth* and *love of liberty*—where was it? And the old *Egyptian spirit*—where was *it* when Greeks and Romans intruded upon that land? What could *replace* this? Not *philosophy*, which had degenerated into *utter sophistry, the art of bickering*, the *peddler's junk* of *opinions without force* or *certainty*, a wooden machine dressed up with old rags that was without power over the human heart, let alone the power that could improve *a ruined age*, a *ruined world!* And now the *rebuilding* of the ruins was to be done *by peoples* who, in *their condition*, still *needed religion*, who could be guided *by it alone*, who mixed the *spirit of superstition* into everything. Yet these peoples found nothing on their *new stage* but what they *despised* or could not *grasp:* Rome's mythology and philosophy [was as useless to them] as its statues and models of virtue. Their *Northern* religion, a *remnant of the Orient formed** *by Northern means*, did not suffice; they needed a *fresher, more powerful religion*. And so—lo and behold!—Providence created it *in a place* where one would have *least expected* to find a replenishment for all the Western world—amidst the bare mountains of Judea! *Just before the overthrow* of an entire obscure people,[10] precisely during its *final, most miserable period*, [the new religion] *arose* in *a manner* that will always remain miraculous; it *survived* and *struggled along* in a similarly strange manner on a *long path* through chasms and caves—onto a stage where it was *needed so much!* Where its effect was *so very, very powerful!* Without a doubt, the most peculiar event in the world!

45/46

It was certainly a great and noteworthy spectacle when, *under Julian, the two most prominent religions*, the *most ancient heathen* and the *more modern Christian* one, fought over nothing less than *dominion over the world. Religion* in the strongest sense of the word—this [Julian] and everyone else could see—was *indispensable* to his *ruined age. Greek mythology* and *Roman state ceremony*—this *he could likewise see*—were *not*, for his purposes, *adequate* to the *age.* Thus he reached for everything he could: for the *strongest* and *most ancient religion* he knew, for the *religion of the Orient.* He stirred up all its *miraculous powers, sorceries*, and *apparitions*, so that

9. Compare Horace, *Odes* III, 2, 13: "It is sweet and proper to die for the fatherland"; also *Do We Still Have a Fatherland?*, 50:11–12; *Do We Still Have the Fatherland of the Ancients?*, 329:29–30.

10. Or possibly "infamous" (*unberühmt*): Herder means the Jews.

it became altogether *theurgy;* he took as much as he could of *philosophy, Pythagoreanism,* and *Platonism* to help him give everything the *fine veneer of reason;*[11] he placed everything on the *triumph-chariot*[12] of the greatest *splendor,* drawn by the two most untamed beasts, *violence* and *fanaticism,* and steered by the finest state-craft—but all in vain! [Julian's creation] succumbed; it had no vitality; it was but the miserable *dressing-up* of a *corpse* that had been capable of *miracles* only in earlier times. The *bare, new Christian religion* prevailed!

One can see that it is a stranger observing the matter, one who might as well be a Muslim or a Mameluke to be writing this.[13] So I shall continue.

It is undeniable that this same religion, created in so peculiar a manner, was *by the intentions of its founder* meant to be (I shall not pronounce on whether this is what it became in the practices of the various ages) the *actual religion of all mankind,* an *impulse towards love,* and a *bond between all the nations* to make of them an *army of brothers*—this was its *purpose* from *beginning to end!* It is just as certain that [this religion] was the *first* (whatever those who professed it may *later* have made of it) to teach such *pure spiritual truth* and such *heartfelt duties;* to dispense *so fully* with *superficiality* and *superstition,* with *frills* and *coercion;* to seek to improve the human heart with such single-mindedness, so *universally,* so *entirely* and *without exception.* All preceding religions, even those of the best times and peoples, were, after all, only *narrowly national,* full of *images* and *masquerades,* full of *ceremonies* and *national practices* to which the essential duties were only ever *attached* and *appended*—in short, religions of *one people, one corner of the earth, one lawgiver, one age!* This one, on the other hand, was evidently just the opposite in everything: the *most honorable moral philosophy,* the *purest theory* of *truths* and *duties, independent* of all legislation and petty local constitutions. In short, if you will, the *deism with the greatest love for man.*

And, therefore, surely the religion *of the universe.* It has been proven by others, and even by *its enemies,* that such a religion could definitely not have sprung up or arisen, or crept in—put it as you

46/47

---

11. *Vernunft.*

12. Compare the triumphant general's chariot, p. 37:32.

13. This stance of historical impartiality may help explain why, at p. 45:5–6, Herder finds it natural to consider Christianity "only as a *ferment, leaven,* to be used for good or bad, and for whatever else one wishes."

will—*at any other time, before* or *after*. The human species had to be *prepared* for this deism throughout so many millennia, *gradually dragged out* of childhood, barbarism, idolatry, and carnality. The powers of its soul had to be *developed* through so many *national educations**—the Oriental, Egyptian, Greek, Roman, etc.—as through *steps* and *entrances*, before even the least beginnings could be made towards opinions, concepts, and the recognition of *the ideal of religion* and *duty* and *the bond between peoples*. Even from a strictly *instrumental* point of view, it seems that the Roman *spirit of conquest* had to *lead the way*, to clear the path everywhere and establish a *political connection* heretofore unthinkable between peoples, and thereby to set in motion *tolerance* and *ideas of a law of peoples* on a scale that would likewise have been unthinkable before! Thus was the *horizon broadened*, thus *enlightened*, and now *ten new earthly nations*[14] *scrambled* towards this bright horizon, *carrying with them* entirely different, new religious *sensitivities* and *needs* and *forging*   47/48
them all *into one* within themselves. Ferment! How strange the manner in which *you* have been prepared and in which *everything* has been prepared *with a view to you!* How *thoroughly* and *widely* everything has been *mixed together!* How long, how powerfully it has been *rising* and *seething*—what else will be *fermented to term?*

Precisely that, then, which is often mocked so wittily and philosophically—"Where has this leaven, called the Christian religion, ever been *pure?* Where has it ever not been *mixed up* with the *dough* of *peculiar, utterly diverse*, and often the *most odious ways of thinking?*"—precisely that strikes me as the obvious *nature of the matter*. If this religion was, as it really is, the *refinement* of the spirit, "a *deism* of *friendship among men*" that was not supposed to become mixed up with *any* one *civil law;* if it was that *philosophy* of *Heaven*, which, precisely on account of its loftiness and unearthly probity, could embrace the entire earth; then I reckon that it was well-nigh impossible for the *fine* scent to *exist*, to *be applied*, without getting mixed up with *more earthly* matters and without needing them as *vehicles*, as it were. Thus the *ways of thinking of each people, its customs and laws, inclinations and abilities:* cold or warm, good or bad, barbaric or cultivated—everything taken just as it was. The Christian religion was only ever able and meant to permeate everything:[15] he who can at all conceive of

---

14. See the list of ten Germanic tribes at p. 43:36–37. Compare also Dan. 7:24: "And the ten horns out of this kingdom are ten kings that shall arise."

15. I.e., to permeate rather than to displace or supersede outright.

divine undertakings in the world and the human realm *other than by worldly* and *human driving forces* is truly made for the abstractions of the *utopian poet* rather than those of the *natural philosopher.* When has the deity ever acted, anywhere *in the whole analogy of nature*, other than through nature? And is it therefore any less deity—or is it not deity precisely by pouring itself out over everything, by manifesting itself so uniformly and inscrutably *through all its works?* Let all the *human passions* act on a human stage—in every age according to that age, and likewise on every continent, in every nation! Religion is meant to accomplish nothing *but purposes for human beings, through human beings.* Leaven or treasure: everyone carries it in his own vessel and kneads it into his own dough! And the finer the scent, the more it would escape if it were left to itself, *the more* does it have to be *mixed* for use. I cannot see any human sense in the contrary opinion.

48/49

Moreover, speaking in a physical and human sense only, *this* very admixture of the Christian religion was perhaps the *choicest* imaginable. [The Church] took care of the *plight of the poor that was growing more desperate by the day*, so that even *Julian* could not deny its merit in this flattering respect. In later times of confusion it became the *sole consolation* and *refuge* from *general distress* (I am not talking about the uses to which the priests invariably put this); indeed, ever since the barbarians themselves became Christians, it gradually became the *real order* and *security* of the world. As it tamed the rapacious lions and conquered the conquerors, what a *comfortable dough* [it became] for *permeating* deeply, for *working* widely and *eternally.* The *small constitutions*[16] *where it was able to embrace* everything; the *great distance between the social classes* that made it something of a *general intermediary;* the *great gaps* in the *feudal constitution*, geared only *towards war*, which left it to *furnish* whatever there was of *science*, the *practice of law*, and *influence* on the *way of thinking*, and thus to become everywhere *indispensable* and, as it were, the *soul* for centuries whose *bodies* were nothing but *martial spirit* and *slavish toil on the land.* Could any other soul but *reverence* have bound together *these* limbs, *animated this* body? If this *body* was adopted in the Council of Fortune, what foolishness it would be to *speculate* about its *spirit* beyond the spirit of the age! All this was, I reckon, the only[17] way of progressing.**

16. Compare p. 47:15.

17. Following the correction proposed at DKV 4:873.

To whom has it not occurred that so-called "Christendom," in every age, took on the complete *shape*, or became an *analogy*, of *the constitution* with which or within which it existed! Just as one and the same *Gothic spirit* permeated the *interior* and *exterior* of the Church, shaping *garments* and *ceremonies, doctrines* and *temples;* sharpening the *bishop's crosier* into a *sword* because everyone was carrying a sword; and creating *church benefices, fiefs,* and *serfs* because that was how things were everywhere. Imagine, through the centuries, those *tremendous arrangements* of *honorary church offices, monasteries* and *monastic orders,* finally even *crusades* and the apparent *dominion over the world*—what a tremendous *Gothic edifice! Overburdened, oppressive, sinister, tasteless*—the earth appeared to be sinking beneath it. But also how *vast, rich, fully developed, powerful!* I am speaking of a *historical Event,* a miracle of the *human spirit,* and clearly an *instrument* of Providence! 49/50

To the extent that the Gothic body with its fermentations and frictions was at all capable of *arousing forces,* much was surely contributed by *the spirit* that *animated* and *bound it together.* If a *mixture of high concepts and inclinations* that had *never been active before* in *this* form and to *this* extent was thus spread throughout Europe, [Providence][18] was certainly *weaving* its web there, too. Without becoming involved here with the various periods of the spirit in the Middle Ages, let us speak of *Gothic spirit* and *Nordic chivalry* in the broadest sense—*great phenomenon* of so many centuries, countries, and situations.

[This phenomenon] continued to be what one might call *"the epitome of all those inclinations that had been developed before by individual peoples and ages."* Indeed the former can still be traced to the latter—but the *active element* that *used to bind* them all *together* and made of them living *creatures of God* is no longer the same at the individual level. *Paternal inclinations* on the one hand and the holy *worship of the female sex* on the other; *inextinguishable love of freedom* and *despotism; religion* and *martial spirit; meticulous order* and *solemnity* and a *peculiar attraction to adventure*—all this flowed together! *Oriental, Roman, Nordic,* and *Saracen* concepts and inclinations: we know *when, where,* and to *what extent* they flowed together and modified themselves. The spirit of the age weaved and bound together the most diverse characteristics—*courage* and *monkery,*[19] *adventure* and *gallantry, tyranny* and *magnanimity*—into

---

18. Following DKV 4:874.

19. *Möncherei,* somewhat mocking; compare *Pfaffentum* at p. 22:28.

the whole that *confronts* us, standing between the Romans and ourselves, like a ghost or a romantic adventure. It was once nature, once—*truth*.

50/51 This spirit of "the Northern *knight's honor*" has been likened to the *heroic times of the Greeks*[20]—and of course points of comparison can be found. But [this spirit] as such remains *unique*, I reckon, in the course of all the centuries! Though *resembling only itself*, in fact, it has been *mocked* so viciously by some because it stands between the Romans and us—*us!* What men we are! Others of a more adventurous mindset have *exalted* it high above everything else. Still I maintain that [this spirit] is no more and no less than "*a singular condition of the world.*" Incomparable to any of the conditions that preceded it, yet founded upon them, and having its *advantages* and *disadvantages* like everything else, it changed perpetually and strove forward—towards *greatness!*

The dark sides of this period appear in all the books. Every classic aesthete who views the regimentation of our age as the ultimate achievement of mankind is given the opportunity to belittle entire centuries for their *barbarism, wretched laws, superstition* and *stupidity, lack of manners*[21] and *bad taste*—in their *schools, country estates, temples,*[22] *monasteries, city halls, guilds, huts,* and *houses.* He may likewise sing the praises of the *light* of our age, that is, its *levity* and *boisterousness*, its *warmth* in *ideas* and *coldness* in *deeds*, its *seeming strength* and *freedom*, and its *real mortal weakness* and *exhaustion* from *unbelief, despotism,* and *extravagance.* All the books by our *Voltaires* and *Humes, Robertsons* and *Iselins* are full of this, and there emerges so beautiful a picture of the enlightenment and improvement of the world from its murky past—via deism and the despotism of souls,[23] that is to say, *philosophy* and *tranquility*—as to make the heart of every lover of his times sing.

All this is true and also untrue: true when, like a child, one compares *one color* with *another*, looking for a light, bright little image (alas, there is so much light in our age!); untrue when one considers former times according to their *very being* and *purposes*, their *pleasures* and *customs*, and in particular as *instruments* within the course of time. For then we can see something *solid* and *binding, noble* and *magnificent* in these seemingly *forced* performances

†20. Hurd, *Letters on Chivalry [and Romance, 1762].*

21. Or morals (*Sitten*).

22. Compare p. 39:41.

23. Compare p. 103:36–37.

and associations, something that we truly *do not feel*, and indeed   *51/52*
very nearly *cannot* feel anymore owing to our—thank God!—
refined manners,[24] our guilds *abolished* in exchange for *indentured*
lands, and our *innate* intelligence and love of all peoples *to the
ends of the earth.* Behold, you mock the days of *serfdom*, the primitive *country estates* of the nobility, the many *small islands* and *subdivisions,* and whatever depended on them; you praise nothing so
much as the *dissolution* of these bonds; and you recognize *no*
greater good, in all that has happened to mankind, than when
Europe, and along with it the world, became *free. Became free?*
Sweet dreamer! If only that were all, and if all that were only true!
But behold, too, how through the condition of those times *things*
were *accomplished,* when all human intelligence might otherwise
have become enfeebled: Europe was *populated* and *built-up*; lineages and families, lord and servant, king and subject were driven
more strongly and *closely* together; your so-called primitive country
estates restrained the *excessive, unhealthy expansion* of the *cities,*
those abysses for the vitality of mankind; the scarcity of *trade* and
refinement prevented *self-indulgence* and preserved simple humanity—*chastity* and *fertility* in marriage, *frugality* and *diligence,* and
community. The *crude guilds* and *baronies* created *prideful knights*
and *craftsmen,* but at the same time *self-reliance, security in one's circle,* a *manliness* standing upon its *center*[25] that could fight off the
worst bane of mankind—the *yoke* of *land* and *soul,*[26] under which
everything has evidently been sinking, with joy and freedom on
our minds, ever since all the islands[27] have been abandoned. It is
only thus that so many *warring republics* and *self-defending cities*
could arise a little later! The forces whose wretched remains you
are living on even today had to be *planted* first, *nourished,* and
raised through friction. Had heaven not sent you these prior barbaric times and maintained them for so long with many a shove
and knock—you poor, regimented Europe devouring or expelling your children—what a *wasteland* you would be with all your
wisdom!

"How could it be incomprehensible to anyone in the world
that light does not nourish human beings, that tranquility and

24. Or morals (as above).

25. An allusion to Herder's theme of the center of gravity that sustains individuals and nations. Compare to 39:5 and note 62 there.

26. I.e., serfdom.

27. I.e., the "many small islands and subdivisions" above.

abundance and so-called freedom of thought can never be the happiness and destiny of all men!" But *feeling, motion, action*—even if they should prove inconsequential (for what has *timeless* consequence on the stage of mankind?), if there will be *knocks* and *revolutions*, if these feelings will at times turn *fanatical, violent,* even *detestable*—as *instruments in the hands of time*, how great their *power* and *effect!* How they nourish the *heart*, not the *head!* How they bind everything together with *inclinations* and *drives*, not with *sickly thoughts*—*reverence* and the *honor of knights*, *boldness in love* and *civic strength*, *constitution* and *legislation, religion!* Nothing could be further from my mind than to defend the endless mass-migrations and devastations, the vassals' wars and feuds, the armies of monks, the pilgrimages and crusades: I only wish to explain them, [to show] how *spirit* breathes in everything, after all! The fermentation of *human forces*, the *great cure* of the whole species by *forced movement*, and, if I may speak so boldly, Fortune's rewinding of the *great wound-down clock*—albeit with great clamor and the inevitable disruption of the weights' calm repose! So the wheels rattled![28]

How differently I view the ages in this light! How much we should *forgive* them when we see them always *wrestling with their faults, struggling for an improvement* truly more visible than that attributed to a certain other age![29] How much *derision* is simply *mistaken* and *exaggerated* since the outrages [of the past] are either dreamt up by the brains of strangers,[30] or else since they were at the time much *milder* and more *inevitable* [than we imagine], or were already being *compensated for* by a corresponding good, or are already discernible to us as means to a *great good* in the future, of which [*those ages*] *themselves were not aware.* Who could read this history and not cry out repeatedly: *inclinations* and *virtues* of *honor* and *freedom*, of *love* and *courage*, of *politeness* and *keeping one's word*—where have you gone? Your *depths* have become *silted up*, your *fortresses* [ground down to] *soft sandy soil* full of *silver grains*, wherein nothing *grows!* Be this as it may: only give us *something* of your *reverence* and *superstition*, your *darkness* and *ignorance*, your *muddled* and *crude customs*, and take our *light* and *lack of faith*, our

28. *rasseln*, a sound commonly associated with chains. Herder is thinking of the kind of mechanical wall clock that is rewound by weights suspended on chains.

29. I.e., Herder's own age.

30. I.e., the brains of strangers to those ages, those unfamiliar with and unsympathetic to the actual ways of those times.

numbed coldness and refinement, our philosophical exhaustion and human misery! By the way: of course the mountain must border on the valley and the *dark, massive vault* could be nothing but dark, massive *vault*—Gothic! What a *giant stride* in the course of human destiny! If we only accepted that *destruction* precedes so that *improvement* and *order* may follow in its wake—a great stride! To cast *such* a light, so *great* a shadow was necessary: the knot had to be pulled *so tight* for development to ensue later. Did there not have to be *fermentation* to produce the *pure, yeastless* drink of the gods? Methinks that this follows directly from "the *favorite philosophy*" of the age. What a splendid opportunity for you to demonstrate how so many edges had first to be *worn down* with force before that *round, smooth, well-behaved thing* which we are could appear! How in the church so many *horrors, errors, vulgarities,* and *blasphemies* had to precede, how all those centuries had to *struggle, scream,* and *strive* for improvement before your *Reformation* or your *light, brilliantly-bright deism* could emerge. The *dark arts of the state* had to run through the full array of all their evils and atrocities before our "*statecraft*," in the full sense of the word, could appear like the morning sun rising from night and mist. So we still have a beautiful painting, *order* and *progression**** of nature, and you, illustrious philosopher, standing upon the shoulders of it all![31]

But I cannot persuade myself that anything under God's dominion is ever *only* means—everything is both *means* and *end,* and this surely goes for the centuries in question, too. Was not the flower of the spirit of the age, "*the spirit of chivalry,*" itself *a product* of all the past, *in the sound form of the North?* Had not *the mixture* of the concepts of *honor* and *love* and of *loyalty* and *reverence* and *courage* and *chastity,* which was now the *ideal,* been unheard-of before? Behold, then, *replenishment* and *progression**** towards greatness* in this very mixture, contrasting with the old world *in which the strength of every individual national character had been lost.* From the Orient to Rome, there was a *trunk:* now *branches* and *twigs* grew from this trunk, none by itself *as solid as the trunk,* but *more spread out, airier, higher!* Despite all barbarism, the *insights* that were treated *scholastically* were *more refined* and *exalted,* the *sentiments* put to *barbaric* and *popish* uses more *abstracted* and *exalted.* From these flowed *morality,* the very model thereof. What other age had ever known *such a religion,* wretched though it

31. This may bring to mind Newton's "standing upon the shoulders of giants." Compare the note to p. 91:31–32.

appeared? Even the more refined elements of the *Turkish* religion, for which our deists have such high regard, only *came about "through the Christian religion."* And even the *most wretched* pedantries of monkery, the most *fictitious* fantasies, show that there was enough *refinement* and *agility* in the world for such things to be *thought up* and *grasped*—that one had truly, keenly begun to breathe such *refined* air. How could *Papacy* have existed in *Greece* or *ancient Rome* considering not only the commonly recognized factors but also, and more importantly, the plain old fact that there was not yet any rationale, any *room*, for such a *refined* system! The "papacy" of ancient Egypt had surely been a far *cruder* and *clumsier* machine, to say the least. Despite all Gothic taste, such *forms of government* had *hardly existed before*—with the idea of *barbarian order*, from *the single element* all the way *up to the culmination*, with the constantly *varied attempts* at *binding* everything *so that it might nonetheless not be bound*. Chance, or rather raw and unimpeded force, exhausted itself *in small variations on the large form* such as a politician could hardly have thought up: a chaos wherein everything *was striving* towards a higher creation without knowing *how* or *what shape* [*things would take*]! The works of the *spirit* and *genius* dating to these times are all of the *same kind*, full of the composite *scent* of all times: too full of *beauties*, of *refinements*, of *invention*, of *order* to remain *beauty, order, invention*—they are like Gothic buildings! And if the spirit extended to the lowliest *institutions* and *practices*—[then] was it not right for the crown of the old tree[32] (not the trunk, which it could be no longer, but the treetop!) to continue to make its appearances during these centuries? Precisely the *disjointed*, the *confused*, the rich *superfluity of branches and twigs:* this made for its *nature!* This is where *the spirit of chivalry* bloomed and where one day, when the storm has blown away the leaves, the more beautiful fruit will dangle.

So many *brother-nations* and *no monarchy* to rule over the earth![33] *Every single branch a whole* now, as it were, that sprouted its own *twigs*—one growing *beside* the other, *intertwined* and *tangled*, each with its own sap. Such a multiplicity of *kingdoms!* So

55/56

---

32. *Stamm.* Herder is returning to the image he introduced a page earlier (p. 54:36 ff.), but he may also be playing on the anthropological meaning of *Stamm*, that is to say, tribe or lineage.

33. Using monarchy in the strict sense of "single rule," Herder writes, "no monarchy on earth." He does not mean to deny that there were kingdoms, however, but only that there was no single, overarching, and unifying authority such as the Roman Empire had provided.

many *communities of brothers living beside one another,* all sharing the same *German descent, one constitutional ideal, one religious faith;* each *struggling with itself* and *its parts,* each *moved* and *driven* almost invisibly but very pervasively by *a holy wind,* the *Papal prestige.* How the tree was shaken! Where were its branches, blossoms, and twigs not thrust through crusades and the conversion of entire peoples? If the subjugation of the world by the Romans had to help acquaint the peoples, though not in the best way, with a kind of "*international law* and *universal recognition of Romans,*" the hand of fortune turned popery, with all its violence, into a machine for [the production of] an "even more *exalted union,* the *universal recognition of all those who were supposed to be Christians, brothers, human beings*"! The tune was surely raised, through missed notes and screeching pitches, to a *higher tone:* a certain number of collected, abstracted, fermented ideas, inclinations, and conditions spread across the world. How the one, old, and simple trunk of the human species sprouted branches and twigs!

At last there followed what we call the resolution, the development: the long, eternal night was enlightened by the *morning* of *reformation* and *renaissance* in arts, sciences, morals! The yeasts sank and there arose *our thought, culture, philosophy!* One began to think as we think today: one was no longer barbarian.

No other point in the development of the human spirit has been described more lovingly! As all our histories, our Preliminary Discourses for the *Encyclopedia of All Human Knowledge,*[34] and our philosophies point towards it;[35] as from East to West, from our earliest beginnings until yesterday, all the threads that have been spun or that flutter in our heads like cobwebs in autumn have known to aim for this as for the *highest pinnacle of human education;** and as this system has already been burnished and praised so lavishly, endorsed so tenderly and settled so completely, I dare not add anything—I shall merely append a few minor *observations.*

56/57

---

34. A reference to d'Alembert's *Discours préliminaire* to the *Encyclopédie.*

†35. Hume's *History of England* and miscellaneous writings; Robertson's *History of Scotland* and *History of the Reign of Charles the Fifth;* D'Alembert's literary and philosophical miscellany; Iselin's *History of Mankind,* Part II, and miscellaneous writings—*as well as whatever else limps and babbles along [in their train].*

[I.] *First of all*, as regards the excessive homage paid to *human reason*,[36,37] I should like to say, if I may, that it was less and less *reason*,[38] but rather a *blind fate* casting and directing things, that contributed to this *universal change of the world*. Either events so great that they *exceeded* all human *powers* and *perspectives* were *thrust upon* mankind, as it were, so that they were mostly *resisted* and so that no one could have imagined their *consequences* as part of any *deliberate plan*; or else the world was changed by small *coincidences, chance finds* rather than *real discoveries*, mere applications of something that one had *long known* but never properly seen or used— or even by nothing more than *simple mechanics*, a new *technique* or *craft*. Philosophers of the 18th century: if this is so, where does this leave your *idolatry* towards the *human spirit*?

Who laid out *Venice* here, under such deep duress and in distress? And who thought through what this Venice, alone in this place, could and ought to be for *all the earth's peoples* throughout a millennium? He who cast these islands upon the morass, who led

57/58 these few fishermen here, was the same one who sowed the *seed* so that there might be an *oak* at that other time and place, who planted a *hut along the Tiber* so that there might be *Rome*, the *eternal* capital of the world. This same one now leads forth the barbarians so that they might *annihilate* the *literature of the entire world*, the *library* at *Alexandria* (so to speak, a foundering continent!), but then leads these very barbarians *to beg for a small remnant of literature, to preserve it*, and to bring it *to Europe* from an entirely *different direction*, via *paths* that no one had *dreamed of* or *wished for*.[39] Another time, the same one lets an *emperor's city*[40] be destroyed by them, so that the sciences, which were not being *sought* there and had long remained *idle*, might *flee to Europe*.

36. *Verstand.*

†37. The glory of the human spirit, its progress, revolutions, development, creation etc. [Herder uses French clichés here, presumably with mocking intent.]

38. Lit.: *Er [der Verstand].*

39. Justinian's closing of the schools of philosophy in Athens, in 529, marked the beginning of the gradual disappearance of certain ancient philosophical texts from Europe. During this period of decline, Arabic scholars continued to study the ancient philosophers, and it was through translations of their works that some of the teachings of the ancient philosophers returned to Europe, in the 13th century. It was during this time that Saint Thomas Aquinas' interest in Aristotle led to a revival of Aristotelianism and to the rise of Scholasticism (compare p. 86; *The Influence of Free Legislation*, 319:9–10).

40. Constantinople.

Everything is grand destiny, *not reflected over, not hoped for, not caused* by human beings. Can you not see, you ant, that you are merely *crawling* on the great wheel of doom?

As we enter more closely into the circumstances behind the origin of all so-called illuminations of the world, our proper subject, [we find] the same thing: *chance, destiny, deity* in all things great and small! What initiated *every reformation* were *details* that never, at the outset, had the great, momentous plan that they would acquire only later. On the contrary, as often as there was a prior, great, and genuinely considered human plan, so often it failed. All your great *church assemblies*—you emperors, kings, cardinals, and lords of the earth!—will never change anything; but that unrefined, unknowing monk, *Luther,* shall accomplish it! And this by *details,* while he himself never so much as thought that far ahead; by *means* that, according to the ways of our age, speaking philosophically, *could never have accomplished such a thing; he himself* accomplishing little, for the most part, beyond *impelling others, awakening* Reformers in all the other countries, standing up and saying "I am moving! Hence there is movement!" Thus came about what has come about, changing the world! How often had such *Luthers* stood up before—and had foundered. Their mouths were stopped with smoke and flames, or else their words found no free air where they resounded. But now it is *springtime:* the earth breaks open, and a thousand new plants spring forth, bred by the sun. Human being, you have always been just a small, *blind instru-* 58/59
ment, [used] almost against your will.

"But why," cries the gentle philosopher, "could not all these reformations have occurred *without revolutions?* If only *the human spirit* had been allowed to take *its quiet course* instead of letting the passions bear new prejudices in the storm of *action* and substituting one evil for another!" Answer: because such a *quiet progression*** of the *human spirit* for the improvement of the world is hardly anything other than a *phantom* in our heads, never *God's course* in *nature.* This seed falls into the earth: there it lies and grows stiff, but now comes the *sun* to awaken it; it bursts open, its vessels swelling violently asunder; it breaks out of the soil—thus the blossom, thus the fruit! Not even the earth's filthy fungi grow as you imagine. The basis of every reformation has always been just such a *tiny seed* that *fell quietly* to the ground and was hardly worth mentioning. People had *long possessed* it: they were *looking at it* but *giving it no heed*—yet now it was supposed to alter *inclinations, customs,* a world of *habits,* to *create them all anew!* How is this possible without *revolution*, without *passion* and *movement?* What Luther said had long been known, but now it was *Luther* who said it! *Roger Baco,*[41] *Galileo, Descartes, Leibniz:* when *they* made their discoveries, it was quiet. There was a *beam of light*, but their discoveries were meant to break through, to move opinions, to change the world; thus there were *storm* and *flame*. If reformers have always also had *passions* that the *matter itself*, the *science*, did not require, the *introduction of the matter* did indeed require them, and the very fact that they had them—had enough of them to break through the present void, which entire centuries had been *unable to do* by their efforts, machinery, and pondering—precisely this is *to the credit of [the reformer's] vocation!*

"[What we have here are] for the most part *simple mechanical inventions* that had long been known, that were available and played with but that now changed the world through a [new] idea and a *use unlike the former.*" Thus, for example, the uses of *glass* for *optics*, of *magnets* for *compasses*, of *powder* for *war*, of the *printer's art* for the *sciences*, of *calculus* for an entirely new *world of mathematics*. Everything took on a new shape. The tool had been changed, a place had been found *beyond the old world*, and so [that world] was *moved forth.***

Firearms were invented, and behold, the ancient courage of the *Theseuses, Spartans, Romans, knights*, and *giants* disappeared—war was transformed, and how much else along with it!

Printing was invented, and how the world of the *sciences* was changed, facilitated and spread, made light and superficial! Everyone can read and spell—and whoever can read is taught.

With the *small needle* on the ocean—who could count the revolutions on all continents that resulted from this? The discovery of lands so much vaster than Europe! The conquest of coasts abounding in gold, silver, gems, spices, and death! Men put into mines, slave-mills, subjection to vice, be it by conversion or by cultivation! Europe depopulated, its most secret powers consumed by disease and luxury. Who can tally this, who describe it? *New customs, inclinations, virtues, vices*—who can count and describe them? The world has been turning these past three centuries by an endless wheel—and what has it been hanging on, what has been giving it its momentum? The *needle's point* of *two* or *three mechanical thoughts!*

41. See Biographical Register. For some short translations of Baco by Herder, compare Suphan 23:219 ff. and 24:100 ff. and 162 ff.

II. It follows necessarily that a large part of this so-called modern education* must itself be *mechanics*, really. Examined more closely, how much this appears as the *modern spirit!* As it has usually been *new methods* that have changed the ways and arts of the world, these new methods *relieved powers* that had heretofore been indispensable, but that now *faded* with time, since every unused power goes to sleep. *Certain virtues* of *warfare*,[42] of *civil life*, of *seafaring*, of *government*—these were no longer needed. Instead there arose a *machine* that *one* alone could direct with a single thought, with a single nod!—for whose sake so many powers are lying dormant! With the invention of *firearms*, what nerves of *raw physical* prowess and *strength of soul* in war were not slackened, what courage, loyalty, presence [of mind] in particular circumstances, what old world's sense of honor exhausted! The army has become a hired machine, devoid of thought, power, or will, that *one man* directs *in his head:* a mere *marionette* of motion, a live wall that is paid to throw bullets and catch bullets. At bottom, so a Roman or Spartan might say, the virtues have been *burned up* within the innermost hearth of the heart, and the wreath of military honor has wilted. And what has taken its place? The soldier as premier hired servant of the state, decked out in hero's livery—behold his honor and vocation! [There] he is—and with no great effort the remnants of *all separate existences* are *exploded:* the ancient Gothic forms of *liberty, estates, property*—that wretched edifice in bad taste!—is shot to pieces and destroyed. What little wreckage remains is confined so strictly that *land, inhabitant, citizen, fatherland* may still mean something occasionally; but *master* and *slave*, *despot* and *liveried servants* of all offices, vocations, and estates, from the *peasant* up to the *cabinet minister,* and from the *minister* to the *priest*—that is now everything. This is called *sovereignty*, refined *statecraft*, the modern *philosophical form of government*— which it really is! The coronets and crowns of recent centuries, what do they rest upon—as the most famous sun-eagle on our coins shows—but *drums, flags, bullets,* and *soldiers' caps always at the ready*.[43]

60/61

42. Or "the science of war"; but elsewhere, Herder consistently speaks of war as an art (*Another Philosophy of History*, 31, 32, 103; *The Influence of Free Legislation*, 308, 311, 315, etc.).

43. From 1745 on, certain Prussian gold coins depicted the state's eagle, together with the sun as a symbol of absolute authority, surrounded by various constellations of military gear including drums, flags, and soldiers' caps. Compare p. 103:27–28.

That the spirit of *modern philosophy* is *mechanics* in more than one way, this is borne out, I should think, by the majority of *its children*. How often philosophy and learning are joined with *ignorance* and *feebleness* in matters of life and good sense! In former times, the philosophical spirit never existed *just for its own sake* but took its start from *practice* and *hastened towards practice* and thus had only the purpose of creating *complete, healthy, active souls;* but ever since it has been standing *alone* and has become a trade—it has been [just that], a *trade*. What small fraction among you recognize logic, metaphysics, morals, and physics for what they really are—organs of the human soul, *tools* to be used in activity, *exemplary forms of thought* that have no other purpose than to give our soul *its own more beautiful shape*. Instead, thoughts are *mechanically* banged *into place* by jesters and illusionists—vagarious fellows fencing with carpet-beaters! Rapiers in hand, they dance on the academic high-wire to the wonderment and delight of all those who, seated around, cheer on the great artists that they may not break their necks. Such is their art. If there is a *business* in the world that you wish to have poorly looked after, just hand it over to the *philosopher!* On paper, how pure, how gentle, how beautiful and great, but hopeless in *execution*—at every step, *marveling* and *bristling* with unseen obstacles and consequences! The child, meanwhile, was truly a great *philosopher:* having learnt *arithmetic* and initiated into syllogisms, figures, and *instruments*, he could often play so successfully that new *syllogisms, results,* and so-called *discoveries* resulted—the *fruit,* the *honor,* the *pinnacle* of the *human spirit!* Through *mechanical play!*

61/62

That was the heavier kind of philosophy—and now the *light,* the *beautiful* kind! Thank God, what is more mechanical than the latter? In the sciences, arts, habits, and ways of life that it has permeated, where it has become the sap and flower of the age, what could be more *mechanical?* What it has cast off its neck like a yoke, after all, is precisely *ancient pedigree,* the *pointless prejudice* about *learning, slow maturation, profound penetration,* and *postponed judgment!* At our *bars of justice,* instead of small, dusty, detailed insights and cases to be treated and examined each one *just as it is,* what *pretty, easy, free judgment* it has introduced to assess and dismiss *everything* on the evidence of *two* cases! From *what is individual,* from what is in the nature of the thing itself,[44] over to the bright and splendid *universal*—instead of being *judge* (flower of the age!),

44. Lit.: *species facti.*

to be a *philosopher.* Instead of hard-earned insights about the needs and genuine characteristics of the land, what an *eagle's view,* what a *view of the whole,* laid out as if on a *map* or a *philosophical diagram,*[45] has been brought to our *political economy* and *political science!* *Principles* have been taken from *Montesquieu's* mouth by and with which *a hundred different peoples* and *corners of the earth* can be spontaneously tallied in two moments according to the *basic arithmetic* of *politics.* Likewise with all *fine arts* and *crafts,* almost down to the least *day labor.* Who needs to climb around, to *toil* strenuously in the depths, as in a vaulted cellar? One can *reason!* With *dictionaries* and *philosophies* that cover them all, without the need to understand a single one, *tool in hand,* they have all become mere abridgments[46] of their prior pedantry—*abstracted spirit!* Philosophy out of two thoughts, the *most mechanical thing in the world.*

62/63

May I prove what a noble *mechanical* thing *modern humor* is? Is there a more *learned* language, a more *periodic form*—that is to say, a *narrower frame* of *thought,* of the *manner of living,* of *genius* and *taste*—than among that people[47] through which, in a hundred guises, [modern humor] has been spread most brilliantly throughout the world? What *spectacle* is more of a marionette of pleasing *regularity;* what *manner of life* more aping of carefree, mechanical *pleasantry, amusement,* and *affected speech;* what *philosophy* a more tired peddling of a few sentiments (and the treatment of all things in the world according to these sentiments)? *Apes of humanity,* of *genius,* of *good humor,* of *virtue*—and precisely because they are nothing more, and are themselves aped so easily, *they are such for all of Europe.*

III. Thus it is surely becoming intelligible toward "*what central point*" the education* [of mankind] has been tending and toward which it has always been directed: "Philosophy! *Thought!* Easier *mechanics! Reasoning* that burrows all the way down to the *foundations* of society, which once simply *stood* and *gave support!*" There again, from ten different angles, I can hardly understand how reasoning[48] could have twisted this so *universally* and *exclusively* into the *pinnacle* and *purpose* of all human education,* all *happiness,* all

---

45. Such as the *Système figuré des connoissances humaines* in Diderot's prospectus and d'Alembert's *Discours preliminaire* of the *Encyclopédie,* as well as in the latter's *Mélanges de littérature, d'histoire et de philosophie.*

46. Lit.: *abrégé raisonné.*

47. The French.

48. *verraisonniert.*

that is *good*. Is the whole body meant to see? Must not the whole body suffer when the hand and foot wish to be the *eye* and *brain*? Reasoning that is spread too carelessly, too uselessly—*might* it not weaken the *inclinations, drives*, and *activity* of life, and has it not in fact weakened them?

63/64   Certainly, this *exhaustion* may suit the spirit of certain countries: exhausted limbs must move along, they have no powers—except, perhaps, for *contrary thinking*. From *fear* or *habit* or *saturation*, and philosophy, every wheel remains in its place; and what are so many great, philosophically-governed herds but heaps thrown together—livestock and timber! They are thinking! Perhaps thinking has been *dispersed* among them, *towards one end:* that they may with every day *feel* more like a machine, according to *pre-set prejudices*, learning to gnash and *needing to move along*. They gnash, but that is all they can do as they refresh themselves with *free-thinking*. Dear, feeble, irritating, useless free-thinking, the substitute for everything of which they would perhaps need rather more—*heart, warmth, blood, being human, life!*

Now let everyone make the calculation. *Light*, infinitely elevated and dispersed, while the *inclination and drive to live is diminished incomparably!* The ideas of a *universal love of mankind, peoples, and enemies elevated* and the warm *feeling of affection for one's father, mother, brother, children, and friends infinitely diminished! Principles of freedom, honor,* and *virtue* dispersed so widely that all *affirm* them most luminously, that in certain countries everyone, down to the least one, has them *at the tip of his tongue*—at the same time that each of them is shackled with the *heaviest chains of cowardice, disgrace, extravagance, servility,* and *wretched aimlessness. Knacks and facilitations*[49] *dispersed without end*, but all of them joined in the hands of *one or a few* who alone are really thinking. The machine, meanwhile, has lost the desire to live, to act, to lead a noble and charitable, joyful human life: is it alive at all anymore? For the whole, as for the smallest part, *only the thought of the master [counts]*.[50]

Is this, then, the beautiful ideal condition toward which we have been formed* through everything, which is *spreading* further and further in *Europe*, which is *swimming out* to all the *continents*, seeking to *regiment* everything so that it may *become what we are*—human? *Citizens* of one *fatherland?* Individual beings who are to

49. Compare p. 68:22.

50. Compare Rousseau, *Discourse on the Sciences and the Arts* I (D: 6–9; *OC* 3: 6–9).

be *something* in the world? It is possible! At any rate, going by numbers and needs, purpose and point, it is all sure to be *political calculation:* everyone in the uniform proper to his place— machines! So there we have those shining *marketplaces* for the   64/65
education of mankind,* *pulpit* and *stage, halls* of *justice, libraries, schools,* and then, in particular, the crown jewel of it all: illustrious academies! What splendor, to the eternal glory of the princes! How great the ends of *the education** and *enlightenment* of the *world, the happiness of men!* Consecrated so magnificently, what do they do, what *can they do? They play!*[51]

IV. So a word about some of the most prominent *means* pursuant to the creative plan of *"educating* mankind"*—the honor of our age! Thus we arrive at a very *practical page* of the book, at least.

If it has not been written altogether in vain, we see that the *formation** and *progressing education*** of a nation* is never anything other than a *work of Fortune:* the result of a thousand *coexisting causes,* the product, as it were, of the *entire element within which [a nation] lives.* And is this—what *child's play!*—a mere matter of recasting this education* with and according to a few *more luminous ideas,* whereupon one may jabber about the very *restoration* of the *sciences?* This book, this author, this mass of writings is meant to *educate;** the product of all this, the philosophy of our age, is meant to *educate.** But what could [education*] mean except the *awakening* or *strengthening* of those inclinations by which mankind is *made happy*—and how far is this from happening! Really, *ideas* yield nothing but *ideas,* greater *clarity, correctness,* and *order* in thinking— but that is all one can count on *with certainty.* As for how everything will *mix* within the soul; or what will *be encountered* and what will *have to be changed;* how *powerful* and *enduring* this change will be; or, finally, how it might *combine* and *clash with* the *myriad incidents* and *contingencies* of *human life,* let alone of an *age* or of an *entire people,* of all Europe, of *all the universe* (as our humility imagines)—you gods, what an altogether different world of questions!

51. The Royal Academy of Sciences in Berlin, founded by Frederick II ("the Great") of Prussia in a bid to rival the Academy at Paris, may appear to exemplify some of the fashionable follies Herder mocks here. Disdain or not, however, Herder repeatedly sought and *thrice* received the Berlin Academy's annual essay prize: writing, in 1770, "On the Origin of Language"; in 1773, on "The Causes of the Deterioration in Taste among the Various Peoples where It Had Blossomed"; and in 1779 "On the Influence of Governments on the Sciences, etc." [see *The Influence of Free Legislation*]. In 1787, Herder was made an honorary member of the Academy.

A man who was introduced to *our age's artificial way of thinking*
would read all the books that we read from childhood on, that we
praise and *according to which*, it is said, we *form** ourselves; he would

gather the *principles* that we all *avow* noisily or tacitly and on which
we expend *some* of our soul's *energies*, and so on. If he hoped, on
this basis, to draw some conclusions about the *whole living, driving
engine* of the age, how *pitifully mistaken* he would be! Precisely
because these *principles* are such *commonplaces, playthings* passed
from hand to hand, *mouth-work* passed from lip to lip, it is likely
that they *can no longer* have *any effect*. Does one *need* that with
which one *plays?* And when one has so much grain that instead of
sowing or *planting* the field, one *dumps out one's stores* on it as upon a
barren, dry granary floor, how can *anything grow roots* or any seed
come up anymore? Will a single seed get *into the ground* then?

Need I seek examples for a truth to which almost everything
bears witness, alas? *Religion* and *morals, legislation* and *common customs:* how flooded they all are with *beautiful principles, demonstrations, systems, interpretations*—flooded to the point where almost
nobody can *see to the bottom* and *stand* upon it anymore. But only
for this very reason does anyone *swim over to the other side.* The
theologian leafs through the most touching accounts of religion, he
learns, knows, proves, and *forgets:* we are all taught to be such theo-
logians from childhood on. The *pulpit* thunders with principles
that we all avow, understand, feel beautifully, and leave on and
beside the pulpit. The same goes for *books, philosophy,* and *morals.*
Who is not tired of reading them? And what writer does not make
it his primary business to *dress things up nicely,* to *coat* his impotent
pill with *sugar?* It cannot be helped that head and heart are
divided: alas, man's condition is such that he will act not according to what he *knows* but according to what *pleases* him. What
good are the most abundant *delicacies* to the sick man whose *ailing
heart* does not *allow* him to *enjoy* them, indeed whose *heart has been
made sick* by this very abundance?

The *purveyors* of this *mode* of education*—in particular the philosophers of Paris—could be permitted their language and their
delusions about educating* "all *mankind,*" that is to say, *toute
l'Europe* and *tout l'Univers.*[52] One knows, after all, what to make of
this language: *the right tone, conventional phrase, beautiful style,* or,
at most, *useful delusion!* But when such methods of the culture of

52. All of Europe and all the universe (see p. 65:30–31, just above). Herder's
capitalization.

letters are discovered even by those with entirely different tools,   66/67
when they are employed to drape the age in a pleasant haze, to
direct *eyes* upon the splendor of this ineffective light in order to
free up *hearts* and *hands*—then the resulting *error* and *loss* is truly
lamentable!

There once was an *age* for which the art of *legislation* was the
only means of educating* nations[53] and where this means, han-
dled in the strangest fashion, was usually supposed to become
simply a *universal philosophy of mankind,* a *codification* of *reason*[54]
and *humanity,* and who knows what else. The thing was surely
more dazzling than *useful.* Certainly, this allowed for "the exhaustion of all *generalities* of *the right and good;* of the *maxims* of *the love
of mankind* and *wisdom;* of the *perspectives* from all *times* and *peoples*
for all *times* and *peoples.*" For all times and peoples—and thus, alas,
not *for* the very people whom this book of law is supposed to serve
as its appropriate attire. What is skimmed off so generally, is it
not mere *foam* that will *dissolve* in the *air* of all the times and peoples? How different [it is] to *provide nourishment* for the blood vessels and sinews of one's people, so that its *heart may be strengthened*
and its *bones and marrow invigorated!*

Between every generally stated truth—even the *most edifying*—
and its *least* application, there is a chasm! To say nothing of the
application in *a single proper place,* for *proper ends,* in the *one best
manner.* The *Solon* of a *village,* who may have done no more than
abolish *a bad habit,* than *set in motion* a *stream of human sentiments*
and *activities,* has done a thousand times more about legislation
than all you *reasoners*[55] for whom everything is *true* and everything
false—a *wretched universal shadow.*

Once upon a time the construction of *academies, libraries,* and
museums was called the *education** of the world—how splendid!
The court assumes the *name* of this academy,[56] this worthy *pryta-
neion*[57] of distinguished men, this [token of] *support* for the precious sciences, this superb *ballroom* for the monarch's *birthday*

53. Compare *The Influence of Free Legislation.*

54. *Vernunft.*

55. *Raisonneurs.*

56. Hoping thereby to benefit from its prestige.

57. The equivalent of a town hall in ancient Greek city-states, which housed
the communal hearth. It was the place where Olympic champions were celebrated
upon their return home and where distinguished citizens were awarded perma-
nent board as a mark of honor. Compare Plato, *Apology* 36d.

celebrations. But what does it do for the education* of *this* land, *this* people, *these* subjects? And even if it did everything, to what extent would this produce happiness? Could these *statues,* even if you were to put them up by every path and post, transform every passer-by into a *Greek,* that he might *look* at them, *care* about them, feel himself *in them* as a Greek would? Hardly! Could these *poems,* these beautiful lectures in the *Hellenic* manner, recreate a time when verses and speeches *were marveled at* and *worked wonders?* I think not! And the so-called *restorers* of the sciences, be they popes or cardinals, did they not always have *Apollo,* the *Muses,* and all the gods enacted in modern Latin verse—knowing that it was all *play? Apollo's* statue could always stand beside *Christ* and *Leda,* for all three had *the same effect*—none! Could this performance, this stage produce *real Roman heroism* and create *Brutuses* or *Catos?* Do you think that your stage or your pulpit would stand? In the noblest sciences, Mount Ossa is piled upon Mount Pelion[58]—great undertaking!—almost without knowing *what for.* The treasures *lie there* and are not used or needed; at any rate, it is clearly not *mankind* that needs them right now.

Once upon a time, everyone stormed after *education,* and education was recast with beautiful *practical knowledge, instruction, enlightenment, facilitation* of comprehension,[59] and of course in early *refinement* to *mannered pleasantries*—as if any of this could *change* or *form* * inclinations. All without considering a single despised means of restoring or *recreating good habits* or even *prejudices, techniques,* and *forces,* thereby forming* a *"better world"* for all. The essay, the plan, was *written, printed, forgotten!* A textbook of *education* just like the thousands we already possess, a *code of good rules* just like the millions we will possess one day—and still the world *will remain as it is.*

How differently the ages and peoples thought about this when everything remained so *narrowly national.* All education* arose from the most particular *individual* need and always *returned there*—so much *experience, action, application of life* in the *most determinate* setting. Here in the *patriarch's hut,* there in a narrow

58. In Greek mythology, the brother-giants Otos and Ephialtes grew arrogant in their strength and sought to challenge the Olympian gods by piling the two Thessalian mountains on top of Zeus' mythical throne, Olympus, the highest mountain in the Greek peninsula. Herder uses this image to identify a great but arrogant and doomed effort to reach heaven. In the Christian idiom, he might have referred to the story of the Tower of Babel (Gen. 11:11).

59. Lit.: *ad captum.*

farming region or a small *republic,* [one was among] *human beings,* 68/69
where one was familiar with everything, where one could feel and
therefore give others something to feel as well, where, heart in
hand, one could speak in full view of things! In this sense it was
an *apt* charge, leveled by our *enlightened* age against the less-
enlightened Greeks, that they never philosophized *in a properly
general and purely abstract manner,* but always spoke in terms of
small needs on a *narrow* stage. What was said was *applied,* and
every word found its *place:* how different, how determined,
strong, and eternal were those better times when one did not yet
speak by words at all, but through *action, habit, example,* and *thou-
sandfold influence!* Now we *speak about a hundred estates,* classes,
times, and human types *at once,* only to say *nothing* about any one
of them: our wisdom is so refined and incorporeal, so *abstract in
spirit,* that it *dissipates* without any use. But then it was and always
remained wisdom of the *citizen,* the history of a [concrete] human
object, a fluid full of *nutrients.*[60]

If my voice had power and space enough, how I would call out
to all those who are working for the education* of mankind: "No
more *commonplaces* about *improvement!* Not *paper culture* or even
institutions—*action!*" Leave it to those who have the misfortune
of being incapable of anything else to *talk* and to *educate** with
their heads in the clouds.[61] Does not the girl's *lover* have a place
better than the *poet* singing about her or the *suitor* courting her?
Beware, lest he who *sings* most beautifully of love of mankind, of
amity among the peoples and faithfulness to the fathers, be plan-
ning to injure it for centuries with the deepest *thrust of his dagger.*
He who seems the noblest *lawgiver*[62] may be the greatest *destroyer*
of his *century!* [Let there be] no talk of inner *improvement, humanity,* and *happiness:* he is just following the current of the age! He
has been made the redeemer of mankind *according to the delusions
of the age,* and he is striving for the brief *wages* of all this—the wilt-
ing laurel *of vanity,* tomorrow's dust and ash. The great, divine

---

60. Compare p. 70:21.

61. Herder's *ins Blaue des Himmels hineinbilden* combines two ideas in a way
that cannot be properly reproduced in English: one the one hand, *ins Blaue* ("into
the blue") is an idiomatic expression for something undertaken without worry,
care, or responsibility; on the other hand, Herder revisits the image, introduced
on the previous page (p. 68:16), of misguided ideals of education as an arrogant
reaching for the heavens.

62. Compare Rousseau, *Discourse on the Sciences and the Arts* II.

work of *educating* mankind—silent, powerful, hidden, eternal*—can have no connection with petty *vanity!*

V. After what I have written, someone will no doubt bring up the platitude that one always praises what is distant and complains about the present; that it befits only children to become so enamored of what is gilded and distant that they would, out of ignorance, give up the apples they hold in their hands. But perhaps I am not such a child. I concede everything *great, beautiful*, and *unique* in our age, and, all my reproaches notwithstanding, I have always held to this ground: "*Philosophy! Spreading brightness!* Astonishing *mechanical skill* and *ease! Mildness!*" To what heights our age has risen in this since the restoration of the sciences, and by what peculiarly *easy* means! How robustly it has *fortified* them and *secured* them for posterity! I think that I have provided *observations* about this, rather than the excessive *declamations*[63] *of praise* that one finds in all the fashionable books, especially the French ones.

Truly a *great age* in terms of *means* and *purpose*: in view of all the preceding trees upon which we are standing, this is without doubt the *highest treetop!*[64] We have *made use* of as much *fluid* from the root, trunk, and branches as our *thin twigs at the treetop could possibly hold!* We are *standing high* above the Orientals, Greeks, and Romans, let alone the ordinary Gothic barbarians! From on high, we thus *look out over the earth!* [We have] all peoples and continents under our shadow, as it were, and when a storm shakes two small twigs in Europe, how the whole world trembles and bleeds! When has all the earth ever been joined so universally *by so few united threads?* When has there ever been more *power* and *machinery* to shake entire nations with the *push of a button*, with the *movement of a few fingers?* Everything hangs from the tip of *two* or *three thoughts!*

At the same time, when has the world been as universally *enlightened* as it is now—and still proceeding towards ever-greater *illumination?* Before, wisdom was always narrowly *national* and therefore reached deeper and attracted more strongly; but how *widely* it casts its rays now! Where is what *Voltaire* writes not read?[65] The *whole world* is well-nigh glowing with *Voltaire's lucidity!*

63. On declamation, see especially *The Influence of Free Legislation*, 309, 310, 318, 320.

64. Compare pp. 54:25, 91:31–35 and *Of the Changes in the Tastes of the Nations*, 157:29 ff.

65. Compare p. 104:11–12.

How this seems to go on without end! *Where are* there no European colonies, and where *will* there not *be* any? The fonder savages grow everywhere of our liquor and luxury, the more *ready* they also become for our *conversion!* Everywhere they are brought closer to *our culture*, by liquor and luxury especially, and before long—God willing!—all human beings will be *as we* are: *good, strong, happy men!*[66]

Commerce and *popery*, how much have you contributed to this great business! *Spaniards, Jesuits*, and *Hollanders:* you philanthropic, selfless, noble, and virtuous nations! How much the *formation* of mankind* owes to you already!

If this is how it goes in other continents, how could it be otherwise in Europe? [What a] disgrace for *England* that *Ireland* remained wild and barbaric for so long: [now] it is *regimented* and *happy*. Disgrace for England that the *Highlanders* went without pant-legs for so long: now they carry [their pants] *on a rod*, at least, and are happy.[67] What kingdom, in our age, has not made itself *great* and *happy!* Only a single one[68] has been disgracing humanity by lying in its midst without academies and agricultural associations,[69] wearing twisted moustaches[70] and therefore fostering regicides. And behold, what *magnanimous France* had already undertaken singly, regarding savage *Corsica*, has since been done by three [countries]—the formation* of twisted moustaches into human beings *such as we are: good, strong, happy* men![71]

---

66. Compare *Ideas*, 19, 2 (DKV 6:818); *Letters towards the Advancement of Humanity*, letters 114, 115, 122, 123 (DKV 7:671–72, 688, 741, 750).

67. Herder seems to be thinking of a supposed strategy for subverting the ban on wearing kilts after the imposition of the Disarming Act of 1746 (DKV 4: 879).

68. Poland.

69. *Ackerbausozietäten*, a form of agricultural organization, taken as shorthand for what were then considered particularly advanced and enlightened forms of production.

70. *Knebelbärte*, a particular style of facial hair deemed embarrassingly old-fashioned by the courtly French arbiters of good taste at the time.

71. Herder is referring to the partition of Poland between Austria, Prussia, and Russia in 1772—viewed as an exercise in regimentation. The "twisted moustaches" symbolize the alleged backwardness and recalcitrance of the Polish aristocrats and their state vis-à-vis the enlightened spirit of the age, and the charge of fostering regicide refers to their conspiracy against the last Polish king, Stanislaus II. On this issue, compare Rousseau, *Constitutional Project for Corsica* and *Considerations on the Government of Poland*.

All the arts we practice, how *high* they have risen! Can one imagine anything above that *art of government*, this system, this science for the *education* of mankind?*[72] The entire and exclusive driving force of our states: *fear* and *money*. Without the least *need* of *religion* (the childish driving force!), or *honor*, or *freedom of the soul*, or *human happiness*. Do we ever know how to *catch* and *transform* the only god of gods, *Mammon*, our second Proteus, and how to *force* him to give us everything we want! Highest, blessed art of governing!

Behold an *army*, the finest original model of human society! All dressed so colorfully and lightly, fed so easily, thinking harmoniously, free and comfortable in all its limbs—moving *nobly*. How bright and piercing the tools in its hands! A *sum of virtues* that are learned with every daily operation—a *model* of *excellence* in the *human spirit* and *the government of the world*. [A model of] resignation!

Balance [of power] in Europe, you great invention *unknown to any previous age!*[73] [Behold] how these great state-bodies, within which mankind is no doubt best cared for, are now rubbing against one another without destroying each other, and cannot ever destroy each other! How we have such sorry examples before us of the poor statecraft of *Goths, Huns, Vandals, Greeks, Persians,* and *Romans*—in short, of all times! And how they proceed on the high road, these water-tons brimming with insects, swallowing everything up in order to create uniformity, peace, and security.[74] Poor

†72. Hume's political writings (essays IV, IX, XXV, XXVI) and his *Hist[ory of England]*. [The first reference is to the fourth volume of Hume's *Essays and Treatises on Various Subjects*, published in 1756. The essays in question are "That Politics may be reduced to a Science (1742)"; "Whether the British Government inclines more to Absolute Monarchy or to a Republic (1742)"; "Of the Original Contract (1748)"; and "Of Passive Obedience (1748)." In the standard 1777 edition of Hume's *Essays*, the respective numbers are III and VII (Part I), XII and XIII (Part II).]

73. Herder is mocking Voltaire's preference for the balance of power in modern Europe over that in ancient Greece, as expressed in his *Historical and Critical Remarks, etc.* (1733).

74. Compare *Ideas*, 8, 5: "It is inconceivable how man could have been made for the state, so that its first establishment would be the necessary seed of his first true happiness: for how many peoples on earth know nothing of a state, and are yet happier than many a crucified state-benefactor . . . On our globe, millions live without states, and even every one of us, no matter how artificial our states, must begin where the savage does if he wants to be happy: that is to say, by struggling for and attaining health and vigor of soul, the well-being of his household and his heart, not from the state, but by his own efforts. Father and mother, husband

city? Tormented village? How blessed we are! For the safeguard-ing of obedience, peace, security, of all the *cardinal virtues* and *blessings: mercenaries, allies, balance [of power] in Europe!* There is and must always be—so blessed are we—eternal *tranquility, peace, security,* and *obedience* in Europe.

So our *political historians* and *composers of historical epics* about *monarchy* are permitted to paint the expansion of this condition over time:[75] "Once, sad times, men acted merely according to their *needs* and *whims;* even *sadder times,* when the power of rulers was not yet boundless; and saddest times of all, when their incomes were not yet entirely *arbitrary*—when there was so little for the *philosophical writer of epic history* to reason about in general, or to *paint on* the full [canvas] of Europe, [because there were] no *armies* capable of *disturbing* distant *borders,* no *princes* who could come forth from their lands in order to conquer, and thus every-thing was geared towards wretched *resistance* and *self-defense!* No *politics;* no *view* to *remote times* and *lands,* no *speculation* reaching for the moon; and thus no connections between countries through these philanthropic side-glances. In short—using the terms of the latest, highest taste—no *social life in Europe.* But since, thank God, the *individual powers* and *parts of the state* have been cast off; since the nobility has been *balanced so gloriously against* the cities and been *outweighed,* as have the cities against the liberated land,[76] and the nobility, cities, and liberated land against the masses; and since all have been steered into the miraculous machine, so that no one knows or may know anything of *justice exercised by oneself, personal dignity,* and *individual self-determination* anymore—since then, how blessed we have become: what *social life* in Europe! Where the monarch has the state so completely in *his power* that [the state itself] is no longer his *purpose,* but that *foreign dealings through it* [are his purpose now]; where [every monarch]

72/73

---

and wife, child and brother, friend and human being—these are the natural rela-tions that make us happy; what the state can give us are tools and artifices—but unfortunately, it can also deprive us of something much more essential, *ourselves"* (DKV 6:333–34).

†75. Thus Robertson's introduction to his *History of the Reign of Charles the Fifth,* of which this is merely a faithful excerpt, with evaluations of his evaluations where appropriate. "It is not things, but the opinions about things that disturb men"— Epictetus. [Despite their billing, the following quotations are not faithful reproduc-tions so much as rather tendentious, even polemical, exegeses. By "introduction," Herder appears to mean all of Robertson's first volume.]

76. Or released (from the bondage of serfdom).

looks so far [ahead], *calculates, consults, acts,* and is *led, moved to enthusiasm* by nods of which he understands and knows nothing;[77] where no state is permitted to pick up as much as a tiny goose feather without being watched, without the most remote cause automatically triggering universal bloodletting in all continents. Great universality! How condensed, *human, dispassionate* are the wars that originate thence, how just, *human, worthy* the negotiations!" How the highest virtue, *resignation,* is thereby promoted among *all individuals*—exalted *social life in Europe!*

And how glorious the means[78] by which one arrived at the point "where the power of monarchy grew in lock-step with the *enfeeblement* of *individual* parts and the *strengthening* of the *mercenaries.* The later and latest history, in particular that of the *French,* which has been leading the way for all of Europe, shows the means by which [monarchy] *broadened* its prerogatives, *increased* its income, *subjugated* its domestic enemies or *controlled* them, and *expanded* its borders. Glorious means and what a *great* purpose: the *scales* of Europe! The *happiness* of Europe! On *these* scales, and with respect to *this* happiness, *every single* grain of sand no doubt means a lot!

"Our system of trade!" Can one think of anything higher than the *refinement* of this *all-encompassing science?* How wretched were the *Spartans,* who needed their *Helots* for agriculture,[79] how barbaric the *Romans,* who locked their slaves into prisons inside the earth![80] In Europe slavery has been abolished[81] because it has

77. An allusion to the power of counselors and other courtiers on monarchs.

†78. Still merely the excerpt from Robertson.

79. Compare p. 37:31–32 and *Do We Still Have the Fatherland of the Ancients?,* p. 332:20.

80. The notorious Roman mines.

†81. Millar about the distinction of ranks, Chapter V. [John Millar, *Observations concerning the distinction of ranks in society* (1771). Chapter V: "The changes produced in the government of a people by their progress in arts, and in polished manners." In Chapter IV, Section 2 ("The usual effects of opulence and civilized manners, with regard to the treatment of servants"), Millar argues for "more extensive considerations of utility" by which the benefits of slavery turn out to be much less than they appear "at first sight." When all circumstances are "duly considered," Millar proposes, "it will be found that the work of a slave, who receives nothing but a bare subsistence, is really dearer than that of a free man, to whom constant wages are given in proportion to his industry."

At *Do We Still Have the Fatherland of the Ancients?,* 336:6–7, Herder suggests that foreign children captured as slaves "must sooner or later become a burden on [the capturers'] own children," but he strikes a rather different note in his review of Millar's *Observations* for the *Frankfurter gelehrte Anzeigen,* no. 77 (25 September

been calculated how much more these slaves cost, and how much less they yielded, than free men. There is only one thing we continue to permit ourselves: to *use* and *trade three continents as slaves,*

1772): 609–14. The following is the conclusion of his review, reprinted at DKV 4:852–53:

Though a little long-winded and self-satisfied about his discoveries, [Millar] demonstrates very well what advantages the *abolition of slavery* has brought for political economy and (according to the fashionable hallelujah to which we have become accustomed) for *all mankind—for all mankind!* Other things are less eye-catching: the *security, tranquility,* and *happiness* of the *ancient German law of property,* for example, which was by no means Polish slavery, and which has been lost in our new constitutions with their *guarantees of mobility;* the *magnificence, daring,* and *invigoration* that was contained, despite all disorder and barbarism, even in the old *feudal order* that has been lost to our *modern ways;* or, finally, the *wretched condition* that was introduced precisely when slavery was abandoned and that has left us all *bound by an invisible chain—shack-led, lashed,* and *emaciated* ten times worse now than the slave who bore a light weight around his ankle—by medal-ribbons, priests' collars, or fancy swords around our waists—by prejudice, luxury, political regulation and miscalculation, and a hundred horrible pestilences of the soul besides. And so we will continue for a long time with nothing but a *one-sided* history of the human species. At last I am forced to admit to an unphilosophical weakness: namely that all these histories of human powers and orders and fates [observed] *without empathy* annoy me. For the great arranger of all things, *everything is good, and human beings are likewise good, in terms of the great scheme, whatever their condition,* be it that of a frog or a behemoth (or so I hope and believe with all my heart). I also grant that it is excellent and quite *divine* for a philosopher to point out *goodness, excellence,* and *wisdom* to us in conditions where the common human eye, our feeling of need and weakness, does not allow us to see it, or not always, anyway. In this business consists the true dignity of philosophy: the human spirit soaring towards the council of the heavenly guardians, whose resolutions are always benevolent, though their conclusions are too great, too lofty, too far-reaching and comprehensive for us poor mortals. To receive, from this source, a whispered word of wisdom out of the philosopher's mouth, is truly a godsend. But then to let all the scenes of human life, good or evil, pass before a cold, indifferent eye *as if they were all equally good;* to touch, at most, upon the *evil* ones with a word, but without also using and as it were gently *prescribing* the *better* ones (which may have preceded or might follow suit, or which may even be present already, though still invisible) for *improvement, awakening, instruction, and consolation;* to write about all the conditions of mankind as if one *were not oneself living in a particular condition right now*—this may well pass for *historical* spirit, *philosophical* spirit, the spirit of *high, insensible, passionless, stoic* or *epicurean gods:* but it should need no repetition to see what is missing, where the *human beings* are missing!]

to *banish* them to silver mines and sugar mills. But these are not Europeans, not Christians, and in return we receive silver and gems, spices, sugar—and secret disease.[82] All this for the sake of trade and for the *mutual fraternal assistance* and *community* among countries.[83]

"The system of trade!" The greatness and uniqueness of the project is obvious! *Three continents devastated* and *regimented* by us, and we *depopulated* by them, emasculated, sunk in luxury, exploitation, and death: what a rich and happy deal! Who could do other than to claim his share in the great *whirling cloud*[84] that is sucking the life out of Europe, than to press for his place within it and to deliver his own children, if not another man's, to it as the greatest *man of trade?*[85] The old name, shepherd of the peoples, has been changed to monopolist,[86] and when the great cloud will one day burst and unleash a hundred tempests, then help us the great god Mammon, whom we are *all serving now!*

"*Ways of life* and customs!" How wretched [the time] when there were still nations and national characters:[87] what mutual *hatred, aversion* to foreigners, *fixation* upon one's center,[88] ancestral *prejudices*, clinging to a *scrap of land* upon which we are born and upon which we are to rot away.[89] *Native* ways of thinking, a *narrow circle* of ideas, eternal *barbarism!* Thank God that all our *national characters* have been erased! We *all* love each other, or rather, none of us *needs* to love any other. We *interact with each*

74/75

82. I.e., venereal disease, and in particular syphilis, thought to have been brought back to Europe from the New World.

83. Compare p. 71:10–13.

84. *Ziehwolke*.

85. At p. 52:33–34 Herder pities "poor, regimented Europe devouring or expelling its children." At *Do We Still Have the Fatherland of the Ancients?*, 336:4–7 he discusses the sacrifice of one's own children for the capture of others as slaves, and at *Governments as Inherited Regimes*, 366:31, he depicts governments as "child-devouring Saturn[s]."

86. In the move from worshipping God to worshipping Mammon.

†87. Hume's writings on various subjects, fourth volume, essay XXIV. [*Essays and Treatises on Various Subjects*, see Herder's above note to p. 71. The essay is entitled "Of National Characters (1748)" and appears as number XXI (Part I) in the 1777 collection.]

88. Compare p. 39:5 and note there.

89. Compare Herder's paragraph at *Do We Still Have the Fatherland of the Ancients?*, 329:32–330:12.

other, completely *indifferent*[90] to each other, *mannered, courteous, blissful!* We may not have a *fatherland,*[91] none who are *dear to us* and for whom we live; but we are *friends to all men* and *citizens of the world.* All the rulers of Europe are speaking French already, and soon we will *all* be doing so. And then—state of bliss!—the golden age shall be upon us again "when *all the world* will have *one tongue* and *language* and there shall be *one flock* and *one shepherd.*"[92] National characters, where have you gone?

"*Way of life* and *customs of Europe!*" How *late* did *youth* mature during Christianity's Gothic ages: barely an adult in one's thirtieth year, one lost *half* one's life to *miserable childhood, philosophy, education,* and *good manners.* What a new *creature* you have made: now we are *mature* in the thirteenth year, but *wilted* by the twentieth through silent as well as clamorous vices. We enjoy life right at *dusk* and in its *brightest bloom.*

"*Way of life* and *customs of Europe!*" What Gothic virtue, *modesty, youthful innocence, bashfulness!*[93] How early we discard the ambiguous, inconvenient cloak of virtue; social gatherings, women (who are most *wanting* in shame, but who also have the least *need* of it), even our very *parents* soon wipe it from our cheeks. Or if not, we travel (the *teacher* of good manners!),[94] and who would bring back the dress of childhood, now outgrown, out of fashion, and indeed indecent? With *brazenness, societal tone,* and *ease* we help ourselves to everything. Beautiful philosophy! "The *delicacy of tastes* and *passions!*"[95] How *crude,* by contrast, the Greeks and Romans remained in their tastes! How little they knew of the   75/76

90. In the German, too, there are two components to this: the lack of interest in each other, but also the absence of any substantial differences that could give rise to such interest.

91. See *Do We Still Have a Fatherland?, Do We Still Have the Fatherland of the Ancients?.*

92. Gen. 11:1–9; John 10:16.

†93. Hurd's *Dialogues on the Uses of Foreign Travel.* [Compare DKV 4:885 about Locke and Shaftesbury debating the modesty of youth and how to protect its premature demise.]

94. An allusion to *Bildungsreisen:* the practice of sending young gentlemen abroad, most conventionally to Italy, to complete and complement their formal educations.

†95. Hume's political essays I, XVII, XXIII. [Once more from the *Essays on Various Subjects,* as above. The titles are "Of the Delicacy of Taste and Passion (1742)"; "Of the Rise and Progress of Arts and Sciences (1742)"; and "Of Simplicity and Refinement in Writing (1742)." All three appear in the first part of the 1777 edition, as essays I, XIV, and XX respectively.]

proper tone for *dealing* with the beautiful sex! *Plato* and *Cicero* could write volumes of dialogues about metaphysics and manly arts *without ever letting a woman speak*. Who among us could suffer through a piece *without love,*[96] even if he *were marooned on a deserted island like Philoctetes!*[97] *Voltaire*—but one should read how seriously he himself warned against imitation. *Women* are our audience, our *Aspasias* of taste and philosophy. We know how to dress *Cartesian* vortices and *Newtonian* attractions[98] in a *corset;* we write history, sermons, and whatever else, *for and as women. The greater delicacy of our taste* has been proven.

"Fine arts and sciences."[99] The ancients were, of course, able to develop some of the cruder ones—thus the wretched, restless form of government: *small republics.* But consider, too, the *crudeness* of *Demosthenes' eloquence,* of Greek *theater,* of famed *classical antiquity* itself. Their *painting* and *music,* especially: nothing but bloated fairy tales and hysterical crying. The *finer bloom* of the arts waited for blessed monarchy! At *Louis' courts,*[100] *Corneille* found *heroes* to copy, *Racine, emotions:* one invented an entirely new species of truth, of sentiment, and of taste—*opera*—of which the fabled, cold, stark ancients had known nothing. Be blessed, *opera,* you gathering point and inspiration to competition for all our finest arts!

It was under blessed monarchy that the real inventions were made.[101] Instead of the pedantic old universities, illustrious academies were invented; *Bossuet* invented a history, *all declamation* and *sermonizing* and *tallying of years,* far surpassing [that of] simpleminded *Xenophon* and *Livy; Bourdaloue* invented his *genre of discourse,* so much better than [that of] *Demosthenes!* One invented a

96. Compare Rousseau's Letter to M. d'Alembert: "Let love be depicted for us as it may: it seduces or it is not love. If it is depicted badly, the play is bad; but if it is depicted well, it overshadows everything that accompanies it." (*OC* V, 51).

97. Compare also Herder's "scenes with song" at Suphan 28:69–78.

98. Descartes and Newton offered competing theories about the shape of the earth. According to Cartesian vortex theory (*Principia* III, §30 ff.), the shape of the Earth was supposed to be prolate, while Newtonian theory predicted the oblate form. The debate was eventually resolved in Newton's favor.

†99. Hume's *Essays,* fourth volume (numbers XVI and XVII); Voltaire's *Age of Louis XIV, XV, XX* and the armies of panegyrists of the new literature. [For essay XVII, see the above note to p. 75. Number XVI is entitled "Of Eloquence (1742)" and appears as essay XIII (Part I) of the 1777 edition. "Of the Sciences" and "Of the Fine Arts" (*beaux-arts*) are the titles of Chapters 31 and 32 in Voltaire's *Age of Louis XIV.*]

100. Louis XIV.

†101. Voltaire's *Age of Louis XIV.*

new *music*,[102] harmony that could do without melody; a *new architecture*, and, believed to be impossible by everyone, a new *column*;[103] and, what posterity will admire most, a *flat architecture*
with all the products of nature—*landscaping!* Full of proportion
and symmetry, full of *eternal* delight and an entirely *new nature*
without *nature.* How blessed we are! The things we could invent
only under monarchy!

Last of all, one began to *philosophize.*[104] And in how *new* a manner: without *system* or *principles*, so that one might always remain
free, at another time, to believe the opposite as well; without *demonstrations*; clothed in *humor* since "dour philosophy has never
improved the world."[105] Then at last—glorious innovation!—
[philosophy arrived] in *memoirs* and *reference books* wherein everyone could read *whatever* and *as much* as he wanted, and thus the
most glorious invention of all: the *Dictionary,* the *Encyclopedia of All
Sciences and Arts.*[106] "Let all books, arts, and sciences one day perish by fire and water; from you and in you, *Encyclopedia,* the *human
spirit* has *everything!*" What the *printing press* became for the sciences, the *Encyclopedia* has become for *printing:*[107] the highest pinnacle of expansion, completeness, and preservation in all eternity.

It remains for me to praise the best thing: our tremendous *religious* progress (for we have begun to catalogue the different *readings* of Scripture!); to praise [our progress] in the principles of
honor, since we have done away with that *ludicrous chivalry* and
have elevated medal-ribbons[108] by turning them into *leashes*[109] for

102. Herder is referring to Rameau's criticism of the ancients for having based
harmony on melody rather than beginning with harmony, which he considered to
be prior.

103. Apparently Louis XIV put out a prize for the inventor of a sixth classical
style of column (after the five orders of classical architecture: Doric, Ionic, Corin-
thian, Tuscan, and Composite).

†104. *Discours préliminaire* of the *Encyclopédie*; Voltaire's encyclopedic depiction
of the human sciences, etc. [Compare note to 57:2–3; here, Herder may be misat-
tributing Diderot's *Système figuré* to Voltaire.]

†105. Hume's *Essays*, first volume, essay I. ["Of Commerce (1752)," which
appears as number I (Part II) in 1777.]

106. Compare p. 57:2–3.

†107. *Discours préliminaire* and *Miscellany on Literature, History, and Philosophy* by
d'Alembert (Part I.IV).

108. Compare Herder's review of Millar's *Observations* (note to p. 74, above).

109. *Leitband.* A kind of leash used to lead small children. Kant uses the word
at the end of the fourth paragraph of his "What Is Enlightenment?"

boys and *presents at court;* and to praise most of all the soaring peak of our *human virtues,* the virtues of our *fathers, women,* and *children.* But who could praise everything in *such* an age as ours? Enough: we are "*the crown of the tree,* swaying in *heavenly air!* The *golden age* is nigh!"

Third Section (Addenda)

The air of the sky is so refreshing that one is tempted to linger too long above the treetops; [let us] descend to the sad ground to take a closer look at what is whole or incomplete, as the case may be.

Great creature of God! The work of *three continents* and nearly *six millennia!* The tender *root* so full of sap; the slender, blooming *shoot;* the massive *trunk;* the entwined, mightily striving *branches;* the airy, wide-spread *twigs*—how everything rests upon every-thing else, how all things grow up out of one another![1] *Great crea-ture of God!* But *for what? Toward what end?*

That this *growing up,* this *progression*** from one to the other is not "*perfection* in the narrow sense of the schoolhouse," this, I reckon, our whole examination has demonstrated. What has become a *shoot* is no longer a *seed,* what a *tree* no longer a tender *shoot.* Above the trunk, there is the *crown* [of the tree]; if every one of its branches, every twig, wanted to be the *trunk* or a *root,* where would that leave the *tree? Orientals, Greeks,* and *Romans* existed only once in the world; they were meant to connect at a *single* point, a *single* spot only, to the electrical chain laid by fortune! Thus, when we want to be Orientals, Greeks, and Romans *all at once,* we can count on being *nothing.*

It is said that "in Europe there is now more *virtue* than ever before in the world." And why? Because there is more *enlighten-ment*—but I believe that for this very reason, there must rather be *less* [virtue].

What, if one were only to ask the flatterers of their age, what is this *greater virtue* of Europe through *enlightenment* supposed to be? "*Enlightenment!* We *know* so much more now, we *hear* and *read* so much that we have become so *quiet, patient, docile, passive.* 'Granted,' 'to be sure,' 'admittedly,' 'and that, too'—always the bottom of our hearts remains so *soft!*" Relentless *sweetening,* that is all there is: we are the *thin, airy twigs* up [in the trees], trembling

1. Compare pp. 54–56.

of course and *whispering* with every gust of wind. But [look] how prettily the *rays of the sun* are playing through us! We stand *so high* above branch, trunk, and root, we *see so far*, and let it not be forgotten, we can *whisper so far* and *so nicely.* 78/79

How could one fail to see that we lack all *vices* and *virtues* of the past because we have none of their *standing*, their *powers* and *vitality*, their *space* and *element!* Which would be no failing in itself, of course, if we did not *lie* and turn it into *praise* and *muddled arrogance*, if we did not deceive ourselves about our *means* of education,* as if they had *accomplished* anything, and about all the collected *junk of our own self-importance.* Why, finally, is our "*one-sided, scornful, lying* caricature [of history]" carried into all the *ages*, thereby mocking and debasing the customs of all peoples and ages so that a healthy, modest, unbiased person would hardly be able to find anything to read in all the so-called *pragmatic histories of the world* but the disgusting jumble of the "*prized ideal*[2] *of his age?*" All the earth becomes a *dung heap* upon which we *crow* and *scavenge for grains! Philosophy of the century!*[3]

"We have no *highway robbers*, no *civil wars*, no *crimes* anymore!" But where, *how*, and *why* would we get them? Given how thoroughly our lands are *regimented*, plastered and violated with highways, and *congested* with garrisons; how *wise* the distribution of our fields, and how vigilant our *wise* justice is—*where on earth* could a poor scoundrel ply his rough trade *even if* he could muster the requisite courage and strength? And *why* should he do so anyway, when, by the customs of our age, he could be *robbing houses, chambers*, and *beds* so much more comfortably—even *honorably* and *gloriously*—in the *paid* service of the state! Why not *allow* himself to get paid instead? Why [choose] the insecure trade for which—and this is the bottom line—he must lack the *courage*, the *strength*, and the *opportunity?* God have mercy on your *new, voluntary virtue!*

Do we have "no *civil wars*" because we are all such satisfied, fully-sated, happy subjects? Or is it not for reasons that often *accompany* precisely the *opposite* [condition]? Do we lack *vices* because we possess such *rapturous virtue, Greek freedom, Roman* 79/80 *patriotism, Oriental piety, chivalric honor*, and all these in the *highest measure*—or, rather, is it not precisely because we have *none* of these, and therefore, unfortunately, also cannot have any of their one-sided, wide-spread *vices? Thin, tottering branches!*

2. Or priced (*Preisideal*).

3. Compare Voltaire's *Philosophy of History.*

Being such, we have the advantage, of course, of our *capacity for* "*that dull, short-sighted, all-despising, exclusively self-satisfied philosophy which accomplishes nothing* and precisely therefore *offers consolation.*" Orientals, Greeks, and Romans lacked this.

Being such, we have the advantage of the *modesty* with which we *estimate our means of education** and *take credit for them.* We owe our *spiritual standing* to the fact that the world has never been so *humane,* so *theologically enlightened;* our *worldly standing* to the fact that it has never been so *humane,* so *uniformly obedient* and *orderly;* our *justice* to the fact that it has never been so *humane* and *peace-loving;* and finally our *philosophy* to the fact that it has never been so *humane* and *divine* as now. Thanks to whom? Everyone points to himself. "We are the *doctors,* the *redeemers,* the *enlighteners,* the *new creators*—the times of mad fever have passed." Well yes, thank God, and the consumptive patient lies so quietly in his bed, whimpers, and *gives thanks.* He gives thanks; but is he really *grateful?* And even if he were, would it not be precisely on account of his *diminishment,* his *pusillanimity,* and the utter *despondency of mankind?* What if, along with pleasure, the very [capacity for] *discerning something better* had been lost? Am I not, in writing this, opening myself to the *most vicious, scornful off-side distortions?* If it were enough for us to *think,* to have *factories, commerce, arts, tranquility, security,* and *order,* and for our governments to have nothing resisting them anymore—then how great the *constitutions of our states* would become! What a commanding view of the surrounding distance, what toying with distant places, distant times! What other age was ever able to do this? Thus speaks our history of the state, of commerce, of art. It reads like satire, and yet it is nothing but *thinking in the expected way.* What point is there in going on? If only it were merely a disease, and not at the same time an impediment that precludes *any antidote!* On the brink of death, but dreaming with opium: why disturb the patient if one cannot help him?

80/81

Instead, on to something that will please the patient rather more. In *this progression by fits and starts,*** our place is of course to be [both] *the end and the instrument of fortune.*

Generally speaking, the philosopher is most like an *animal* when he wishes to be most like *God:* and so it is when it comes to optimistic appraisals of the *perfection* of the world. Would that everything went in a nice *straight line*, with every *subsequent human being* and every *subsequent generation* being *perfected* according to *his* ideal in a *beautiful progression*** for which he alone was able to provide the *highest exponent* of virtue and happiness! It would always be around him that everything would be gathered *at last:* he the final, highest link, where everything *comes to an end.* "Behold the enlightenment, virtue, happiness to which the world has ascended! *Behold me* ringing the bell from on high, the *golden tongue*[4] tipping the scales of the world!"

And the wise man failed to consider what even the faintest *echo* from heaven to earth ought to have taught him, namely that *man* is likely always to remain *man*—nothing but a *human being* by the *analogy*[5] *of all things.* Human beings in the form of angels and demons are *but the characters of fiction,* for man is always something in between: both *defiant* and *despondent, striving* in *need, wearied* by *indolence* and *abundance* alike, a *nothing* when he lacks *opportunity* and *exercise,* but *almost everything* when he gradually *makes his strides*** through them. Man—*hieroglyph*[6] *of good and evil* with which *history is filled.* Man—never other than a *tool.*

[The wise man also] failed to consider that this concealed *dual creature* could be, and given the structure of our world, *almost had to be,* modified a *thousand* times over; that the *climate* and *circumstances of an age* will create *national* and *worldly virtues,* flowers that grow and flourish almost without effort under *one* sky, but elsewhere die out or *languish* miserably (thus the *physics of history, science of the soul* and *politics* about which our age has already fantasized so much and over which it has been brooding!); that all of this not only *could,* but *had to* exist, but that on the inside,   *81/82* beneath the much-changed husk, the same *kernel of being* and *capacity for happiness* could be stored and can indeed be expected, based on all human experience, to be [preserved for the future].

Moreover, he failed to consider that it would show infinitely greater solicitude on the part of the *father of all*[7] if there were in all mankind, *in all the world* and *all the ages, an invisible germ of*

---

4. In German, that which tips the scales is often referred to as a "little tongue [that is, a little flame] on the scales" (*das Zünglein an der Waage*).

5. Compare p. 41:29.

6. Compare p. 21:1 ff.

7. Literally All-Father (*der Allvater*). A little further down, at p. 86:4, Herder will be linking this term directly to the Old Germanic mythology, and to Odin in particular, who is commonly designated thus.

receptiveness to happiness and virtue that, developed in *different* ways, might appear in different forms, but [that would remain] *one* and the same *measure* and *mixture of forces* on the inside.
Finally, he failed to consider—omniscient creature!—that where the human species is concerned, *God might have a greater overall plan* than what an individual creature is able to comprehend; because nothing ever leads towards anything merely *individual*, and certainly nothing runs towards the *philosophers* and *throne-sitters* of the 18th century as its *finishing line;* because all the scenes, in which *every single* actor has only that part to play which allows him to strive and be happy, *all scenes* together make a *whole*, a *major presentation* of which the *individual, self-centered actor* cannot *know* or *see anything,* but which the *spectator with the right* perspective, in *calm anticipation* of the *complete sequence,* can indeed see.

Behold the entire *universe from heaven down to earth*—what is a means, what an end? Is not everything a means towards *a million ends,* everything an end by *a million means?* The chain of omnipotent, omniscient Good contains thousands of entwined meshes: every link of this chain hangs in its proper place as a *link*, yet none can see *where the chain [as a whole] hangs in the end.*[8] Each feels itself, in its delusion, to be the *center point;* each feels the points that *surround* it only *insofar* as it directs its rays or waves upon them.[9] Fine delusion! But the great line that encircles *all* these waves, rays, and seeming centers—*Where?—Who?—Why?*

Would the history of the *human species* with all its *waves* and *successive ages* be any different, any other than just this *"blueprint of omnipotent wisdom"?* If a *simple house* will reveal the *"design of God"* in even the least of its components, how could it be otherwise with the *history of its inhabitants*—the one merely decoration, the depiction of *a* scene, just a view; the other, *"endless scenes* of *drama,* God's *epic* through the *millennia, continents,* and *human races,* a *thousand-faced fable* full of a *great meaning!"*

[Who could deny] that this *meaning,* this *full view,* must lie outside the reach of *mere human beings!* You insect on the ground, take another look at heaven and earth: do you find *yourself* to be the exclusive center and end of all the *simultaneous* motion in the universe, dead and alive; or are *you* not yourself contributing (*where, why,* and *when*—who ever asked you this?) to *higher ends*

---

8. Compare *Do We Still Have a Fatherland?*, 51:8–9 and *Do We Still Have the Fatherland of the Ancients?*, 336:25–27, 337:28–34.

9. Compare p. 39:5 and note there.

that remain unknown to you—ends to which the morning-star and the little cloud by his side are contributing, as are you and the worm that you are just stepping on? All this is undeniable and inscrutable in the great, all-encompassing, *all-uniting world* of a moment: in the great, all-encompassing *world to come*, in all the *occurrences* and *further developments* of the human species, in that *drama* full of the *wisdom* and the *knots* of its creator—can you expect anything less or different? So what if it were a *labyrinth* to you, with a hundred locked gates and a hundred open ones? This labyrinth is "a *palace of God*, [designed] for *his* satisfaction, perhaps for *his* enjoyment, *not* for *yours!*"

The whole world, *one moment* in the sight of God, is an abyss—an abyss wherein I am lost on all sides. I behold a great work *without name*, yet everywhere *full of names*, full of *voices* and *forces!* I do not feel [as if I were] at *the place* where the harmony of all these voices would be gathered in one ear; but what abbreviated, confused echoes I can discern from where I am standing—that much I know and can hear for sure—are harmonious in their own way: songs of praise, they too, resounding in the ear of the One for whom *space* and *time* are nothing. The human ear lingers a few moments, hearing but a few sounds and often no more than the displeasing, *discordant notes* of *tuning;* for this ear arrived just in time for the tuning and may, alas, have stumbled upon a storm raging in a water glass. The enlightened *man of later times*, meanwhile, takes himself not only for *one who can hear everything* but for no less than the final *summation* of all *sounds*, for the *mirror* of all *the past* and the *representative* of the *purpose* behind the *composition* of *all scenes!* The precocious brat does his bad-mouthing; if only it were the *last remaining echo* of a *dying breath*, or else part of the tuning! *83/84*

Am I an eagle on the mighty tree of the *father of all*,[10] the crown of which reaches beyond the heavens, the roots of which burrow beneath the worlds and below hell itself? Am I the *raven* on his shoulder that brings *daily tidings* of the worlds to his ear?[11] What minute *leaf's fiber* from this tree might I be? A little comma or dash in the book of the worlds!

†10. A great presentation of the Nordic *Edda*.

11. In the Norse mythology, Hugin and Munin—Thought and Memory—are two ravens sitting on the shoulders of Odin, the "All-Father" whose throne rises above the twelve other great gods of the Norse pantheon. Every morning, the ravens bring news of what had been passing in the world during the previous day and night.

Whatever I may be, a call from heaven to earth [assures me] that like everything else, so I, too, must have *some* meaning in my place—with *powers reserved for the whole* and with a *feeling* of happiness that adequately reflects the *scope* of these powers! Who among my brothers enjoyed *privilege before he existed?* And if the purpose and harmony of the household demanded that he be made *gold*, I a *clay pot*—I but a *clay pot*, too, in my *purpose, sound, duration, feeling*, and *competence*—then is it for me to challenge the craftsman?[12] I have not been *passed over*, nor *preferred* over anyone; the sensibilities, activities, and competences of the human species have been *spread around*. Here the stream runs dry, there it sallies forth. He to whom much is given, of him shall much be required.[13] He who is refreshed by abundant senses will also have to struggle with abundant senses: I do not believe that *in the light of all history*, any *single* thought could produce stronger feeling than this one by what it *expresses* and *withholds*, by what it reveals and what it *covers with the blanket of heaven!*

That [such a thought] might appear [in such a light], this is the goal, at least, towards which my wish is running [along] the great *Olympic racetrack!* If there is any regard in which our age can be used for something noble, it is "by its *lateness*, its *height*, its *view*"! [Consider] what, through millennia, has been *prepared* with a view to [our age]; or what *preparations*, in a higher sense, it has been making in its turn for yet another! [Consider] all the steps leading *towards* it and *away from* it! Philosopher: if you wish to honor and put to use the height attained by your age, the *book* of [its] *prehistory* lies before you! *Secured* with seven seals, it is a *wondrous book of prophecy:* the *end of days* awaits you![14] Read!

84/85

There [lies] the *Orient*, the *cradle* of the human species, human *inclinations*, and all *religion*. Let religion be *despised* and faded in all the cold world: its Word, the spirit of flame and fire, is still traveling thence.[15] With *paternal dignity* and *simplicity*—which

---

12. Compare Romans 9:20–21: "Shall the thing formed say to him that formed it, 'Why hast thou made me thus?' Hath not the potter power over the clay, of the same lump to make one vessel unto honour, and another unto dishonour?"

13. Compare Luke 12:48.

14. The imagery of Apocalypse; compare Rev. 5:3.

†15. The despised book—the Bible!

continues, in particular, to draw "the heart of the *innocent child*"—the childhood of the *species* will always retain its power over the childhood of *every single individual:* the last *minor* will still be *born* in the first *land of the morning.*[16]

The Greeks marked the youth of all so-called fine literature and art. What lies beyond may be too deep, too childish for the sight of our age; but they, right at the dawn of world events, what *effect* they have had on all their *posterity!* The *most beautiful blossoms* of the *human spirit*—of *heroic courage,* of *patriotism,* of *feeling free,* of the *love of art,* of *song,* of *poetic tone,* of *narrative pitch,* of *rhetorical thunder,* of the *beginnings* of all *civic wisdom*—such as there are now, belong to them. Set up in their place, having been given their sky, land, constitution, and a fortunate point in time, they formed,* created, named. We are still forming* and naming after them—it was their age that accomplished [things], though *one time only!* When the human spirit sought with all its powers to awaken their age *a second time,* the spirit had turned to dust, the shoot remained ash. Greece never returned.

The Romans were the first *gatherers* and *distributors* of the fruits that had grown elsewhere and now fell ripe into their hands. They had to leave blossoms and vital fluids in their place, it is true: but they still had *fruits* to distribute—*relics* of the *primeval world* in *Roman garb,* in the *Roman manner,* in the *Roman tongue.* What if everything had come directly *from Greece* instead—*Greek spirit, Greek learning,* * *Greek language?* How different everything would be in Europe! But it was *not meant to be.* Greece, on its lovely archipelago, still so far removed from the North, the human spirit within it still so lean and delicate—how could it have *wrestled* with all the other peoples of the world and *forced* them to succeed it? How could the crude Northern *husk have held* the fine *scent of Greece?* So *Italy* became the *bridge:* Rome as the *intermediate period* during which the *kernel* was hardened and *distributed.* Even the *holy language* of the *newly Christian world,* with all that became attached to it, was *Roman* during an entire millennium and throughout Europe.

85/86

Even when Greece was set to have its impact upon Europe a *second time,* it could not do so *directly: Arabia* became the silt-filled canal; *Arabia,* the subplot for the history of Europe's education. Perhaps *Aristotle* was indeed destined to rule single-handedly over

16. Compare note at p. 16:27.

his centuries[17] and to give rise to the *worms* and *moths of decay* of the *scholastic way of thinking* everywhere, which is how things turned out; but what if fate had instead decreed that *Plato, Homer,* all the *[ancient] poets, historians,* and *orators* have their effect much earlier? How utterly different things would be! But it was *not so decreed;* the circle was meant to pass over there. The Arab religion and national culture reviled these *flowers,*[18] though they might not have *flourished* in Europe, either, in those times whose spirit agreed so well, on the contrary, with *Aristotelian pedantry* and the *Moorish tastes. Fate!*

What had *grown* throughout the preceding *ages of the world* was only meant to be *dried* and *run through the wine press* in Europe: but from there it was to be spread *among the peoples of the earth.* How peculiar [it seems], then, that the nations hastened *towards the site of their labors* without knowing *how* or *why!* Fortune called them to their business in the vineyards, by and by, each at its assigned hour.[19] Everything that might have been thought up had already been *discovered, felt, devised;* here everything was now cast into *method,* into the *form of science.*[20] And thus only the newest, coldest mechanical *inventions* were added and applied on a large scale. The *machines of cold, European-Northern abstraction*—what *great tools* in the hands of Him who guides everything! There lie the seeds, [dispersed] among almost *all the nations* on earth—or at least they are *known* and *accessible* to all [nations], who will receive them when their time has come. Europe has *dried* them, *threaded* them on to a *string, preserved* them for all time. Strange globe! What you *were turned into* on this globe, you *little Northern continent,* once no more than a void of *groves* and *icebergs!* What else are you *yet* to *become?*

86/87

The so-called *enlightenment* and *education* of the world* only ever touched and kept its hold on a *narrow strip* of the *globe.* Nor could we change anything about its course, status, and gyrations without

17. A reference to the revival of Aristotelianism in the 13th century. Compare p. 58:3–6.

18. This comment may have been motivated by a misconception about the destruction of the library at Alexandria. Compare our note to *The Influence of Free Legislation,* 319:9–10.

19. In the parable at Matt. 20:1–16, the laborers are called to the vineyard at different times of the day until the eleventh hour, but everyone is paid the same at the end of the day.

20. Compare p. 59 ff. above.

everything [else] changing at the same time. What if nothing but the *introduction* of the *sciences*, of *religion*, or of the *Reformation* had gone *differently*, for example? [What if] the Northern peoples had mixed *differently* or migrated *differently?* [What if] the *papacy* had not been needed as *a vehicle for so long*—and ten times more questions besides! Dreams! That is not what happened, and in hindsight we can always find some reason *why* it did not happen— though a minor reason, of course!

We can also see why no nation *following upon another,* even if it had *all the same accessories,* ever *became* what the other had *been.* Let all their *means of culture* be identical: *the culture [itself] can never be the same,* because it is devoid of the various *influences* that shaped the older, now *altered* nature. The *Greek sciences* that the Romans appropriated became *Roman; Aristotle* became an *Arab* and a *scholastic.* And the *Greeks* and *Romans* of *modern times:* what a *wretched affair! Marcilio*[21]—you are [supposed to be] *Plato? Lipsius*—you, *Zeno?* But where are your *Stoics,* your *heroes* that *did* so much then? All you modern *Homers, orators,* and *artists*—where is your *world of wonders?*

Nor has this education* ever *retraced its steps* into *any country,* so that it might, *for a second* time, become what it *had been earlier.* The course of fortune is relentless and stern: the curtain has already fallen on *that* time, *that* world; the *ends* that they were meant to serve have become obsolete. How could today become the day before? When *God's course among*[22] *the nations* is advancing with giant strides, how would *human powers* be able to *beat back a childish path?* No *Ptolemy* could recreate *Egypt;* no *Hadrian, Greece;* nor *Julian, Jerusalem! Egypt, Greece,* and *Holy Land*—how miserably you lie there with your bare mountains, with no trace or voice of the *genius* who once walked upon you and spoke to all the world. And why? [Because] *he has finished speaking;* [because] *his imprint upon the ages is complete;* because *the sword is worn out*[23] and *the empty scabbard lies broken on the ground.* That would be the answer to so much useless doubt, admiration, and questioning.

 87/88

---

21. Marcilio Ficino.
22. Lit.: under.
23. Compare Matt. 10:34: "I came not to send peace, but a sword."

"[Behold] *God's course*[24] *across*[25] *the nations!* [Behold] the *spirit* of *laws, times, customs,* and *arts* as they *followed* one upon the other, *prepared, developed,* and *displaced* one another!" If only we had a *mirror* of the *human species* reflecting faithfully, fully, and with feeling for *God's revelation.* Though there have been plenty of preliminary labors, all we have are husks and clutter. We have crawled through and ransacked our *present* age, in almost all the nations, as well as the *history* of almost all prior times—almost without any notion of *why* we should have rummaged through them. The historical facts and explorations, the discoveries and travel reports lie before us, but who will sort through and examine them?

"*God's course across the nations!*" By the hand of one man alone, *Montesquieu's* noble, gigantic work[26] could never have become what it was meant to be: a *Gothic* edifice according to the *philosophical taste of its age—esprit!*—and often no more than that. [Everything] torn from its spot and place and spilled out upon *three* or *four marketplaces* beneath the banner of *three miserable platitudes*— [mere] *words!*—and *empty, useless, indefinite, all-confusing esprit-words* at that! A work that stumbles dizzily through the ages, nations, and languages, circling them like the Tower of Confusion,[27] and inviting everyone to hang his scraps, riches, and hat on *three puny nails.* The history of all peoples and ages, this great, living work of God *with all its ramifications,* turned into a pile of rubble with three protruding peaks and capsules—though of course also with some very noble, worthy materials. [So much for] *Montesquieu!*

88/89

Who will recreate for us the temple of God in its *progression*[28]

24. *Gang.* This has to be seen in relation to *Fortgang* (progression), Herder's interpretation of the course of advancement in human affairs (see A Note on the Texts and the Translation).

25. Lit.: over (cf. note 22). The reversal of prepositions may be significant in that "under" is used in the context of the sword; "over," in that of the arts.

26. Herder is referring to Montesquieu's famous *The Spirit of the Laws* (hence the play on *esprit*). Montesquieu declared the giant tome his entire life's work and swears that its completion "nearly killed" him (xi). The "three miserable platitudes" are Montesquieu's three principles of government—virtue, honor, and fear—that define the democratic or aristocratic, monarchical, and despotic forms of government, respectively (I, iii).

27. The Tower of Babel (Gen. 11:1–9).

28. *in seinem Fortgebäude:* a variation on Herder's theme of *Fortgang* that applies it literally to the progressing construction of a building.

through the ages? The earliest ages of *mankind's childhood* have passed, but plenty of *remnants* and *monuments* remain. The greatest remnants: the *father's* own *instructions* to his children—*revelation*. Dare you say, human being, that it is *too old* for your overclever, senile years? Just look around you: the greatest part of the earth's nations continue to be *in their infancy;* they continue to speak *that* language, to uphold *those* customs, to be examples of *this* degree of formation.* Wherever you may travel among so-called savages, listen and you will hear the *sound of scriptural explanations—living commentaries on revelation blowing in the air.*

The idolization that the *Greeks* and *Romans* have been enjoying for so many centuries, the often *fanatical zeal* with which everything of theirs has been sought out, put on display, defended, and extolled—what great *preparatory works* and *contributions!* [But] we will know and appraise you [properly], you *Greeks* and *Romans,* only after the spirit of excessive adoration has been dampened and the bias sufficiently tempered that leads everyone to *caress his* [favorite] people like a Pandora.

A path appeared branching off to the *Arabs,* towards a world of monuments by which we might know them. Though for very different purposes, monuments of *medieval history* have likewise been found, and some of what remains hidden in the dust will no doubt be discovered soon, perhaps within the next half-century. (If only everything could be so reliably expected from our enlightened times!) Our *travel reports* are multiplying and improving: everyone who has nothing to do in Europe is running *around the world in a kind of philosophical fury.* As we are collecting *"materials from all the ends of the earth,"* we will one day discover among them what we are seeking least: *discussions of the history of the most important world,* the *human* world.

Before long, our age will open some eyes: soon enough, it will drive us to seek out *wells of ideas*[29] [to slake] the thirst of the desert. We will learn to appreciate ages that we now despise—the feeling of a *universal humanity* and *happiness* will become keen. The prospect of a higher *existence in the present* than our [merely] *human one* will emerge from the rubble of history and will reveal a *plan* to us where we were only able to see *confusion* before [and where] everything has its proper spot and place. *History of mankind* in the noblest sense—you shall be! Until then, let the great teacher and

89/90

---

29. *idealische Brunnquellen.* This expression also appears in Herder's letter to Johann Kaspar Lavater of 18 June 1774 (*Briefe* 3:100, line 27).

lawgiver of kings[30] *lead* and *mislead*. He has provided such a fine example of how to gauge everything with two or three words, to *lead on* everything towards two or three *forms of government* whose origin and whose strictly limited *scope* and *timeliness* are readily visible. How pleasant, nonetheless—and this, too, is fate—to be able to follow him, in the spirit of the laws of *all times and peoples*, as he moves beyond the confines of his own people! One often holds the *ball of threads* in one's hand for a long time, delighting in one's ability to *tug* here and there, and leaving everything even more *tangled*. Fortunate[31] is the hand that might enjoy unraveling[32] the tangle by gently and patiently pursuing a single thread—how widely and evenly the thread runs! *History of the world:* it is towards this that kingdoms and bird nests small and large are striving.

All our age's events take place *at high altitudes* and *strive for great distances*. I reckon that this is the *compensation* for the diminished *strength and feeling of joy* with which we are left *as individuals*. Thus [we receive] real *encouragement* and *strengthening*.

You, *Socrates* of our time, can no longer accomplish what Socrates did, for you lack the small, narrow, bustling, crowded *stage*, as well as the *simplicity, customs*, and *national character* of [his] times—his *fixed sphere!* As a *world citizen*, and no longer a citizen of *Athens*, you must naturally lack a *view* on what you ought to do in Athens, a *secure sense* of what you are doing, and a *feeling of joy* about what you have accomplished—[you lack] your daimon![33] But behold, if you will act like Socrates, humbly *striving against prejudices* and spreading *truth* and *virtue* to the best of your ability, with honesty and love and without shrinking from sacrificing yourself—then the *breadth* of your sphere may compensate for your more *indeterminate* and *misguided* beginnings. Hundreds will read you and fail to understand; hundreds will yawn; hundreds, despise and mock you; hundreds will prefer the dragon fetters[34] of

90/91

30. Montesquieu, as the play on the title of his work below will confirm.

31. Or adept (*glückliche Hand*).

32. *entwickeln:* also used by Herder in its other meaning (to develop) in the context of argument or analysis.

33. Compare Plato, *Apology* 31d.

34. I.e., fetters strong enough to restrain even dragons. The exact source of this expression is obscure, but the theme of dragons subdued at the hands of mythical heroes is especially common in regional German folk tales.

habit and remain as they are. But consider that this may well leave *hundreds* more among whom [your efforts] will bear fruit; long after you have turned to dust, *future generations* will still read and make better use of you. Not just the *world*, but also the *world of the future* is your Athens. *Speak!*

The *world present and future!* An *eternal* Socrates, still *acting*, and not the *dead bust* with its poplar wreath[35] that we call *immortality*. [Socrates] spoke clearly, vividly, within narrow bounds, and his words fell into just the right hands. *Xenophon* and *Plato* wrote him into their *memorabilia* and *dialogues:* mere *manuscripts* that, luckily for us, escaped the flood of time, unlike so many others. Thus whatever *you* write, word for word, should be *worthy of the world and eternity*, because—by your materials and possibilities, at least— you may well be writing *for all the world and all eternity.* Think of the hands into which your writings may fall! In the circle of what worthy *men* and *judges* you ought to speak, to teach virtue with such brilliance and clarity as was beyond even Socrates and all his age; to encourage a *love among all men* that would, if it were possible, *indeed* be *greater* than that uniting *lovers of the fatherland* and *citizens;* and to spread happiness even in conditions and *situations* for which those under the thirty *saviors* of the fatherland, who also had *their statues*, were hardly a match![36] *Socrates of all mankind!*

Teacher of nature,[37] how much more you can be than *Aristotle* or *Pliny!* How much more accessible the wonders and works [of nature] are to you, and what *aids*, unknown to them,[38] you have at your disposal to open the *eyes of others!* What heights you are standing on: remember *Newton!*[39] What a single *Newton* did for the human spirit as a whole, and what this did in turn—what it

35. Herder may mean to mock the substitution of German poplar for Greek laurel as symptomatic of a deeper falsification of antiquity.

36. Herder is suggesting that a latter-day Socrates would have to contend with circumstances even more adverse to human happiness than those facing Socrates under the Thirty Tyrants. Thus he writes to Hamann, in early March 1781, "The Thirty Tyrants of Socrates' day have multiplied into millions, and at all levels of society confusion is so rife that there are neither colors nor words to describe it" (DKV Notes 892; *Briefe* 4:177).

37. The modern scientist.

38. Aristotle, Pliny, etc.

39. Considering that Herder has already introduced the image of the "illustrious philosopher, standing upon the shoulders of it all" (54:24–25), he may be thinking of Newton's famous observation, made in a letter to Robert Hooke dated 5 February 1676, that if he had seen further than others, he had done so "by standing on the shoulders of giants."

changed, what fruit it bore!—to what heights he raised his entire species! You are standing upon [these] heights![40] Instead of struggling to reduce God's great creation to the narrow dimensions of your head (theories about the *origins of the universe*, of the *animal*

91/92   *species*, of the *forms*,[41] etc.[42]), just follow the *stream* of *the divine power* and strive to feel it deeply and faithfully in all its forms, shapes, and creations; make others feel it, and serve the Creator rather than yourself! Messenger of glory throughout the kingdoms of creation, it is only from *this height in time* that you could *fly towards heaven*, discover and speak so *comprehensively* and *nobly* and *wisely*, and refresh human hearts, as mere puddles could not, with the innocent, mighty, universally benevolent view of God. This is what you are doing for the world present and future! Of course [you are] only *one* among all the discoverers and explorers [in history], *a single small name!* But [you are working for] *the world present and future*, and [your work is] so exalted, so glorious that *Pliny* and *Aristotle* could not equal it. Angel of God in your time!

How many are the *means* that a doctor and expert in the nature of man has at his disposal today: a hundred times more than *Hippocrates* or *Machaon!* Compared to these, he is surely *a son of Jupiter, a god!* If only he were to become such [a god] in respect, too, of all the feeling of those more human times—a god, discoverer, and savior to him who is ailing in body or soul! Thus he might save a *youth* who, meaning to cut the first roses of life, may have been surprised by a fire-snake[43]—perhaps *single-handedly* returning [this youth] to himself, to his parents, and to the future generations that live or die through us, to the world and virtue! Or he might assist a man worn out by his meritorious toils and sorrows, presenting him with the sweetest reward that he can still enjoy *now*, often the only thanks given for his life: a *cheerful old age*. He might be able to keep him from the grave for *a few more years*—as perhaps the *only bulwark* against the hundreds of accidents to which humans are prone before they close their eyes at last. All that is good in these years is *his*,[44] all the consolation and good cheer spread by this resurrected

---

40. Compare pp. 54:25, 70:18–20, and *Of the Changes in the Tastes of the Nations*, 157:29 ff.

41. *Formenbildung*.

†42. Buffon.

43. Most likely a discreet hint at syphilis—the "secret disease" mentioned at p. 74:19.

44. The doctor's.

man, *his!* In times when one saved man can accomplish so much, and when, on the other hand, the most innocent human beings might die so wretchedly in so many ways—how [godlike] you are in such times, you *doctor with a humane heart!*   92/93

Need I go through all the ranks and classes of *justice, religion,* the *sciences,* individual *arts?* The *higher* each stands *among its kind,* the *more far-reaching its effect,* the *better* and *dearer* [it is]! Precisely because *nothing but your free will* made you act thus, because nothing *required* or *forced* you to be so good and great and noble within your rank and class; precisely because you were not *roused* [to action] at all, but on the contrary, pressured on all sides to become merely a *mechanical servant* of your art and to put any kind of *deeper sensation* to sleep; and because, in some strange cases, you may even have been crowned with thorns rather than laurels—precisely therefore, your *hidden, tested* virtue is all the more pure, quiet, and divine. It is greater than the virtue of other ages when, *prompted* by *encouragements* and *rewards,* it was, in the end, merely a *civic prop* and a magnificent adornment of the *body*—[whereas] yours is the very *lifeblood of the heart.*

How I would have to talk to do justice to the merits of those who truly are the *pillars* of our age, or the *hinges on which everything turns! Rulers, shepherds, caretakers* of the peoples—their power, together with the driving forces of our age, is very nearly *omnipotence!* Must not their very *look,* their *perspective,* their *wish,* their *silent, passive way of thinking,* let alone their intelligence, inform them that theirs has to be a nobler purpose than to appropriate and *toy* with their herds as with machines, however glorious the aim; that it must also be their end to *graze* their herds and, what is more, to care for the *greater whole* of mankind. You *rulers, shepherds, caretakers* of the *peoples,* the scepter of omnipotence in your hands: think how *much more* you can do—with only *a little human effort,* in [only a few] years, by nothing more than *intention* and *encouragement*—than that mogul on his golden throne can, or than that despot on his throne of human skulls ever will! He who allows himself to be overcome by political intentions may have as base a soul, despite his eminent rank, as that lentil-thrower who was perfectly happy casting his lentils, or the flute-player who can do nothing but hit his stops.[45]

45. A popular image for useless skill, employed also by Hamann. Originally found in Quintillian and apparently disseminated in modern times through Pierre Bayle's *Dictionnaire historique et critique,* the anecdote tells of a Macedonian who

I would rather talk to you, shepherds of your flock, father, mother, in your humble hut! You, too, have been deprived of a thousand *encouragements* and *enticements* that once made your *fatherhood* your *heaven*. You cannot decide for your child, who is marked early, perhaps already in the cradle, with the honorable fetter of freedom—the highest ideal of our philosophers. You cannot raise him for the paternal hearth, for the paternal customs, virtue, and existence—all along you lack a *circle*, and as everything is confused and in flux, you also lack the *most helpful driving force* of education, *will*.[46] You have to worry that as soon as [your child] has been torn from your hands, he will at once sink into the age's great sea of lights—the abyss! A sunken jewel, the irretrievable existence of a human soul! A tree covered in blossoms, torn too early from his[47] maternal soil, transplanted into a world of storms that even *the sturdiest trunk* can barely survive, perhaps even planted *upside down* there, by the crown instead of his roots, with the sad roots [dangling] in the air. Expect him, before long, to stand there withered and hideous, his blossoms and fruit on the ground. But do not despair before the leaven of the age: whatever may threaten and impede you, *instruct!* Make your instruction all the *better, more secure, more solid*—[fitting] for all the *social ranks* and *disappointments* that might be thrust upon [your child], for all the *storms that await him!* You must not remain idle: for good or for bad, you must instruct; and if for good, what *greater virtue*, what *greater reward* could there be than the paradises of *easier purposes* and a *more unified formation?** How much more than ever the world now needs *individuals* instructed in simple virtue! Where *all customs are the same*, all equally *level, right*, and *good*, what need is there for any *effort?* Habit educates,* and virtue subsides into mere habit. But here [we have] a shining star in the night, a diamond underneath a pile of clay and limestone! One human being among hordes of apes and political larvae—how much his quiet, divine example can do to further education!* [How many] *waves around* and *after* him may spread into the future! Think how much purer and nobler *your virtue* [is], and how many more and greater *teaching aids* [you have at your disposal], inasmuch as you and your youth are not *driven* by external *forces!* Think also how much *higher* the virtue

---

could throw a lentil through the eye of a needle and who was rewarded by Alexander with a dish of lentils.

46. Compare note to p. 39:5 and references given there.
47. The child lost to the sea of light, now likened to a tree.

[is] to which you are raising him than that to which *Lycurgus* and *Plato* were able and allowed to raise [their people]. The best age for *quiet, taciturn* virtue, which is so often *misunderstood* and is yet so *high* and is spreading itself *so far and wide!* This much strikes me as altogether certain: the less *complete* and *great* goodness there may be in our age, and the harder it shall *become for us* to attain the *highest virtue,* and the *quieter* and more *concealed* it *may* be forced to become, *the higher and nobler* it shall be *where it will prevail,* perhaps even becoming a virtue *infinitely useful* and *pregnant with consequence* one day! As we are commonly prone to *resignation* and to *disavowing our own part,* and as we cannot often expect *immediate rewards,* we strew our seeds *across the wide world* without looking where they are falling and taking root, or whether they are yielding any *good* fruit. It is nobler to sow with a view to *what remains concealed* and *all-distant,* without expecting to be called to harvest—thus the all-distant harvest is sure to be all the greater! Entrust your seeds to the gentle breeze of the zephyr, which will carry them all the further, until one day all the shoots to which the *nobler part of our age* has quietly and tacitly contributed shall be awakened. How blessed are the times on which my eyes are fixed!

It is from the tree's *highest branches* that the *fruit* [can be seen] blossoming and sprouting—marvel from up there at the beautiful *foresight* of *God's greatest works!* If *enlightenment* does not always seem to benefit *us,* if we are losing the *depth* and *embeddedness of a river* as we are expanding our surface and breadth, then this is surely because we, already a small sea, are on our way [to becoming] a *great ocean.* From all over the world, [we have gathered] nearly as many *connected insights* as our universe could offer us: a *knowledge* of *nature,* of *heaven* and *earth,* of the *human species;* but the *spirit* of all this, its *substance* and *fruit,* awaits *future generations.* The *age* has *passed* when Italy formed* its language, customs, poetry, politics, and arts while struggling with confusion, oppression, sedition, and betrayal; but *what was formed** outlived its age, continued to exert its influence, and became Europe's *pre-eminent form.*[48] The *wretchedness and misery* under which the age of the

---

48. Lit.: "*erste Form* Europens." Herder means the extraordinary cultural influence of the Italian Renaissance throughout Europe.

95/96   great French king[49] had groaned *came, in part, to an end: the purposes* for which he wanted and needed everything [are] forgotten or else are left languishing, the idle puppets of vanity and disdain. The sea of medals on his breast and the walls where he resided are exposed before the thoughts of anyone, whether or not he may care to think about *what Louis cared to think about.* But the *spirit of the arts* that was refined [by these means] still remains. The measurements made with the *herbalist's, money changer's, or jeweler's scales,* or with the *carpenter's level,* or by the *journeying surveyor,* all these remain long after everything has crumbled that once *contributed* to them, once *suffered* on their account, or was once *their purpose!* The future strips us of our *husk* and takes the *kernel.* The *small twig* may not benefit from this, but from it hangs the *lovely fruit.*

What if, one day, all *the light* that we are casting out into the world like seeds and with which we are now blinding so many eyes, causing so much *misery* and *gloom,* were everywhere to become *mild life-light* and *life-warmth?* The piles of *dead* but *bright insights,* the fields of bones scattered *around us, above* and *below us* (*whence? what for?*) would be *revived, fructified.*[50] What a new world! What bliss to enjoy one's handiwork therein! *Everything,* down to our *inventions, entertainments, suffering, fate* and *chance,* seeks to raise us above the *cruder sensuality of prior ages,* to *accustom* us to a *higher [level of] abstraction* in our *thinking,* our *wills,* our *lives* and *actions*—[which is] by no means always pleasant for us, and often disagreeable! Beyond the *sensuality* of the Orient, the more beautiful sensuality of the Greeks; and beyond this, the power of Rome: how poorly we are consoled [for their loss] by our *tedious abstract consolations* and the *maxims* that are often all we have left by way of *motivations, driving forces,* and *conceptions of happiness.* The child is cruelly weaned of every last bit of sensuality. But behold the *higher age* that *beckons!* Not even a fool could deny that if certain kinds of more *refined motivation,* more *eminent, heavenly virtue,* and more *abstracted delight in worldly bliss* were indeed *attainable* for human nature, then they

49. Louis XIV.

50. The dread of history reduced to a graveyard of knowledge—described with imagery drawn from Ezek. 37:1–14—is one Herder shared with Hamann. Thus Hamann wrote in the second of his *Hellenistic Letters:* "The field of history has . . . always appeared to me as a wide field full of bones. *And lo, they were very dry . . .*" (DKV 4:893). Compare *Letters Towards the Advancement of Humanity,* 116 (DKV 7:700).

would be immensely *exalting* and *ennobling!* Perhaps there are *many* currently *perishing* on this cliff. Perhaps, or rather quite certainly, there are infinitely fewer men today who possess this *Fénelonian virtue* than there were once *Spartans, Romans,* and *knights* who represented the sensuous bloom of their *world's* and their *age's spirit.* The wide highways are becoming *ever narrower* 96/97 footpaths and *steep inclines* where only a few can venture—but they remain *heights* that *strive for the summit!* What conditions [would prevail] on the winding snake-path of Providence if, one day, our skins and impediments were sloughed off and a *rejuvenated* creature were to arise in a new spring of life! A *less sensuous* mankind, more *like* itself, now fully *engulfed in the world* and containing *within itself* that *vital force* and principle for which we *strive* with such effort—what a creation! And who could deny its likelihood and possibility? The *refinement* and *purifying progression*** of our *concepts of virtue,* from the most *sensuous times of childhood on and up through all of history,* is *evident;* its *dissemination* and *far-ranging progression*** is likewise *evident*—and all this *without purpose, without design?*

It is well known that the *concepts* of *human freedom, sociability, equality,* and *universal happiness* have *come to light*[51] and *spread out.* The consequences may not be immediately beneficial to us; often the bad may appear, at first, to outweigh the good. However!

Have not *sociability* and *casual intercourse* between the sexes *eroded* the honor, decency, and discipline of both parties? All around the world, the locked [doors] have been *burst open* for class, money, and pleasantries? But what suffering this has meant for *the first bloom* of the male sex and for matrimonial and motherly love and child-rearing, the noblest *fruit* of the female sex! How far has the damage *spread?* What an abyss of irredeemable evils when the very sources of amelioration and recovery, of youth, vitality, and improved education are *blocked!* The slighter twigs that are flitting about so playfully cannot do other than to *wither* right in the sunshine on account of their premature and feeble *life-play*—irreplaceable loss, perhaps *beyond remedy* by all political means! From the perspective of the love of man, this *could not be deplored enough*—yet, for the hand of Providence, even this remains an *instrument.* Let a hundred poor creatures collapse with parched tongues, groan with thirst, and succumb around the first source of life, of fellowship and joy—the source itself, which

51. *sich aufklären.* Compare p. 11:6.

they mistook so tragically, is still purifying![52] In later years, perhaps *overdoing things again,* they[53] may seek *other fruits of delight* by *dreaming up new worlds* and [presuming to] *improve* the *world* with their *woe.* Weary *Aspasias* form* [their own] *Socrateses, Ignatius* his *Jesuits,* and the *Epaminondases* of all times stage their *battles at Leuctra. Heroes* and *philosophers, wise men* and *monks* of such *ethereal, eminent* virtue, such *soaring zeal* and *merit*—how many of them [have become such] for *this reason* alone![54] Let him who would ponder and [try to] calculate the benefit for the world do so: he is dealing with many instances whose tendency is not often *in doubt.*[55] Fortune will reach its destination, even over millions of corpses!

Freedom, sociability, and *equality,*[56] such as they are *germinating* everywhere now, have brought about many evils through their thousand-fold abuse, and they will continue to do so. *Anabaptists* and other *fanatics* devastated Germany in *Luther's* times; now we have the general *confusion* of the social classes, the *upward drive* of the low-born seeking to replace their *withered, proud,* and *useless* superiors and soon becoming even *worse* than they. The strongest, most necessary *fundamentals* of mankind are being *abandoned;* the great mass of debased *vital fluid* is running very low. And whether the guardians of this great body *look on, cheer on,* and *press on* because of a *temporary increase in appetite* or a *seeming gain* in strength, or whether they put up the most vehement resistance instead, they will never *displace* the grounds for the *"progressive*** refinement* and the *upward drive* towards *reasoning, abundance, freedom,* and *insolence."* The slightest comparison will show how unspeakably the *true, voluntary respect* paid to the *public authorities,* to elders and social superiors in the world, has deteriorated *just over the past century.* In manifold ways, our lesser and greater great men are continuing to do their part: *barriers* and *border posts* are torn down, so-called *prejudices* of *class, education,* even *of religion,* are trod underfoot and mocked to their further detriment.

52. That is to say, the power of love is undiminished by those who seek it in the wrong place, or by the wrong means.

53. Those who have been disappointed by love.

54. Because their amorous disappointments drove them towards "other fruits of delight."

55. The calculation of the benefits for the world in individual cases may be doubtful, in other words, but the general direction of all these cases taken together is not.

56. A remarkable anticipation of the motto of the French Revolution.

Through *one and the same education, philosophy, irreligion, enlightenment, vice*—and finally, as our encore, through *oppression, thirst for blood*, and the *insatiable greed* that will *awaken* hearts and *arouse* 98/99 their self-regard[57]—we are all made what our philosophy praises and cherishes so. How blessed we are, after all the confusion and misery: *blessed are we*, as we are all made equally *master* and *servant, father* and *child, youth* and the most foreign *maiden*—we are all made *brothers!* The gentlemen prophesy like Caiaphas, but of course it is upon their own head, or the heads of their children, [that their prophecy will fall] first![58]

Even if our "*government of men*" had gained nothing but a *beautiful facade*—the *respectable appearance* and *image*, the *language*, the *principles and convictions* and the *order* that every book today professes and every young prince, as if he were a living book, has at the tip of his tongue: *Great Progress!*** Let anyone try to read *Machiavelli* and the *Anti-Machiavelli* side by side:[59] the philosopher and friend of man will *revere* the latter, willingly overlooking the *untouched* and decaying parts that have been *covered* with flowers and greenery, as well as the *open wounds* whose depths no one has been eager or willing to *probe*. "What a *book!*" he will say, "What a *prince*, who would think like the book, who would *admit, acknowledge, know, act* in accordance with casual convictions—what a prince for the world present and future!" Yet the reign of diseases other than crude, savagely cruel *madness* may be *just as oppressive* and indeed more *pernicious*, because they *proceed by stealth*, because they are *praised* rather than *exposed*, and because they will burrow into the very *marrow* of our *bones* and *devour the soul*. The universal dress of *philosophy* and *love of mankind* can be made to disguise *persecutions—violations* of the true, personal freedom of *men* and *countries, citizens* and *peoples*—such as *Cesare Borgia* himself could only dream of. But as all this is in keeping with the *presumed principles of the age*, with all the *trappings* of *virtue, wisdom, love of mankind*, and *prudent care for peoples*, it not only *can*

57. Or self-feeling (*Selbstgefühl*).

58. Compare John 11:49–53.

59. Here and throughout this paragraph, Herder is alluding to Frederick the Great, whose *Antimachiavel*, a lofty defense of morality in politics, was edited by Voltaire and published in 1740. (In the second edition of 1741, the French text was accompanied by a translation of Machiavelli's *The Prince*. Hence Herder's reference to reading the two side by side.) Herder charges that Frederick's ruthless power politics, in the first Silesian campaign of 1740 for example, expose his rhetoric for a sham and mere dissimulation. Compare p. 100:5.

but almost *has* to happen—and I do not wish to sing the praises of *facades* as if they were *deeds*. There is no doubt that even *Machiavelli*, in our age, *would not have written as he wrote*, and *Cesare* would not, in another setting, have been *permitted* to act as he once did. At bottom, it is only alterations in the *dress* that are at issue here;[60] still, it would be a blessing if *these changes* were made, and everyone *in our day* who *wrote* like *Machiavelli* were stoned. But I retract; for he who writes on behalf of virtue, though more wickedly than Machiavelli, will never be *stoned*. He writes *philosophically, with wit, in French,* and, needless to say, without *religion*—thus, "like one of us." And he *discredits* his own writings!

99/100

Even on the *poisonous, debauched* tree of that *exuberance in thinking* which goes with certain *conveniences* of *wealth* (let real prosperity be as distant as it may!) some good *fruits* are growing! Do you not believe that all the sense and nonsense that is today said so unabashedly *against religion* will have splendid consequences one day? Abstracting from *explanations, justifications,* and *proofs* of religion that often do not prove much, what great man would prophesy a coming age *of superstition* because ours exhausted itself in *such stupid unbelief?* But however it may turn out (and it would be tragic if only *superstition* could alternate with *unbelief* and if the endless, wretched cycle did not get us any further!), *religion, reason,*[61] and *virtue* must inevitably *gain*, sooner or later, by the ridiculous attacks of their opponents! It is certain that humor, *philosophy*, and the *freedom to think* were unwitting and unwilling *scaffolds* for this new throne: but one day, when they are still standing, the *cloud* will suddenly be *dispersed*, and the sun in all its glory will illuminate the entire world.[62]

The *great scale* and *universality* on which all this runs, we discover, can apparently be another *unrecognized scaffold*. The more *means* and *tools* we Europeans invent to enslave, cheat, and plunder you other continents, the more it may be left to you to *triumph* in the end! We forge the chains by which *you* will pull *us* [one day], and the *inverted pyramids*[63] of our constitutions will be

60. The "dress of *philosophy* and *love of mankind*" from above.

61. *Vernunft*.

62. Compare *Letters towards the Advancement of Humanity*, letter 10: "No fog, no hypocrisy, no order—or rather, disorder—that is built upon delusion can last indefinitely; the thickest darkness will give way to light" (DKV 7:766).

†63. Sir Temple likened a certain form of government to this image! [William Temple's *Essay upon the Original and Nature of Government (1680)*, vol. 1 , p. 105 ff., compares the stability of political constitutions to that of certain shapes in

righted on your soil—*you with us*. But enough: it is evident how
everything is moving *towards greatness!* We are encompassing the   *100/101*
globe by any means, and whatever shall follow will probably never
be able to *narrow* its *base* again. We are approaching something
new, if only through *decomposition*.

Just where will we be led by the fact that our way of thinking is
getting more *refined* with regard to both good and evil, and that
our stronger, more sensuous principles and driving forces are
thereby *being ground down* without the mass of men having either
the *desire* or the *strength* to put up resistance or to put something
else in their place? The *powerful* sensuous *bonds* of the old republics and ages have long been *dissolved* (this is the triumph of our
times!), and *everything* is *gnawing* on the finer bonds of our times:
philosophy, free thinking, abundance, and an *education* towards all this
that is *spread* more and more *deeply* and *widely* from link to link.
Most of the driving forces behind our politics have already been
made to *condemn* or *despise* even *calm wisdom*, and [we all know]
how ancient are the reproaches and scruples to which the conflict
between Christianity and the ways of the world has given rise on
both sides! Since *weakness* cannot end but in *weakness*, then, and
since the *excessive straining* and *ill use* of the *last reserves of waning
strength* can hasten nothing but complete *collapse*—but it is not my
place to *prophesy!*

Even less [would it be my place] to prophesy about "what *could,
would,* and would almost *have to* offer the sole *source of new vital
energies* and *replenishment* on such an *expanded* stage; whence a *new
spirit* could and would draw all the *light* and the *humane disposition*
towards which we are working, so as to bring us *warmth, permanence,* and *universal bliss.*" No doubt I am speaking of what are still
distant times.

My brothers, let us work with brave, cheerful hearts even *right
underneath the cloud*,[64] for we are working towards *a great future*.

---

architecture. For Temple, the least stable form of government, comparable to an
inverted pyramid, is the one with the greatest number of participants, that is to
say, democracy (DKV 4:895).]

64. The cloud in which God goes before the Israelites on their way through
the desert; see Exod. 13:21, Num. 9:15–23, 1 Cor. 10:1–2. Herder also uses this
image in a letter to Johann Friedrich Kleuker, dated 13 November 1777:
"Patience! No grumbling or foolishness: just wait. It is God who calls us, not we,
and I know from personal experience that things go awry whenever we want to
call ourselves somewhere. What use is all the effort and striving, which is pride at
bottom, or the premature struggling of a child in the womb that is not ready to be

And let us imagine our goal to be as *pure*, as *bright*, as *untainted* as we possibly can, for we are treading in *treacherous light*, at *dusk*,

101/102   and through *fog*.

When I envisage the deeds [of that great future]—or rather, when I detect the silent features of deeds done from *a spirit* that is *too great* for the frame of its age and that passes by *too quietly* and *modestly* to attract *shrieks of praise* as it *sows* in the dark—[I see] seeds that begin *with a small germ*, like *all God's works* and creations, yet whose first, tiny shoots already reveal, by their lovely appearance and smell, their special future as *God's concealed creation*. And what if these were the beginnings, specifically, of the *noblest plant of mankind*, of *education,* instruction*, the *invigoration of nature* in its *neediest nerves*, of *love of mankind*, *sympathy*, and the *happiness of brothers?* Holy plants, is there anyone among you so changed that he would not be gripped by visions of a *better future* and that he would not give thanks—be he small or great, *king* or *servant*—to your Creator in his quietest evening, morning, and midnight devotions? All *merely physical* and *political purposes* will fall apart like shards and corpses. It is the *soul* that remains, the *spirit, that which fills the whole of mankind;* and blessed is he who is given much from that pure, incorruptible source of life!

It is nearly inevitable that the very height and wide range attained by our age must also give rise to ambiguities regarding the *best* and *worst* of deeds, which would not happen in narrower, less elevated spheres. Almost nobody knows anymore what effects his actions are having: everything is an ocean with wave upon wave roaring who knows where and with what violence! How should I know where I will get with my *little wave?* It is not only enemies and detractors who will often be able to cast the beginnings of even the *most effective, most excellent* man in a dubious light; fervent admirers, too, in their *colder hours*, may see *fog* and *twilight* around him. The points on a radius are already *so far removed* from the center[65]—*where* are they going, and *when* shall they *arrive* there?

---

born? Grow in the quiet over there, *underneath the cloud*, and emerge as a tree." (*Briefe* 4:47, lines 8–13. Our emphasis.)

65. Compare note to p. 39:5 and references given there.

We all know what the reformers of all ages have been reproached for: that whenever they took a *new step*, they always left gaps *behind*, stirred up dust and tremors *ahead*, and trod innocents *underfoot*. This is most visibly and doubly true of the reformers of the recent centuries. *Luther, Gustavus Adolphus, Peter the Great:*[66] *what three* have made *greater* changes in modern times, with *more noble* intentions? But have the consequences of their deeds, especially the *unforeseen* ones, all been unequivocal *blessings* for their successors? Anyone familiar with the *ensuing* history will surely have his doubts.

The monarch[67] whose name our age bears and deserves to bear—more than that of the age of "Louis, whom his century has preserved for us!"[68]—what a *recreation of Europe* he has been able to instigate from his little corner in thirty short years! In the *arts of war* and *politics*, in his *treatment of religion* and the *institution of laws*, as the *Apollo* of the *Muses* and as a *private citizen under the crown*[69]—always he appeared as the very model of monarchy. Such *good* he did, dispersing *enlightenment*, a *philosophical spirit*, and *moderation* everywhere *from his throne!* The ludicrous Oriental *ostentation, decadence*, and *luxury* that before had often been the courts' only glittering adornment—fiercely *crushed* and *chased away! Indolent ignorance, blind zeal*, and *superstition*—everywhere mortally wounded! *Frugality* and *order, discipline* and *industry, fine arts* and a so-called *taste for thinking freely*—all raised to such heights! The age bears his image, just as it wears his uniform—an age, no doubt, that sings his highest praises. All the same, this very coin, heads flipped over,[70] will one day show *something more* and *rather different* about what resulted from the creations of this friend of man and philosopher. Perhaps it will show how, by the natural law of the inadequacy of all human actions, *enlightenment* must also spread a corresponding, luxuriating *fatigue of the heart;* how *frugality* must also carry *poverty* as its sign and in its train; how *philosophy* fosters blind, short-sighted *unbelief*, while with *freedom of thought*

66. Compare *Do We Still Have a Fatherland?*, 51:28 ff.

67. Frederick the Great.

68. From Friedrich Gottlieb Klopstock, "Ode to Mr. Gleim" (1752), lines 47–48.

69. Frederick was fond of pronouncing himself no more than the first citizen or subject—even the first servant—of the state.

70. Compare p. 61:21–3. As is still the case in many countries, one side of the coin would depict the head of state—in this case Frederick—hence the expression "heads." That this side is turned down may be of symbolic significance.

comes *enslavement of action*, the *despotism of souls under chains of flowers*.[71] Along with great heroes, conquerors, and martial spirit, something *deadened* also appears, as with the Roman constitution that made armies everything and had to spread ruin and misery everywhere. [Perhaps it will] show what *must* be the consequences of *love of mankind, justice, moderation, religion*, the *well-being of the people*—all taken to *some extent* as *means to be attained*—for *their times*, for *kingdoms with entirely different constitutions* and *regimes*, for all the *world present* and *future*. Will the scales *hover?* Will one side *rise* or *fall*—and which one? What do I know?[72]

"The writer *of the century*"[73] who without disagreement or dissent *held court* over his age—was read, studied, admired, and what is more, *obeyed* from *Lisbon* to *Kamchatka*, from *Zemlya*[74] to the *colonies* of *India*. What this great writer has been able to do—*for the benefit of the age*, too, no doubt—by his *language*, by his manifold talents of *presentation*,[75] by his *ease*, by his *sweeping ideas* on beds of flowers—and most of all by *being born into such an auspicious place* for *availing himself* of the world, of his predecessors and rivals, and of his age's opportunities and occasions, its prejudices and most popular foibles, and especially of the most advantageous weaknesses of his age's most beautiful brides, the *rulers* of all of Europe! He spread the *light*, the so-called *philosophy* of *humanity, tolerance, ease* in *thinking for oneself*, the *gleam of virtue* in a hundred charming *guises*, *little human inclinations diluted* and *sweetened;* as a writer he stands at the summit of the age, no doubt! But at the same time what wretched *recklessness, weakness, uncertainty,* and *chill!* What *shallowness, lack of design, distrust* of *virtue*, of *happiness*, and *merit!* What was *laughed off* by his wit, sometimes without any such *intention!*

71. Compare 51:27; Rousseau, *Discourse on the Sciences and the Arts* I: "the Sciences, Letters, and Arts, less despotic but perhaps more powerful, spread garlands of flowers over the iron chains with which they are laden" (D: 6; *OC* 3:7).

72. Although *"Was weiß ich?"* is a common expression in German, this may well be an allusion to Montaigne's famous dictum, which he had struck on a medal: "'What do I know?'—the words I bear as a motto, inscribed over a pair of scales" (Michel de Montaigne, *Essays*, ed. Donald M. Frame [Stanford: Stanford University Press, 1958], 393).

†73. Voltaire.

74. The far reaches of Russia: the Kamchatka peninsula in the Russian Far East and Novaya Zemlya, the continuation of the Urals into the Russian Barents Sea.

75. Or, more specifically, his ability to dress things up nicely (*Einkleidung*). Compare p. 66:25: "[W]hat writer does not make it his primary business to *dress things up nicely* . . . ?"

Our gentle, pleasant, and necessary bonds have been *dissolved* with a shameless hand, yet those of us who do not reside at the Château de Fernay[76] have been given nothing at all *in their stead.* And by what *means* and ways did he achieve even *his best?* Into whose hands will he deliver us with all the philosophy and the *pretty dalliance of a way of thinking* without *morals* and *solid human feeling?* We all know about the great intrigues for and against him, and we know how differently *Rousseau* preaches. Perhaps it is good that *both of them* preach, *far apart from one another* and perhaps in some ways *canceling* each other *out.* Such is the end of many human beginnings: the lines cancel each other out, but their final points stand! *104/105*

Of course no great spirit through whom fortune effects *change,* with everything *that he thinks and feels,* can be judged according to the *common measure* of any *mediocre soul.* There are *exceptions of a higher type,* and nearly all that is *remarkable in the world* happens *through* these exceptions. The straight lines merely run their course, and everything would be left in its place if the deity did not also thrust *extraordinary human beings—comets—*into the calm *orbits around the sun,* letting them fall and at their lowest point *raising* them again to heights where no eye on earth can follow them. It is only for God, or for the fools among men, to enter every moral or immoral effect of an action, be it ever so *distant* and contingent, into a calculation of the *merits* and the primary intentions *of the actor!* Otherwise, who would face more *accusers* throughout the world than the first and only *actor,* the Creator himself?[77] But my brothers, let us under no circumstances abandon the poles around which everything revolves: *truth,* the *recognition* of *goodwill,* the *happiness of mankind!* Most important of all, given the *utmost elevation of the sea* upon which we are now floating through *treacherous* and *foggy light* that may be more dangerous than *pitch darkness,* let us be diligent in our search for the stars, those reference points for all *direction, security,* and *tranquility,*[78] so that we may keep our course with *faithfulness* and *vigor.*

The whole that appears *as a whole* in each of its particulars must be a great one! But in every particular, there is always an *indistinct*

---

76. Voltaire's residence near Geneva.

77. Compare p. 84:20–21.

78. *Ruhe.* A strikingly positive evaluation in light of Herder's scathing passages about *Ruhe* earlier in the text. Compare the note to 44:28–29.

oneness that alone reveals itself and points towards the whole.[79] There, even *minor* connections can have great *meaning*, and yet entire centuries are mere *syllables;* nations, mere *letters,* and perhaps no more than punctuation marks that mean nothing by themselves but mean *so much* for the easier comprehension of the whole. What are you, *O single human being,* with all your inclinations, abilities, and contributions? In you, perfection is supposed to have *exhausted* all its *aspects?*

The very *limitations* of my earthly point of view, the *blindness* of my glances, the *failure* of my ends, the *riddle* of my inclinations and desires, the *defeat* of my powers by the whole that is *a single day,* [let alone] *an entire year, nation, or age*—precisely this assures me that *I* am nothing, whereas the *whole* is *everything!* What a work it is, *this whole* containing so many shadowy clusters of *nations* and *ages, colossal figures* with barely a *perspective* or *view,* so many *blind instruments* that are acting in a *delusion of freedom* and yet do not know *what* or *what for,* that are unable to *survey anything* and yet *are taking part* as eagerly as if their *anthill* were the *universe*—what a *work!* Even the *slightest* of its *stretches* that we can survey contains so much *order* and *confusion,* so many *knots* and *beginnings* of *disentanglement*—so many safeguards and guarantees for the exuberant glory of the universal. How miserably *small* it would have to be if I, *a fly,* could see it all! How little *wisdom* or *great diversity* [would there be] if one who is *stumbling* through the world, who has such trouble holding on to a *single thought,* were never to get *entangled!* [Who am I] on such a stretch, which is nothing, really, but where there are still *thousands of thoughts* and *seeds striving simultaneously;* or in *half a musical bar* of [only] two beats, but where the *heaviest tones* may be winding *towards the sweetest disentanglement*—who am *I* to judge, when I am just *crossing* the great ballroom and eyeing some far corner of the great concealed painting in the dimmest of lights? Given what Socrates said about the writings of a mere human being,[80] one as constrained as he by the *limited powers of man,* what am I supposed to

---

79. Compare *Letters towards the Advancement of Humanity,* letter 123: "The *tendency of human nature* comprises an entire *universe* within it, whose inscription is: 'None for himself alone, each for all; thus you are all worthy and happy, one for the other.' An infinite diversity striving towards a unity that resides in all, and that advances all. Its name (which I will repeat over and over again) is reason, fairness, benevolence, *the feeling of humanity*" (DKV 7:750).

80. According to Diogenes Laertius' *Lives of the Philosophers* (II.22:5–8), Euripides presented Socrates with the writings of Heraclitus, and asked him what he

say about the *great book of God* that extends *over all the worlds and times*, when I am barely a single letter in that book and when, looking around, I can scarcely see three more letters?

[We are] infinitely *small* in relation to the pride that wants *to be everything, to know, do, and form* it all*, but infinitely *great* in rela-   *106/107* tion to the *pusillanimity* that does not dare *to be* anything at all! Both are nothing but *individual instruments* for the plans of an *immeasurable Providence.*

What if we were one day to arrive at a *perspective* that would allow us to survey the whole of our species? [To see] how far the chain will reach that was at first drawn *so slowly* between the peoples and continents, but that then wound its way through the nations with *so much clanking*, and that would finally, gently but *firmly bind, draw together,* and *lead away* these nations—whereto? Then we shall see the *ripe harvest* of the seeds that we dispersed among the peoples *through a blind sieve* and whose *strange* shoots, *manifold* blossoms, and *ambiguous* promises of fruit we once observed. Then we shall get to taste *for ourselves* what *delicacies* were finally brought forth for the *universal education* of mankind* by the cloudy, unsavory *leaven* that has been fermenting for so long. You fragment of life, what did you amount to? "How great a darkness shrouds our days"![81] Blessed is he who even then will have no regrets about his life's fragment!

For now we see through a glass, darkly; but then face to face: now I know in part; but then shall I know even as also I am known. And now abideth faith, hope, charity, these three; but the greatest of these is charity.[82]

---

thought of them. Socrates replied that he found both what he had understood and what he had not understood excellent.

   81. Lit.: "*quanta sub nocte iacebat nostra dies,*" from Lucan, *The Civil War* (or *Pharsalia*), Book IX, lines 13–14.

   82. Herder gives the Greek text of 1 Cor. 13:12–13.

Selected Political Writings

On Nations, Cultures, and Ages

OF THE CHANGES IN THE TASTES OF THE NATIONS THROUGH THE AGES

A FRAGMENT (1766)

DKV *Werke* vol. 1, p. 157 line 4–p. 160 line 19

Once a man saw trees being planted for posterity and cried out: "Always we must do things for our descendants; I wished that our descendants would also do something for us!" This silly man, who did not consider that he was himself a descendant, that he owed everything to his ancestors, and that future generations would be a part of him, should have thought ahead a few centuries, putting himself in the position of the descendants who would enjoy these trees. Now what would they be able to do for him, their ancestor? Think of him! What could they do for their descendants, however? Work for them!

Thus every human being in every age stands in the middle. He can assemble the faded images of his ancestors around him; he can summon up their shadows and make a feast for his eyes as he lets them rush by. But can he also cast a prophetic eye on future times, beyond his grave, watching his children and grandchildren wander over his ashes, as it were? The view of the past is secured by history; the prospect of the future is darker—but even this shadowy darkness is pleasurable.

When one casts a glance ahead and behind from such philosophical heights;[1] when one conjures up the spirit of an extinct age from its ashes; when one compares different, successive ages with each other and believes that one can see a continuous thread,

---

1. On the perspective from these "philosophical heights," compare also *Another Philosophy of History*, 54:25, 70:18–20, and 91:31–35.

157/158 a coherent whole—what, then, would be more natural than to wonder whether this chain of changes, which has been running along so evenly for many centuries, should be broken by us? Should it not keep running along beyond us? When one gathers together the many changes of the past, when one sees what altering power the arm of time possesses and how it has been employed, then does not the audacious look ahead become a little more excusable? Perhaps these will be the results of change behind our backs: so things changed before us, so they will change after us.

If, meanwhile, this prophetic glance were to prove deceptive, the examination of past generations would still be all the more useful. The spirit of change is the kernel of history, and he who does not direct most of his attention to picking out this spirit, putting together in his mind the tastes and character of each age, and traveling through the different periods of world events with the piercing perspective of a wanderer eager for instruction; he sees only trees instead of men, like the blind man,[2] and ruins his stomach on history as on a dish of husks without kernels. Thus the greatest historians attained such heights by noting these changes through the ages, by also thinking as they told their story, by leading their readers around so that they might not only see but also learn. If *Voltaire* has some merit as a historian, it is with a view to his often apt remarks on the spirit of events. The greatest man in this regard, however, is in my opinion the *historian* of *Britain*, *Hume*, a writer who understands the difficult art of applying the pragmatic tricks of *Tacitus* or *Polybius* to the taste of our times.

No doubt my introductory remarks are too long for this one little treatise. If it were well received by the public, however, it
158/159 should be merely the precursor for similar reflections *on the spirit of change in the various ages.* When philosophy is guided by history and history is enlivened by philosophy, then it is doubly entertaining and useful.

Some people who are ignorant about history and know only their own age think that present tastes are the only ones and so necessary that anything besides would be unthinkable. They think that

2. Compare Mark 8:24: "And [the blind man] looked up, and said, I see men as trees, walking."

everything they find indispensable on account of their habits and education must have been indispensable at all times, and they do not know that the more comfortable we are with something, the newer it is likely to be. Commonly, pride is joined to such ignorance—two siblings who are as inseparable as envy and stupidity. Their times are the best because that is when they are living and because other ages have not had the honor of their acquaintance. These people are like the Chinese who, because they knew no one else, considered their country the square of the world and who painted the corners of this square with hideous grimaces and monsters, which were supposed to portray us, the pitiful inhabitants of the rest of the world. We laugh at the Chinese, and yet how often does it seem like one were [living] in China when one hears the opinions of persons who know the world only by the corner in which they are stuck and by the *Hamburg Correspondent*.

Two looks at history will dispel this prejudice. Time has changed everything so much that it would often take a magic mirror to recognize the same creature in so many shapes. The very *shape* of the earth has changed, its *surface* as well as its *position*; the *blood*, the manners of *living* and *thinking*, the forms of government, the tastes of the nations have [all] changed. How families change as well as individuals! If our great ancestor Adam, or Noah, or the other progenitors of every people were to rise [from the dead]—heaven, what a sight this would be for them!

None of these changes is as difficult to explain as the variation *159/160* in *tastes* and *manners of thinking*. How could that which a nation holds at one time to be good, beautiful, useful, pleasant, or true be considered bad, ugly, useless, unpleasant, and untrue by it at another time? And yet this does happen! Are not truth, beauty, and moral goodness the same at all times? Surely—and yet one can observe how the same principles for which everyone would at one time have sacrificed his last drop of blood are at other times cast into the fire by the very same nation; how fashions that some years ago everyone found beautiful are soon after extinguished; how reigning practices, favorite conceptions of honor, merit, and utility can dazzle one age [as] by a magic light; how a [particular] taste in this or that science can set the tone for a century; and how all this nevertheless dies out with that century! We should almost go mad with such skepticism, putting no more trust in our own tastes and feelings!

DO WE STILL HAVE A FATHERLAND? (1765)

Second Section of Herder's
"The Public and the Fatherland"[1]

DKV *Werke* vol. 1, p. 48 line 11–p. 53 line 6
(Cf. Suphan 1, pp. 21–6)

The public of the ancients has in a way been lost for the *state*, the *orator*, the *writer*; so is the *fatherland* also extinct, then, that *fatherland* whose name was the pride of *Rome*, the center of Sparta, and the motto of *Athens, Thebes, Crete?* Has the *love of the fatherland*, which called the young man there to the *field of battle* and to his *death*, which gave sweetness to the word *freedom* and roused him to the most selfless, *patriotic deeds*, which made a public laurel wreath the brilliant object of all his aspirations—has this great driving force now ceased to function?

I would rather not dare venture upon the special *districts* of the legislator-like *Montesquieu* to investigate the driving forces behind the various forms of government today. I would perhaps have to take Crevier for my guide, and that would lead to quarreling.[2] I shall only examine the matter *in general*, since I will consider the old and the new states together. Do we no longer have a fatherland with regard to *honor, utility, freedom, courage*, and *religion?* I

48/49 shall answer these questions in reverse.

Religion for the Greeks and Romans was almost only *political*. The writings of Cicero about the nature of the gods illustrate the

---

1. "Publikum und Vaterland": a presentation Herder gave on the occasion of the inauguration of a new court building in Riga, where he was working for the cathedral school.

†2. Of all Montesquieu's opponents, Crevier is the only one who deserves respect, namely for his *Observations sur le livre: de l'Esprit des Loix.*

state of their religious doctrine, since he was himself an *augur*[3] who wrote publicly. Without wishing to rack our brains with *Shaw* and *Warburton* about the Orphic and Eleusinian mysteries, about *symbols* and *hieroglyphs*, we see that their *protector-gods* and their religious worship, their oracles and ceremonies were nothing but a sacred fog and sacrificial smoke to dull the eyes of the people, the bridle and bit with which to direct them.

We do not have such a *religion of the fatherland* that would retain its value only as far as a city's walls and that would change along with the air in a different region. Whatever *Montesquieu* and his admirer *Beaumelle*, whatever *Bayle*, *Rousseau*, and *Diderot* may say about the relationship of our religion to the state, it still remains the most certain of truths and a solid lesson of experience—even if *Grotius*, *Pufendorf*, *Haller*, and *Mably* did not write about it and the younger *Herr von Moser* does not wish to preach about it—that an honest, reasonable religion is the foundation of thrones and states, the pillar of city halls, palaces, and huts, and indeed that our godly *religion* makes for our happiness both here and beyond the grave. Likewise *trade* and *commerce* have made our age more tolerant of foreign religions so long as they do not undermine the central pillars of the state or oppress the liberties of the cities. *Holland, England,* and other countries have flourished this way: an inquisition in a place of trade is like a messenger that on the one hand invites guests with the utmost subservience and on the other drives them away with a brotherly whipping.   *49/50*

Secondly, do we have a fatherland for which the warrior might fight, *spill blood, die*? Certainly! If he is more than a dead mercenary who sells his *courage*, his *blood*, his *life* for cash in the manner of the *slave trade*, then the words *fatherland, king, queen* will ring for him with the sound of victory that makes his blood vessels glow, invigorates his heart, and strengthens his hand by his nerves and his chest with an iron armor. For a patriot, it is sweet and honorable to die for the fatherland,[4] not only where the law and hundreds rule but also where it is ruled by the law and an individual—but one who is the father or mother of a happy people. The little book *Of Death for the Fatherland* speaks here on my behalf.[5]

---

3. A reference to Cicero's *De natura deorum* and *De divinatione.*

4. Compare *Another Philosophy of History*, 45:17; *Do We Still Have the Fatherland of the Ancients?*, 329:29–30.

5. Thomas Abbt's *Vom Tode für das Vaterland* (1761).

Thirdly, do we have a fatherland whose sweet surname is *freedom?* Yes! But we think differently about the word *freedom* than the ancients. For them *freedom* was an untamed insolence, a dare by those who wished to control the rudder of the state all by themselves, the obstinacy of those who would not suffer anyone above them. In our age all states have sunk into balance; those who cannot protect themselves require protectors, fathers. The character of our people is no longer the *brazen wildness* of the ancients but rather a finer and more moderate *freedom:* the freedom of *conscience,* of being an honest man and a Christian; the *freedom* to enjoy one's hut and grapevine quietly, to own the fruits of one's sweat, in the shadow of the throne. The *freedom* to be the creator of one's own happiness and comfort, to be a friend to one's dear friends and the father and governor of one's children—this is the *freedom,* that moderate *freedom* for which every patriot wishes today; this is the jewel that *Riga* received from the hands of its most just *queen,*[6] which it enjoys so excellently and with all due gratitude.

Finally, is there still a fatherland in our times, the love of which might move us to selfless sacrifice? Do we know anything anymore of the passion of the ancients in vying for the love of our fatherland, for its honor and reward as a patriot's most beautiful wreath? Who will answer "No" to this question whose blood feels nobly also towards his superiors, whose heart in his chest beats warmly for his brother, who wants to be a link in the chain of the whole, and joyfully so?

Only a *Helvétius* who finds none but selfish drives in man, a *Mandeville* who would turn us into mere *bees,* a *Hobbes* who inscribes enmity on every man's forehead, a *Machiavelli* who created that monster of the despot who sucks the blood [of the people] through tax-collectors, *vampires* and *leeches;*[7] only such base and cold misanthropes rob us of the gentle sensation of patriotism. It is a bad soul that allows itself to be robbed, that tears itself from its fatherland and follows the Ptolemaic system in making its own lump of clay the center of the whole.

50/51

6. Under Catherine the Great, Riga enjoyed a considerable degree of independence.

7. Herder seems to be ignoring Chapter XVII of *The Prince,* where Machiavelli argues that the prince will avoid being hated "if he abstains from the property of his citizens and his subjects" because "men forget the death of a father more quickly than the loss of a patrimony" (Niccolò Machiavelli, *The Prince,* trans. Harvey C. Mansfield, Jr. [Chicago: The University of Chicago Press, 1985], p. 67).

Of course we do not sacrifice ourselves blindly anymore:[8] the times are past when armies of warrior-knights would rush to the sword for a statue in their honor and a wreath upon their bloodied hair; when youths would shout the word *"Fatherland!"* right in the thick of battle, like those crazed heroes crying out for the invisible princess for whom they were sacrificing themselves; those times are past, but has the fire of love for the fatherland been extinguished along with them? Was *Peter the Great* not a true patriot when he, the name and marvel of our century, became the father of his old—and the founder of a new—fatherland? Why did he not rule in the leisurely manner of his forebears? What put the great thought in his head, alone deserving of a *Petread,*[9] to tear his children, against their will at that time, away from their inherited disgrace? What embers turned him into a foreigner, a student? What made him wrap his arms around the tombstone of Richelieu and cry: "Great man! If only you were alive, I would give you half my empire, but teach me how to rule the other half!" What was it that raised him ever higher, through all the tempests and setbacks, and only spurred him on even more? O great father of your fatherland! From your patriotic spirit ten sovereigns could be made, and we would revere them all.

    If one took from a king or queen the sweet thought that he or she is working for a *fatherland*, ruling his or her *children*, nothing would be easier than for him to turn into *Machiavelli's* portrait of the prince and for her to turn into *Mandeville's* machinelike queen of the bees. If one took away the vitalizing words "for[10] the *fatherland*" from a *judge* or from any other man of the *public authorities* who is required to subordinate his private affairs to the public, to forgo his own power, to yield up his own interests and those of his family to the interests of the whole—would he not then be a fool if he donned a small laurel wreath rather than a green *Jewish skullcap,*[11] if he took the judge's seat rather than seeking out gold mines and church riches so long as nobody was watching? If one abandoned the word *fatherland*, many quiet and noble deeds of

51/52

---

8. Compare *Letters towards the Advancement of Humanity*, letter 13: "The noisiest patriots are often the most hard-hearted, narrow-minded egotists; the most ardent defenders of liberty are the coldest souls, often born slaves to self-interest and self-regard: the swiftest eagles in words and phrases, but the earth's laziest mules in their deeds" (DKV 7:773).

    9. Presumably a heroic epic along the lines of the *Iliad* or the *Aeneid*.

    10. Following the correction at DKV 4:926.

    11. I.e., to seek financial gain.

amity would disappear. He who carries so many stones because they bear the inscription *"fatherland"* would shake them off; he would tread on the burdens that he took upon himself out of patriotic pride. If there is no *fatherland*, beyond the *land of one's birth*, that one might earn for oneself by one's contributions, then the foreigner must despair if he labors as a patriot and sacrifices himself while the native-born fool esteems his sacrifice no more than he does a bet in a game of cards. Where does all this leave that magnanimous disposition which is not *for lease?* No, *fatherland*, you driving force of worthiness, you wise man's enthusiasm and sweat's laurel wreath!

52/53

DO WE STILL HAVE THE FATHERLAND OF THE ANCIENTS? (1795)

Second Part of a Text Appended to Herder's 57th *Letter towards the Advancement of Humanity*

DKV *Werke* vol. 7, p. 329 line 6–p. 338 line 5
(Cf. Suphan 17:311–9)

For the Greeks and Romans, the word "fatherland" was sweet and worthy of honor. Who is not familiar with passages from their poets and orators in which the sons of the fatherland dedicate to it, as to a mother, their childlike love and gratitude, their praises, wishes, and sighs? He who finds himself removed from it yearns to return; with hope or with sorrow he looks in its direction, receiving the winds blowing from there as messengers of his beloved. Having returned to the fatherland, he embraces it and tearfully kisses its soil. He who dies at a distance bequeaths his ashes to it, wishing even for an empty tomb of memory among his people. To live for the fatherland was for them the highest glory; to die for it, the sweetest death. He who helped raise the fatherland by his counsels and actions, who rescued it and adorned it with the wreaths of glory, earned for himself a seat among the gods; he was certain of immortality in heaven and on earth. He, on the other hand, who insulted the fatherland or dishonored it by his actions, who betrayed it or made war on it, thrust a sword into the bosom of his mother; he was a murderer of father, child, friend, and brother. "The fatherland must be dearer to us than we ourselves."[1] "It is sweet and honorable to die for the fatherland."[2]

1. Cicero, *De finibus bonorum et malorum* III, 64.
2. *Another Philosophy of History*, 45:17; *Do We Still Have a Fatherland?*, 50:11–12.

And so forth. Do we, too, have this fatherland of the ancients? And what are the bonds of love that tie us to it?

329/330   The soil of the country, on which we are born, can hardly tie this magic bond all by itself. It would, rather, be the heaviest of all burdens if man, viewed like a tree or a plant or a beast, would *have to* belong, inherently and eternally, with all his soul, body, and powers, to the land where he was born. There have been and still are enough harsh laws about such servitude and serfdom, and so forth. [Meanwhile] the whole course of reason,[3] of culture, even of industry and of utilitarian calculation, leads towards a gradual unshackling of these slaves, born of a mother's womb or of the mother-earth, from the hard scrap of land that they are expected to fertilize with their sweat in life and their ashes in death, and instead ties them with more gentle bonds to a fatherland.

When nomadic peoples were still roaming the earth, dwelling in deserted places for periods of time and burying their fathers there, the ground of the land held by these peoples, at that time or in the past, gave rise to the name *land of the fathers*. "We shall await you at the graves of our fathers," one would call out to the enemy: "Their ashes, too, we shall protect as we defend our land." Thus the holy name emerged, and not as if human beings had sprung from the soil. Only children can love the fatherland, not serfs born of the soil or slaves captured like wild animals.

What first invigorates us in the fatherland is not the earth beneath our feet but the air we breathe, the father's hands that hold us, the mother's breast that feeds us, the sun we see, the siblings we play with, and the friendly natures that are good for us. Our first fatherland, therefore, is the *father's house*, a *father's field*, *family*. It is in this small society that the first and foremost friends of the fatherland live, as in an idyllic circle; the land of our early youth lives by just such idylls. Let the soil or climate be what it may: the soul yearns to return there, and the further this small society in which we were raised was from a *state*, the less ranks and classes of men were separated within it, the fewer obstacles there

330/331   are to the imagination that yearns to return to the bosom of this fatherland. It was there that we heard and understood the first tones of love; it was there that we committed ourselves to friendship for the first time and felt the first buds of tender attraction between the sexes.[4] We saw the sun, the moon, the sky, the spring

3. *Vernunft.*

4. Compare *Another Philosophy of History*, 97:20 f.

with its trees, blossoms, and fruit that were then so sweet to us. The course of all the world was displayed for us; we saw the seasons roll along, we struggled with dangers, with grief and joy—we grew into the world like summer and winter, as it were. These impressions, moral and physical, remain engraved upon our imagination; the tree's tender bark received them, and if they are not eradicated by force they will die only with the tree itself. Who has not read of the sighs and sorrows with which even the Greenlanders left behind the land of their youth and that accompanied them as they strove, through all the dangers, to make their way back from the culture of Europe? Whose ears do not ring with the sighs of the Africans who were torn away from their fatherland, where they had lived in simple *small societies*, in an idyllic land of youth.

The states—or rather *cities*—of the Greeks, to whom the name of the fatherland was so dear and precious, followed right after these *small societies*. Legislation favored them and originally derived all its energy from them. It was the *land of the fathers* that one protected; it was companions from one's youth—siblings and friends—for whom one yearned. The league of love into which young men entered was approved and made use of by the fatherland. One wished to be buried with one's friends, to enjoy things together, to live and die with them. And since the noble ancestors of these tribes had built the community to which they belonged with the protection of the gods, marking it with their troubles and toil and sealing it with their blood, so the bond of such laws was sacred to their descendents as a *moral fatherland*. For the Greeks esteemed nothing more than the achievement of those *civil institutions* that had turned them into Greeks and by which they had been raised above all the barbarians of the world. The gods of *their* land were the most beautiful gods; their heroes, legislators, poets, and wise men were immortalized in institutions, songs, monuments, and celebrations. Their public places and temples were resplendent with all this. The victory of the Greeks over the Persians alone made their land, their constitution, their culture and language the crown of the universe for them. The Greeks were floating in the ether of such ideas when they so often used the name of the fatherland nobly, but also often abused it. Several cities shared in this glory, each in its own way. And how Rome thought of herself as the queen of all the world, the gathering place for all victory and glory, this Roman history shows.

It would be foolish to wish to return to the times of Greece or Rome. This youth of the world has passed, as has the iron age of the times of Roman rule, and we would hardly gain much of what we really desire by trading, even if such an exchange were possible. Sparta's zeal for the fatherland oppressed not only the Helots, but also its citizens, and, with time, the other Greeks as well. Athens was often hard on its citizens and colonies, which needed to be concealed with sweet phantoms. Finally, the Romans' love of their fatherland proved pernicious not only for Italy but for Rome itself and for the entire Roman world. We shall therefore seek out what *we* ought to respect and love about the fatherland, that we may love it worthily and purely.

1. Is it that once upon a time gods climbed down from the heavens and assigned this land to our fathers? Is it that they gave us a religion and established our constitution themselves? Did Minerva conquer this city in a contest?[5] Did Egeria inspire our Numa with her dreams? A vain glory, for we are not our fathers. If, on Minerva's hallowed ground, we cease to be worthy of the great goddess, if Numa's dreams no longer accord with our times, then may Egeria rise once more from her spring and may Minerva bring new inspiration as she [once more] comes down from the heavens.

To speak plainly, it is good and glorious for a people to have great ancestors, an advanced age, and illustrious gods of the fatherland, so long as [the people] are thereby roused to noble deeds and inspired to worthy convictions, so long as the ancient discipline and teaching remain suitable to them. Where [this discipline and teaching] is scorned by the people themselves, however, it has outlived itself or is abused: "What good, you proud Pontic Mast," cries Horace to *his* fatherland, "what good is your noble descent to you now? What good are the painted gods on your hulls?"[6] A glory idly possessed and lazily inherited from our ancestors soon makes us vain and unworthy of them. He who fancies himself to be courageous, noble, and upright by birthright easily forgets to prove himself such. He misses the chance to reach for a wreath that he thinks he already possesses by inheritance from his ancestors.[7] It is by such a mania of pride—about the

332/333

5. The goddess Athena (Minerva) defeated Poseidon in a contest over Attica and became the protectress of Athens.

6. Horace, *Odes* I, 14. Herder's own translation of this ode about the ship of state is reprinted at Suphan 26:219 ff.

7. Compare *Letters towards the Advancement of Humanity*, letter 13: "We grow the fonder of all the old junk of glory and prestige the more tattered it becomes and the less it belongs in our age. When the sword has been lost, the hilt and scabbard are displayed all the more lovingly" (DKV 7: 773).

fatherland, its religion, lineage, ancestry—that Judea, Greece, Rome, and nearly every ancient, mighty, or holy state has perished. Our respect and love is due not to what the fatherland may once have been, but to what it is now.

2. Hence [the proper object of our respect and love], apart from our children, relatives, and friends, can only be the institutions [of our fatherland], the good *constitution* under which we would most like to live with what is dearest to us. Physically, we praise the location of a place whose healthy air is good for our body and spirits; morally, we consider ourselves to be happy in a state where under a lawful freedom and security we do not make ourselves blush, where we do not waste our efforts, where we and those dear to us are not abandoned but are free to do all our duties as worthy, active sons of the fatherland who are recognized and rewarded in the eyes of the mother. The Greeks and Romans were right [to think] that no other human achievement exceeds that of establishing such a union, or of strengthening, renewing, purifying, and preserving it. To think, to work, and (blessed lot!) truly to accomplish something not only for the common cause of those dearest to us but for all those who descend from us and for the entire, eternal fatherland of mankind—what, compared to this, is a single life but a day's work of a few minutes and hours? *333/334*

Anyone aboard a ship caught amidst the tidal waves of the sea will feel the common bond of mutual aid for the preservation and rescue of the ship. It was the word *fatherland* that rendered the ship seaworthy at the shore; [he who boards it] cannot, must not, stand idly by as if he had remained on land, counting the waves— unless he were to fling himself overboard, surrendering himself to the wild waves of the sea. Duty calls him (for all his companions and loved ones are on the ship with him) that he may help and cry out for help whenever a storm looms, a danger threatens, the wind turns, or another ship skids towards a collision with his own. Quietly or loudly [he does his part] according to his station, be he a simple sailor, the helmsman, or the ship's captain. Duty, the welfare of the entire ship, calls him. He cannot save himself on his own; he must not dream of punting in choice company at the shore, which is out of his reach, but must rather put his hands to the task and thereby become, if not the ship's savior, then at least its loyal companion and guardian.

How did it come about that estates of men once highly respected gradually came to be despised, having sunk into disgrace and still sinking today? Because none of them were concerned with the common cause, because all lived by the privileges of their estate, its property and honor. They slept calmly through the storm like Jonah, and they met with the same fate as Jonah. O that men whose eyes can see will not believe in *Nemesis!* Every breach or neglect of duty entails not an arbitrary but a necessary punishment that accumulates from generation to generation. If the cause of the fatherland is holy and eternal, then every failure to promote it must by its very nature be atoned for, and vengeance is accumulated with every rotten dealing or generation. You are not to brood over the fatherland as you were not its creator, but you must join in aiding it wherever and however you can by encouraging, rescuing, improving—even if you were to be a goose guarding the Capitol.[8]

3. Should we not, therefore, in the very spirit of the ancients, consider the voice of every single citizen an expression of the freedom of the fatherland, a holy ostracism, provided that it also appears in print? Perhaps the poor man could do nothing but write, or he would probably have done something better; would you rob him who is sighing of the breath that goes out into the desolate emptiness? But still more valuable to the intelligent man are the nods and glances of those who see further ahead. They wake [men] up when all are sleeping; they sigh, perhaps, when all are dancing. But they do not only sigh; they produce better results by simpler equations, by virtue of an unquestionable art. Do you want to silence them because you calculate only according to the common arithmetic? They keep silent easily and continue to calculate; but the fatherland counts on these silent calculators. A *single* step ahead that they pronounced to good effect is worth more than ten thousand ceremonies and words of praise.

Is our fatherland not supposed to need this art of calculation? Let Germany be courageous and upright. Courageously and uprightly it once let itself be led to Spain and Africa, to Gaul and England, to Italy, Sicily, Crete, Greece, Palestine. Our courageous and upright ancestors[9] bled there—and are buried there.

8. According to Livy's *History of Rome*, Gauls who had found a passage to the Capitol managed to climb the hill so quietly that neither guards nor dogs heard them. They did, however, wake the geese that were sacred to Juno. The noise made by the geese awoke Manlius, who in turn alerted others and repelled the attack (I, 5.47).

9. I.e., the German peoples during the times of the Great Migration.

[But] courageously and uprightly, so history shows, the Germans were [also] willing to fight each other for a price, within their fatherland and outside it, friend set against friend, brother against brother; the fatherland was torn apart and remained forsaken. Should not something more than courage and uprightness therefore be necessary to our fatherland? Light, enlightenment, a public spirit; the noble pride not to be governed by others, but to govern oneself like other nations have done since time immemorial; to be Germans on their own *well-defended* land.

4. The glory of a fatherland in our time can hardly be that 335/336 wild *spirit of conquest* anymore which stormed like an evil demon through the histories of Rome and of the barbarians and of many a proud monarchy. What kind of mother would sacrifice her children—like a second, worse Medea—in order to capture foreign children as slaves who must sooner or later become a burden on her own children? How miserable is the child of the fatherland that is given away or sold, that is made to die by the sword, or to devastate and murder, in order to satisfy a vanity that bears advantage for no one! In our time and before the judgment of an even stricter posterity, the glory of the fatherland can be no other than that this noble mother provide her children with the security, activity, cause for free and charitable exercise—in short, the upbringing—that makes for her own protection and utility, dignity and glory. All the peoples of Europe (other parts of the world not excepted) are now competing with each other in terms not of their physical but of their *mental and artistic powers*. When one or two nations are making such progress, in a short time, as once required centuries, then other nations cannot, must not, long to go back by centuries lest they come to grievous harm. They *must* move forward along with those [leading the way]: in our times one cannot be a barbarian any longer; as a barbarian one gets deceived, trodden on, despised, abused. The world's epochs form* a chain whose pull no individual link can resist in the end, even if it wanted to.

A *fatherland's culture* belongs here and so, within it, does the culture of language. What roused the Greeks to their glorious and most difficult works? The voice of duty and of glory. Whereby did they deem themselves more excellent than all the other nations on earth? By their cultivated language and what was planted among them by means of it. The imperatorial language of the Romans commanded the world, a language of law and action.

Whereby has a neighboring nation[10] won so much influence on all Europe's peoples for more than a century now? Other causes aside, the primary and most excellent reason is its *national language*, one *developed** in the highest sense of the word. Anyone who delighted in [its] literature thereby joined its empire and participated in it. [Those who were dominant] formed* and deformed; they commanded, they impressed. And the language of the Germans, which our ancestors considered the language of the tribe, the core,[11] the hero—should it now pull the victory chariot of others, as if vanquished, while thrusting out its chest about the plodding style of its imperial officers and princelings' courts?[12] Throw it away, this oppressive adornment, you matron confined against your own will, and be what you can be and once were: a language of reason,[13] of vigor and truth. You fathers of the fatherland, honor her, honor the gifts that she brought you, unbid and unthanked and yet deserving of praise. Shall every art and deed by which many would like to come to the aid of the fatherland first sell itself outside the country like the lost son, entrusting the fruits of hard work or genius to a foreign hand, so that you may have the honor of receiving it from there? Methinks I can see a time coming . . .

   Let us not prophesy, however, but only observe, in conclusion, that every fatherland has a *moral tendency* even in its sweet name. It hails from our forefathers, and the name *father* brings to mind the *days of our youth* and its *games*; it reminds us to think of all the accomplished men that came before us, of all the worthy men whose fathers we shall become. It forges all mankind into a chain of continuous links that are to one another brothers, sisters, betrothed, friends, children, parents. How else should we think of ourselves on earth? Must one fatherland really have to rise up against another, nay against *every* other one, while all of them link their members together by the same bonds? Does the earth not have room for us all? Cannot one country lie quietly beside the others? Cabinets may deceive each other; political machines may be moved against each other until one blows the other to pieces. But *fatherlands* do not move against each other like this;

---

10. France.

11. *Kernsprache*. Presumably connected to Herder's image of husks and kernels.

12. Where the greatest efforts were being made to imitate the French.

13. *Vernunft*.

they lie quietly side by side and assist each other as families do. *Fatherlands against fatherlands* in bloody struggle—that is the worst barbarism of the human language.[14]

14. Compare *Letters towards the Advancement of Humanity*, letter 119: "Could any spectacle be more detestable to a higher being than two armies facing each other and murdering one another with impunity? . . . [T]he terrible word 'war,' which one pronounces so easily, [ought] not only to become loathsome to men, but they should barely dare to name or write it, shuddering as they would before a ghastly brain-fever, pestilence, famine, the trembling of the earth, Black Death" (DKV 7:720).

ON THE CHARACTERS OF
NATIONS AND AGES (1796)

Herder's 88th *Letter towards the*
Advancement of Humanity[1]

DKV *Werke* vol. 7, p. 493 line 25–p. 495
(Cf. Suphan 18, pp. 56–59)

How I am struck with fear when I hear an entire nation or age
characterized by a few words:[2] for what tremendous differences
are contained in the word *nation*, or in *Middle Ages*, or in *ancient
and modern times!* I find myself similarly embarrassed when I hear
talk of the *poetry of a nation* or of an *age* in general terms. The
poetry of the *Italians*, the *Spaniards*, the *French*—how much, what
variety does it comprehend within itself! And how little does he
often conceive it, or know it even, who characterizes it most ver-
bosely!

493/494

When I used to read my *Dante* and *Petrarch*, *Ariosto* and *Cervantes* and sought to acquaint myself with each of these writers
from within, as my friend and teacher, then it pleased me to consider him as one *unique*. Towards this end I sought out everything
that lies within him and everything around him that had contributed to his intellectual formation* and deformation. The entire
world of literature before and after him disappeared from my
sight; I saw only him. And yet I was soon reminded of the whole
series of ages that had preceded and succeeded him. He had
learned and taught; he followed others, others followed him. The

1. An abbreviation of the title given this letter in the table of contents for the
seventh collection of letters, DKV 7:438.

2. Compare *Another Philosophy of History*, 32:20–30.

bond of language, of one way of thinking, of the passions, of content tied him to many, eventually even to all, writers—because he was a *human being,* he composed for *human beings.* Inadvertently, we are therefore led to examine what place—forward or backward—everyone will take relative to those like himself, inside or outside his nation, and what place *his* nation will take relative to *others;* and thus an invisible chain pulls us into *Pandemonium,* into the *Realm of the Spirits.*

If poetry is the blossom of the human spirit, of human mores—I would even say: the *ideal of our way of imagining,* the *language* of the collective desire and longing of mankind—then, I should think, he is happy to whom it is granted to pick that blossom from the crown of the tree of the *most enlightened nation.* It is surely no small advantage of our *inner life* that we are able to speak not only with the Orientals and the ancients, but also with the noblest spirits of Italy, Spain, and France, and that we are able to notice with each [of them] how *he* sought to robe his heart's concepts and desires, those most ardent within *him,* in the most worthy fashion and to present them to the world present and future in an agreeable, even enrapturing, fashion. Enraptured with your sweet and bitter reveries, you poets, we stroll with you in a world of magic and hear your voices as if you were alive. Others tell of themselves and of others; you transport us into yourself, into your world of thoughts and sensations of suffering and joy.

Alas, how small is our world! How often do sensations and thoughts repeat themselves! The circle of all human composing and striving is a narrow one; all our interest is tied into but a few knots.   *494/495*

Now in *this* regard, of course, one cannot understand the history of the art of poetry—that is, the *history of human imaginings and desires,* and, if I may say so, of the *sweet delusion of mankind,* of the *most ardently expressed passions and sensations of our species*—in a general or *great enough* sense. Just as entire nations have one language in common, so they also share favorite paths of the imagination, certain turns and objects of thought: in short, one *genius* that expresses itself, irrespective of any particular difference, in the best-loved works of each nation's spirit and heart. To eavesdrop in this pleasant maze, to tie up that Proteus—whom we commonly call *national character* and who surely expresses himself no less in the writings than in the customs and actions of a nation—and to make him talk: that is a high and fine philosophy. In works of poetry, that is, of the imaginative faculty and of the sensations, such a philosophy is most safely practiced, since it is in these that the *entire soul* of the nation shows itself most freely.

It is also thus with the *spirit of one or more ages*, however much this label comprises, since every age has its tone, its color, and there is a peculiar pleasure in aptly characterizing these in contrast with other ages. The so-called *Middle Ages*, for example, seem noteworthy to me not only in their fairy tales, in the good faith and superstition governing them, but also in the entire direction in which the European way of thinking was then proceeding. This delusion is closer to our hearts than the mythology of the Greeks and Romans; we may have acquired some of its traits through innate inclinations and ways of imagining, while we have certainly inherited others in the remnants of our fathers' habits.

GOVERNMENTS AS INHERITED REGIMES[1] (1785)

Part II, Book 9, Chapter 4 of Herder's *Ideas on the Philosophy of the History of Mankind*[2]

DKV *Werke* vol. 6, p. 362 line 6–p. 372
line 3 (Cf. Suphan 13:375–87)

The natural state of man is the state of society, for within it he is born and brought up; he is led towards it by the awakening drive of his fine youth, and the sweetest names of mankind—father, child, brother, sister, beloved, friend, provider—are all bonds of natural law that occur in the condition of any original human society. With these, then, the first governments among human beings were also established: regimes of the family without which our race cannot persist, laws that nature gave and also limited sufficiently through herself. Let us call these regimes *the first degree*

---

1. Lit.: "Governments are established regimes among men, mostly through inherited tradition." Apparently, Herder discarded three earlier versions of this chapter. (Compare Suphan 13:448–59 for materials from these abandoned drafts.) In a letter to Hamann, dated 23 April 1785, Herder reports on the trouble the chapter had been causing him: "Certain chapters of this book required a frightful effort, especially the morbid dregs on government by which the whole wretched thing . . . hangs—and I am still not satisfied. After I had condemned the first essay to the dungeons on my own, I asked our friend Goethe to read the second for the censors, and he returned it to me with the comforting verdict that not one word of it could stand. The third essay did not turn out any better, and so I am still hoping for a good Pentecostal revelation . . . to make a clean cut through this Gordian knot. So it goes when one's stomach is full of spoiled political juices" (*Briefe* 5:121, lines 61–70).

2. *Ideen zur Philosophie der Geschichte der Menschheit.*

of natural governments; they will at any rate always remain the highest and final such degree.

This is where nature ended her foundation of society and left it to the reason[3] or the need of man to base higher edifices upon it. In all the corners of the world where individual tribes and races have less need of one another, they also concern themselves less with each other; they have thus never thought of large political edifices. Such are the coasts of fishermen, the pastures of shepherds, the forests of hunters; where the paternal and domestic rule ends, there further connections between human beings are mostly based on contract or commission only. A nation of hunters, for example, goes out on a hunt: if it requires a leader, then it elects the most skillful one as leader of the hunt, who is thus obeyed by free choice and for the communal purpose of its business only. All animals living in herds have such leaders; during travel, defense, attack, and any communal business of a group generally, such a king of the game is necessary. Let us call this condition the *second degree of natural government:* this occurs among all peoples that merely follow their need and live in the state of nature, as we call it. Even the elected judges of a people belong to this degree of government, for the brightest and best are elected to their office as to a business, and with that business, their rule, too, comes to an end.

362/363

But how different things are with the third degree, the hereditary governments among men! Where do the laws of nature end here, or where do they begin? That the worthiest and brightest man was elected judge by the disputants resulted from the very nature of the matter, and if he proved himself as such a one, he may have stayed in office to his gray age. But then the old man dies, and why is his son judge? That the brightest and worthiest father sired him is no reason, since neither brightness nor worthiness have been bequeathed to him. Even less would the nation be obliged by the nature of the business to recognize him as such because it had once elected his father as judge for personal reasons: for the son is not the father. And if the nation wanted to go so far as to commit all its unborn by law to recognize him as such, and it made a contract in the name of their common reason[4] and for all time that every yet unborn descendant of that lineage should upon his birth be recognized by all as the natural judge,

3. *Verstand.*
4. *Vernunft* (here and just below).

leader, and shepherd of the nation, that is, as the bravest, worthiest, and brightest among the entire people, then it would be difficult to reconcile such a hereditary contract with reason, let alone with justice.[5] Nature does not bestow her noblest gifts by family, and the right of blood whereby one unborn is supposed to have the right to rule over another once they are both born—this, for me, is one of the darkest formulations of the human language.

There must be other reasons that introduced hereditary governments among men, and history does not keep these reasons from us. Who gave Germany, who gave the cultured part of Europe its governments? War. Hordes of barbarians descended on this part of the world; their leaders and nobles distributed countries and human beings among themselves. Hence principalities and fiefdoms sprang up, hence the serfdom of the subjugated peoples. The conquerors were in possession, and whatever was altered in this possession since that time was again decided by revolution, war, agreement of the powerful, thus always by the right of the stronger. On this royal road history proceeds, and the facts of history cannot be denied. What brought the world under Rome? Greece and the Orient under Alexander? What founded and subsequently shattered all great monarchies, all the way up to the heights of Sesostris and the fabulous Semiramis? War. Conquests by force took the place of right, which later became right only by the passage of time[6] or, as our theorists of state say, by tacit contract; yet tacit contract in this case means nothing but that the stronger takes what he wants, and the weaker yields or suffers what he cannot change. And thus the right of hereditary government, as that of nearly any other hereditary possession, depends on a chain of tradition[7] whose first claim was staked by luck or power and that was then extended, sometimes with kindness and

5. *Recht*, which can mean law, justice, or right, depending on the context.

6. *durch Verjährung*: the legal doctrine whereby crimes can only be prosecuted for a limited time (statute of limitations).

7. Compare Herder's elaboration from an earlier draft: "It would be but a sad consolation if we lay down upon the thorny pillow of tradition thinking that it was roses injuring our heads: for even if our fathers had given us guardians with a good intention, their good intention and our obligation to heed it are voided entirely upon the addition that this guardianship, and thus our nonage, is to last forever. None but the weak will agree to be put in eternal chains; none but a half-wit will sign a hereditary contract by which he and his heirs would sacrifice all reason and rights of mankind to an arbitrary master" (DKV 4:1030–31; compare Suphan 13:456).

363/364

wisdom, but more usually, yet again, by mere luck or greater power. Successors and heirs received what the progenitor had seized; and that to those who had, ever more would be given so that they might have in abundance,[8] this requires no further explanation: it is the natural consequence of said first possession of countries and human beings.

One should not assume that this applies only to monarchies, as monsters of conquest, while the first states originated differently, for how in the world would they have originated differently? As long as a father ruled over his family, he was father and allowed his sons also to become fathers whom he sought to guide only by his counsel. As long as a number of tribes chose their judges and leaders by free deliberation and for a particular business, these officeholders remained only servants of the common cause, appointed heads of the assembly; the names Lord, King—self-appointed,[9] arbitrary, hereditary Despot—were, to peoples of such a constitution, something unheard-of. But where a nation fell asleep and gave its father, leader, and judge free reign, finally even handing him, in a grateful stupor, the hereditary scepter on account of his meritorious services, power, wealth, or for whatever other reasons, so that he might watch over them and their children as a shepherd over his flock—what relationship could be conceived here other than weakness on the one side, overwhelming power on the other, thus the right of the stronger? When Nimrod slays beasts and afterwards enslaves human beings, he is a hunter either way.[10] The leader of a colony or horde, whom human beings followed like animals, would soon help himself, in ruling over them, to man's right over animals. Thus it was with those who cultivated the nations: as long as they cultivated them, they were fathers, educators of the people, handlers of the law for the common good; as soon as they became self-appointed or even hereditary sovereigns, they became the more powerful ones whom the weak served. Often a fox took the place of the lion, and thus the fox was the more powerful, for strength is not just the force of arms; craftiness, cunning, and artful deceit will in most cases accomplish more than such force. In brief, the great differences between human beings in gifts of the mind, of good fortune, and of the body have spawned subjugations and despotisms on earth, according to the

8. *Fülle*. Compare Matthew 13:12.

9. Or high-handed (*eigenmächtig*).

10. Compare Genesis 10:6–10.

differences in region, manner of life, and age, despotisms that
have, unfortunately, in many countries merely succeeded one
another. Warlike mountain peoples, for example, flooded the calm   *365/366*
plains; made strong and kept courageous by climate, hardship, and
deprivation, they therefore expanded as lords of the earth until
they were themselves defeated, in milder regions, by opulence and
subjugated by others. Thus our old Earth[11] has been subdued, and
her history has turned out a sorry painting of manhunts and conquests: almost every little border, every new epoch, has been regis-
tered in the Book of the Ages with the blood of the sacrificed and
the tears of the oppressed. The world's most renowned names
were stranglers of mankind, executioners wearing crowns or
reaching after them; and, what is even sorrier, it was often the
noblest human beings who stood, forced by necessity, upon this
black stage of their brothers' enslavement. How did the history of
the world's kingdoms come to be written with so few reasonable
end results? Because she was led, in most and in the greatest of her
events, with few reasonable end results: since it has not been
humanity but passions that have assumed power over the earth
and that have driven its peoples, like wild animals, together and
against each other. Had it pleased Providence to have us governed
by higher beings, how different human history would be! But it
has usually been *heroes*, that is, human beings thirsting for honor,
adept wielders of power, or cunning and enterprising men, who
have tensed the thread of events according to the passions and
who wove it as Fortune would have it. Even if no other point of
world history revealed the baseness of our species, the history of
the world's governments would demonstrate it, according to
which our earth, in its greatest part, should not be called Earth,
but rather Mars, or child-devouring Saturn.

What now? Shall we accuse Providence of creating the parts of
our globe so unequally and of also distributing her gifts so
unequally among human beings? The complaint would be pointless and unjust, since it runs counter to the obvious purpose of
our species. For the earth to become habitable, there had to be
mountains on it and hardened mountain peoples living on their   *366/367*
ridges. Now when these poured down upon the opulent plain and
subjugated it, the opulent plain for the most part deserved such
subjugation, for why did it allow itself to be subjugated? Why did

11. Herder writes "our old *Tellus*": the Roman goddess of the planted fields
and of motherly earth.

it slacken, at the breast of nature, in childish opulence and foolishness? One can take it for a principle of history that no people is oppressed but that which wants to be oppressed, which thus deserves slavery. Only the coward is a born servant; only the dumb one is destined by nature to serve someone brighter; thus he is comfortable with his station, and he would be unhappy if he were asked to command.

Besides, the inequality of human beings by nature is not as great as it becomes through education, as the condition of one and the same people under its diverse types of government shows. The noblest people quickly loses its nobility under the yoke of despotism: the marrow in its bones is crushed, and as its finest and most beautiful gifts are abused for lies and deceit, for crawling slavery and opulence, is it any wonder that it finally gets accustomed to its yoke, kissing it and adorning it with flowers? As deplorable as this fate of human beings in life and in history may be, there is nearly no nation that rose again from the abyss of a habitual slavery without the miracle of a complete palingenesis, and therefore this misery is clearly not the work of nature, but of human beings. Nature leads the bond of society to families only; beyond that, she left our species the freedom to organize itself and to construct the finest work of its art—the state—as it pleased. If human beings organized themselves well, they would do well; if they chose or tolerated tyranny and foul forms of government, they would have to bear their burden. The good Mother could do nothing but teach them through reason,[12] through historical tradition, or finally, through their own feelings of pain and misery. Thus it has been the inner degeneration of the human kind alone
367/368   that has given space to the vices and degenerations of human governments, for does not the slave, under the most oppressive despotism, always share with his master in rapine, and is the despot not always the greatest slave?

But even amidst the worst degeneration, the tirelessly kind Mother does not abandon her children and knows how to sweeten the bitter potion of human oppression through oblivion and habituation. Wherever the peoples keep themselves alert and vigorous, or where nature feeds them only with the hard bread of labor, there no soft sultans can exist; the rough country, the hard way of life are fortresses for their freedom. Where, on the other hand, the peoples fall asleep in [nature's] softer lap and tolerate

12. *Vernunft.*

the net that is cast over them, there at least the consoling Mother comes to the aid of the oppressed with her milder gifts: for despotism always presumes a kind of weakness and consequently a number of comforts that were either gifts of nature or products of art. In most despotically ruled countries, nature feeds and clothes human beings almost without effort, so that they may likewise resign themselves to the hurricane that thunders by; afterwards they may drink the breath of her refreshment—without thought and dignity, yet not entirely without delight. Quite generally, the lot of man and his destiny for happiness in the world is tied neither to ruling nor to serving. The poor can be happy, the slave can be free in his chains; the despot and his instruments are usually, and often for generations, the most unhappy and unworthy slaves.

Since all the propositions that I have touched upon so far need to receive their proper elucidation from history herself, their refinement remains bound up with her thread. For now, let me be permitted some general views:

1. A ready but wicked basic proposition about the philosophy of human history would be that "man is an animal that needs a master and that expects the happiness of its final destiny from that *368/369* master or from a connection with him." Reverse the proposition: a man who needs a master is an animal; as soon as he becomes a human being, he no longer needs any actual master. For nature has appointed no master over our species; only beastly vices and passions make us require the same. A woman requires a man, and a man requires a woman; the unformed child needs parents for instruction, the patient needs a doctor, the disputant needs an arbitrator, the crowd needs a leader: these are all natural relations that lie within the concept of the thing. The notion of needing a despot who is also a man does not lie within the concept of the human being: the latter must first be considered weak to need a protector; immature, to need a guardian; wild, to need a tamer; and odious, to need an avenging angel. All human governments thus arose out of necessity and are there on account of this continuing necessity. Now, just as it is a bad father who raises his child so that he may remain a lifelong minor in lifelong need of an instructor, as it is a wicked doctor who nourishes sickness so that he may become indispensable to the miserable all the way to his grave, so let us apply this to the instructors of mankind, the fathers of the fatherland and their charges. Either the latter are simply incapable of improvement, or else should not all the millennia

during which human beings have been governed have made it
apparent what they have become and to what purpose the former
have raised them? The remainder of this work will demonstrate
these purposes very clearly.

2. Nature raises families; the most natural state is therefore
also *one* people, with one national character. Through the millennia, this national character is maintained within a people and can
be developed most naturally if its native prince so desires, for a
people is as much a plant of nature as a family, only with more
branches. Nothing, then, seems to run so obviously counter to
the purpose of governments as the unnatural expansion of states,
369/370   the wild mixture of all types of races and nations under one scepter. The human scepter is much too weak and small for such contrary parts to be implanted[13] into it; pasted together, they become
a fragile machine called the machine of state, without inner life or
sympathy of the parts for one another. States of this kind, which
turn the name Father of the Fatherland into such a burden for the
best of monarchs, appear in history like those symbols of the
monarchies in the prophet's vision[14] where the lion's head is
united with the dragon's tail and the eagle's wings with the bear's
claws into one unpatriotic state-structure. Like Trojan horses,
such machines close ranks, vouching for each other's immortality,
since without national character there is no life within them and
only the curse of fortune could condemn the forcibly united to
immortality. For the very statecraft that brought them into being
is also the one that plays with peoples and human beings as with
lifeless bodies. But history shows sufficiently that these instruments of human pride are made of clay, and like all clay on earth,
they crumble and dissolve.[15]

3. Just as communal assistance and security are the main purpose of all associations of human beings, so none but the natural
order, where each is that which nature ordered him to be, is also
the best for the state. As soon as a sovereign seeks to take the Creator's place and to create by his own arbitrary will or passion what
the creature should not be according to God, such a despotism that
would command the heavens will be father to all disorder and to

13. Lit.: injected, or implanted, as one would a vaccine.
14. Compare Rev. 13:2: "And the beast which I saw was like unto a leopard,
and his feet were as the feet of a bear, and his mouth as the mouth of a lion: and
the dragon gave him his power, and his seat, and great authority."
15. Compare Dan. 2:31–45.

inescapable misfortune. Since all human estates fixed by tradition work in a certain way against Nature, who has confined her gifts to no rank, it is no wonder that most peoples, after having passed through all types of governments and having experienced the burdens of each, finally despaired and fell back upon the one that had turned them altogether into machines, namely, despotic-hereditary government. They spoke like that Hebrew king when he was presented with three evils—"Let us rather fall into the hand of the Lord than into the hand of man"[16]—and abandoned themselves, for better or for worse, to the grace of Providence, awaiting whom she might send as their sovereign. For the tyranny of aristocrats is a hard tyranny, and the commanding people is a true Leviathan. All Christian sovereigns therefore call themselves rulers *by the grace of God* and confess, thereby, that it was not by their own merit, which anyway does not exist before birth, but by the approbation of Providence, which allowed them to be born into that place, that they obtained their crowns. The corresponding merit has to be earned by their own labors, by which, likewise, they have to justify the Providence that found them worthy of their high office, for the office of prince is no less than that of a God among men, a higher genius in a mortal form. Those few who understood this distinguished calling sparkle like stars in the infinitely dark, cloudy night of common sovereigns, refreshing the lost wanderer on his sad walk through the political history of mankind.

370/371

Would that another *Montesquieu* gave us a taste of the spirit of the laws and governments on our round earth, if only through the best-known centuries![17] Not the empty names of three or four forms of government, which are, or remain, nowhere and never the same; nor clever principles of the state, since no state is built upon one verbal principle, let alone one maintained immutably in all the state's conditions and ages, nor yet the disjointed examples from all nations, ages, and regions of the world, from which confusion the genius of our Earth himself could not form* a coherent whole; rather, nothing but a philosophical, lively depiction of civil history in which, however uniform it may appear, no scene occurs twice, and which completes the painting of the vices and virtues of our species and its sovereigns, always changing with places and times yet ever the same, in a frightfully instructive fashion.

371/372

16. Thus David at 1 Chron. 21:13: "[L]et me fall now into the hand of the Lord; for very great are his mercies: but let me not fall into the hand of man."

17. Compare *Another Philosophy of History*, 88.

THE INFLUENCE OF FREE LEGISLATION ON THE SCIENCES AND ARTS (1780)

First Question, Third Section of Herder's Essay
"On the Influence of Governments on the Sciences,
and of the Sciences on Governments"[1]

DKV *Werke* vol. 9/2, p. 307 line 14–p. 321 line 8
(Cf. Suphan 9:324–37)

Much as Homer praises monarchy, he also proves himself a minstrel and herald of liberty. Nothing in him is veiled, incomprehensible, or oversized but what has to be so: everything has its measure, place, recognizability, and character. Even the miraculous in him is human; his repetitions, sweet and childlike. The beautiful outline, the felicitous Greek view in the description of his heroes, the wisdom and humanity by which he moderates even raw passions and scenes—all these characterize not the servant-slave, but the minstrel of nature, of humanity and liberty. Greece was the first land[2] that gradually tore itself loose from its petty tyrants and, with a *new* government, also brought forth *new* sciences and arts.

Lycurgus drew his people together around the stern principle of *sacrifice and love for the fatherland*. The sciences, too, had to respect these bounds, and even the *laconic* language[3] was formed

1. "Vom Einfluß der Regierung auf die Wissenschaften, und der Wissenschaften auf die Regierung." One of Herder's prize-winning essays, honored by the Berlin Academy of Sciences in 1779, but published in 1780. Compare our note to *Another Philosophy of History*, 65:7.

2. Compare *Another Philosophy of History*, 34:26.

3. Literally, the language of the Laconians (Spartans), but also terseness in expression more generally.

accordingly. Wealth, plays, and opulent verse disappeared. Useless orators, sophists, and windbags banished themselves: they *307/308*
found no air in Sparta. The *art of war* was their science and exercise, the flute[4] was their instrument, and Tyrtaeus their poet.
Sparta is the most powerful example not only of how much a state
must *choose, mold,* and *check* the sciences, but also of how it *can*
check them, for how opposite to Athens was Sparta! And yet it
may have been Lycurgus who collected Homer's rhapsodies in
Asia and gave them to the Greeks.[5] To his Sparta he did not give
them, at least not for a model.

Solon went an entirely different way, seeking to pair *riches* with
liberty, opulence with *patriotism,* leaving deliberation to the nobles
and all decision to the people and thereby making of his republic,
as Aristophanes says, an old man who was wise at home and childish in public or, as we may want to say, who could be wise for himself but had to be decent, beautiful, and eloquent in public.
Inevitably, with this constitution Solon stirred up all that one
could call *popular science:* oratory, poetry, philosophy, arts; *oratory,*
for the orator was a demagogue, and the state itself supported
orators. All public business that came to the people was discussed,
and on the moment's impression the matter was decided. What a
field this was for eloquence! What a school! Business, expeditions,
the weal and woe of the state were discussed—not words—for an
immediate decision [to be taken], not to be forgotten and
ignored; seriously, not out of old habit and in jest. The orator
spoke to his people, to a circle he knew—not for strangers and
despots—to the Athenian people, a lot educated* in the world's
finest language through poetry, songs, arts, and drama; not for
Scythians and Lombards. Can one compare any other eloquence,
circle of orators, or constitution of speaking to this one (the
Roman somewhat excepted)? And, in particular, compare to it
things that are of the most disparate kind: speeches and compli-
ments before despots, chatter before a people that is no people,
about matters that are not material, without point or purpose? *308/309*
Bring us an Athens, and Demostheneses and Pericleses will come
into being of themselves.

It was just so with the *theater* of the Greeks: it served democracy, as did the speeches. The people were supposed to be flattered

4. The *aulos,* a wooden flute especially popular in Spartan military music.

5. According to Plutarch's *Lives,* Lycurgus discovered the works of Homer in
Ionia and rearranged them so that they would yield moral and political lessons.

about freedom, and thus tragedy became the tyrant's strangler, the
voice of liberty. They were supposed to be nourished and educated* by old heroes and their deeds and fates, made to feel their
Greek excellences and the glory of their tribe. That is why they
lived out their ancestral myths so magnificently on the stage.
[Tragedy] had originated as religious festivity; soon it became a
need for the idle state thirsting for entertainment. Commerce and
prosperity thrived in Athens and were meant to thrive there
according to the plan of the founder. Thus all [kinds of] *entertainments, muses,* and *graces* moved in so as to amuse the born lovers of
music, dance, song, joy. Even though Solon, who was himself a
poet, expressed his displeasure at the first play he saw and foretold
its evil consequences, it was still his *constitution* and the *nature* of
the people that prepared the ground for it. An Athenian theater
cannot emerge again but under similar circumstances.

The *philosophy* of the Greeks flourished through interaction in
the circles of Hellenic society and was closely connected to its
oratory, sophistry, statecraft, poetry, and declamation. As is well
known, Socrates in particular led the wisdom of the orators,
poets, and sophists of his time down from its height. His ironic
genius and conversational good humor stripped the stage of its
armor,[6] the orators of their chatter, and the sophists of their false
political wisdom, in order to teach the people (the circles of
youngsters and the houses where he spoke) true popular wisdom
and the wisdom of life. Of course such a Socrates belonged only
in Athens, where the people were prepared for such things and
receptive to such conversations. To raise questions about such
matters in a Socratic manner within our own societies would be to
309/310   insult them.[7] Thus we rarely get the tone of such conversations
right in our books, because it is so foreign to us in everyday life.
So much Socratic reason,[8] in so little time, among so few persons,
in so light and natural a manner! We would rather have proofs
instead, impudent judgments, declamations; there we think we
have really got something! Of course the Greek lightness, and
especially the Athenian, also meant that everything turned all too
soon into vacuous chatter about systems and word-stuff. The phi-

6. See Plato's *Laches.*

7. One might object that Socrates' role as the "gadfly of Athens" was meant to
provoke and that enough offense was taken for him to be put to death by the citizens of the very city that is supposed to have been so uniquely receptive to his
wisdom.

8. *Vernunft.*

losophers became peddlers of words, sophists of vacuous systems, and it is a peculiarity of fate, and of the unfortunate worship of everything Greek and ancient, that we have discovered infinitely more in some of their words than they themselves probably put into them. Much of their philosophy was *conversational hypothesis*, Greek wisdom.

Since the *history* of a people is a reflection of the constitution of its senses and government, the *description* of that history must be the same. Surely the Athenian constitution could therefore also deliver the *best* historians. Xenophon and Thucydides were themselves military commanders, men of public affairs; only such can write of war and of the business of the state. In Athens all was closely related: philosophy and public service, the art of rhetoric and grammar. It was thus a single spirit—one and the same Hellenism—that lent such a light, silver clarity and golden dignity to their style, their speeches, their reflections and that was able to unite the most varied talents with the greatest simplicity. In later times, too, it was men of the state and of war—in short, men of public affairs—who restored history and here and there renewed the Xenophonic spirit of looking at the state and at history. Happy republic for the sciences, where Socrates' student was also military commander and statesman!

Without wishing to concern myself specifically with the other states of Greece, I cannot pass over the overall effect that the *number* and *diversity* of the *competing Greek cities and states* had on the sciences. So many cities and republics close to each other, *310/311* connected to each other through language, by the honor of the Greek name, and partly by their tribal type and constitution, inevitably had to compete with each other, more or less, in what was considered the glory of their race. And since, besides the art of war and military power, it was the freedom of the fatherland, the *love of the sciences* and *fine arts* that was glorified thus, no state remained a complete stranger to the Muses, at least. One competed with statues and buildings, plays and poets. Since the common games of Greece gathered together all that was flourishing and noble as it were, so one competed there in more than the fight of the games themselves. It was there that Herodotus read his *Histories* and acquired a follower;[9] there artists displayed their works to the admiration of all Greece. The games presented an occasion for song and arts; the most beautiful lyrical wreath worn

9. Thucydides.

by a Greek was wrought, likewise, by the hand of all Greece. So
many cities, so many peoples, so many victors and their eternally
glorious lineages, so many gods and heroes interwoven with these
lineages are the leaves and blossoms in this wreath. Who will
return to us an Olympia with its games and victories, an assembled Greece with its interests, its glory, its language? Even fat
Thebes managed to produce a Pindar.

It is evident from all this that Greece's own sciences and arts,
which have been surpassed by no other age and in which [the
Greeks] have now for two thousand years surpassed all other ages
and peoples, were *daughters of their legislation, their political constitution,* in particular of *liberty,* of *work for the common good,* of *universal striving and shared zeal.* I am not disregarding national
character, language, climate, location,[10] chance events of history,
and much else besides; all this was required for establishing the
Greek constitution, was conjoined with it, and stood faithfully by
its side. Meanwhile history shows that as soon as freedom was
311/312   lost—language, climate, the genius of the people, abilities, and
character remained!—the spirit of the sciences was as good as
lost. Their poetry was lost; theater became a vacuous pastime for
its defeated, idle people. Demosthenes was their last voice of liberty; Aristotle and Theophrastus [were] their last philosophers.
The former was exiled,[11] and after the death of the latter, a law
was passed that no one was to teach philosophy in public anymore
without the permission of the Senate, and consequently all philosophy was, as it were, exiled for some time. The teachers of
their sciences soon became grammarians, sophists, writers, and
what sciences migrated now to Asia, to Egypt, arrived there like
transplanted flowers in a foreign land, missing their native soil.
Under the Romans, the sciences returned to Athens, but not
alive; they were sold like seeds for whose cultivation and use the
seller holds the instructions. The most well-meaning Roman
emperors could not recreate Greece in Greece: the freedom they
gave to Athens was a mere shadow, and the science and oratory
that grew out of it, a shadow of a shadow—no more than the echo
of better times. Mount Athos has plenty of monks now, but no
orators, poets, and philosophers; all the provinces' most beautiful

10. Compare Aristotle, *Politics* 1325b33–1328a21; Montesquieu, *The Spirit of
the Laws,* III.

11. Aristotle left Athens for Chalcis in 323 BC, but the circumstances are in
dispute.

ruins no longer awaken any artist in the spirit of the ancients. Why no longer? The air, the climate, the education,* the character of the Greeks remains the same, but they lack the constitution, the government, without which they can never be what they were. The spirit animating their talents and limbs is gone; talents and limbs are dead.

So how did [the spirit] animate these [talents and limbs]? Just *how* did the Greek form of government *affect* talents, sciences, arts? All I can say is: *by itself,* by the very fact that such a *form of government*, such a *constitution* at such a time *existed*. Look at this plant: how does it grow? Whence its blossom, its flourishing? It stands upon its own soil, in its natural place. Air, weather, season are all favorable to it; that is enough. Whatever it is meant to be lies within it and will eventually emerge by inner energy.[12] Soil and air provide it with nutrition and fluids; the sun, with warmth; the wind, with motion. Now it will become what it is meant to be. The plough does not make the land rich; fragrant water does not make the flower blossom. What is supposed to grow must grow naturally, and it is likewise with the world's finest flower, science, freedom of the soul. What Athens did was to *nourish* its poets, orators, philosophers, to *set off their electrical fire* by its motions and institutions. Its academy was called *glory, Greek name, fatherland, liberty.* Thus sang the poet, spoke the orator, wrote the historian and wise man. They were Greeks, they were citizens, they scorned the satraps, despised the barbarians, and always believed themselves to be promoting the state's best through their science and its exercise. Was not Demosthenes greater than Philip for a time? Was not Pericles in his circle more than a king of slaves? The wreaths, the statues that the poets received—what was greater than these wreaths? Did Alexander receive any other reward for his deeds but that the Athenians should praise him? [There were] those who truly loved and served their fatherland, beyond the common glory and popular judgment: Theseus, Thales, Lycurgus, Solon, Socrates and Aristides, Phocion and Plato, and so many other glorious men, each great in his art, in his business, in his science. Following closely one upon the other, or else side by side, they called each other to action by their respective example, competing and surpassing each other. Through speech and deed, song and science they took turns carrying the scepter of Greece's liberty, uniquely resplendent in their triumph even

312/313

12. Compare Aristotle, *Physics, Politics.*

beyond the great king,[13] up to the ranks of the immortals. What such souls could deliver! What they could become! Did they need voices of encouragement when everything was calling out to them, when their fatherland's entire constitution was the medium of their science, their art? Did they need pay when they were being paid everywhere, when glory, esteem, immortality, honor was the most beautiful pay? Where finally, when it came to pay-

313/314 ment, one of Pindar's odes, one of Phidias' sculptures, or one of Demosthenes' speeches was worth [so much] more than today? But I do not wish to compare, for the difference of the ages permits no comparison. Athens was impoverished by the theater, and the common treasury of Greece almost along with it.[14]

This brings us to another type of republic, that of the Romans.

"Rome was nursed by the she-wolf to a warrior's pride"—and it is well known that there was little room for the sciences during its first five centuries. What Numa introduced, what was adapted from the neighboring Etruscans, was urgently *required* by their *strict religious practices* and their *martial spirit:* the same goes for their various *laws, rights, diaries,* and *songs about their ancestors' deeds.* Rome was to be considered a martial tribe, a city of war that did not wish, like Sparta, merely to protect itself, to defend itself, to make no conquests, and not even to pursue the enemy. Rome's principle was not to have any unconquered enemies but rather to pursue them even after their defeat and in peacetime and to arm itself for ruling the world. The *introduction of the sciences* among [the Romans] followed the same pattern. They arrived *vanquished,* as it were, and sought refuge and security at the bosom of the mother of all conquests. Rome's first poets were foreigners, freed slaves, servants; their theatrical productions, crude entertainments or mercenary work. The Senate debated whether one should allow the Greek orators and philosophers into Rome, and Cato, himself no barbarian, concluded "No," straightaway! So long and so well did Rome get by without Greece's sciences! Indeed, it was part of the story that Rome made itself Rome, the conqueror of the world, without these sciences. It pushed and was pushed, thus not having the time to write, to philosophize, to study.

314/315 Even when Rome took up to the sciences, it was really only those that nourished and supported the *constitution of the state and*

13. Alexander the Great.

14. Compare Rousseau, *Letter to M. d'Alembert.*

of war that fell upon fertile soil. The poets of the theater were paid in money, like servants, and for many reasons having to do with the state and the character of the Romans, their drama never became the world's foremost. To be a great actor was not part of the greatness of the Roman; nor was it, for a long time, even to feel the spirit of the play. We know how much, even in Caesar's day, it pained that nobleman whom Caesar forced to take the stage, and how he could not get over the disgrace, as it were.[15] *History*, on the other hand, the *art of rhetoric, practical philosophy, manly* and especially *instructive poetry*, the *art of war*, the *science of the law*—these were branches of knowledge of which, in due course, even the noblest Roman was not ashamed. Indeed, precisely because such renowned and active men studied them, [these sciences] acquired dignity, solidity, greatness—truly the most innocent greatness of the Romans. I have never begrudged Scipio's people the destruction of Rome's unfortunate rival, the city and republic of Carthage. Yet I should think that their name shines forth more beautifully in their personal virtues and in that Scipio's noble men were also the first to combine their bloody laurels with the olive branches of the Muses; in that Scipio Africanus had the father of Roman poetry at his side and considered Lucilius worthy of his friendship, Terence worthy of his collaboration; in that Fabius and Publius Scipio were not ashamed of splendid Polybius and that by their example they awakened among other noble youths—Laelius, Furius, Tubero, Scaevola—a love of Roman science. Never again would so many great men, in so few years, know each other as they followed and pushed one another up the peak of the world, most of them great and true Romans in more than one way, in speech and in deed, in the business of war and the deliberations of peace, in their active love of the sciences and their knowledge. Cato and Scaevola, Laelius and Scipio, Cornelia and the Gracchi, Crassus and Antonius, Hortensius and Cicero, Atticus and Nepos, Sallust and Varro, Sulla and Caesar, Hirtius and Brutus—each in his own way gave the Roman language its majesty, wealth, and vigor, so that their word also became deed, their thought strength and decorum. The conquerors of the world, the judges over the fate of all nations, crowned

315/316

15. Decimus Laberius, a famous mime, was forced by Caesar to compete on stage in 46 BC despite the fact that this meant the loss of his aristocratic rank. Though restored to his rank and amply compensated, he complained bitterly of the disgrace he had suffered (DKV 4:1161).

themselves with a beautiful wreath, the wreath of science and practical wisdom.

It is evident from this what it was about the Roman constitution that actually made possible such a short but bright and worthy period for the sciences, namely, in part the *need of the state* at *that high level of public affairs* and in part the delightful *example of its noblest men and families.* How vital were the matters that the Roman *orator* addressed! To speak in favor of the great Pompeius against a Caesar, Sulla, Antonius—what a business! To deliberate about the needs of war and about plans for peace that kings were begging for, on which the welfare or perdition of an empire, of half a continent depended—what a business! To speak, to write, to form opinions or record history under the pressure of events and amidst the clash of human powers—what heights, what times! To be Scipio's companion or one's own historian if one were a Sulla, Caesar, Lucullus, Brutus; to be the historian of a Rome that had such men whom, still living, one might gaze upon—I should think that there the spirit of *deeds* had to become part of the spirit of *words* and that the majesty and power, the brevity and seriousness of the Roman *constitution* would also have had to inform the manner of its writers. "As someone is, so he will act; as someone acts, so he will write." The ease of Caesar's victories is also recognizable in his manner of writing, and the spirit of Lucullus and Sulla would be similarly recognizable if we still possessed their memoirs. But ah, how much fortune begrudges us the works of the Greeks and Romans! Pieces are lost for which we would trade all the new libraries of wasted paper: most of the works of Aeschylus, Sophocles, Pindar, Menander; so much of the writing of Polybius, Diodorus, Ennius, Cato; the essays of Laelius and Scipio, Hortensius and Atticus, Sulla and Lucullus, Varro and Caesar—as well as so many of the writings of other noble Romans that would surely bear witness to their souls! Even when Varro, Cicero, and Caesar wrote about language and grammar, they could not write other than as Varro, Cicero, and Caesar; and such people have only lived once in the world. To be merely their friend, their companion, let alone their competitor or rival—the very idea precludes almost all comparison. Scipio and a German prince! Caesar and the mayor of some speck on the map! These Romans were themselves historians, orators, enthusiasts in the sciences who could not and did not want to be judged any differently than anyone else stepping into the arena with them. [Contrast] the men of more recent times: so often incompetent patrons

316/317

who praise what they do not understand and reward with their pennies what would embarrass the wise man. Anyway, almost nothing in history equals the causes or effects of the brief period of blossoming in the Roman sciences. As conquerors of the world the Romans adorned themselves with the *loot* of science; active and enthusiastic, they soon ascended to the greatest heights, for they stood at the pinnacle of the ages, as it were. Just as quickly, however, the spirit of science also withdrew from them; it had remained for them only an adornment, only a cloak for their triumphs. Where science was part of the freedom and constitution of the state instead, it sank along with the latter.

Whenever else *imitations* of Roman greatness appeared (mere *shadows of their constitution* and *manner of acting*), traces of the Roman manner of thinking and writing could also be found again. The parliaments of France and England are no match for the Roman Forum; yet in both, splendid displays have appeared of the arts of rhetoric and statecraft in deliberating about laws and events. The best history has at all times been the one written by the heroes and statesmen themselves; only through the memoirs of such men has the true story been revived again for more recent times. Comines, Sully, Clarendon, Retz, Thuanus, Turenne, Montecuculi, and so forth, are witnesses. After the restoration of the sciences, the spirit of true history was awakened again by the contemplation of Roman history, as Machiavelli's reflections about Livy show, as well as so many others about Sallust, Caesar, and Tacitus. Nothing in the world, however, is further removed from the spirit of Roman science than the modern language of our schools and its tedious Latin phrases. A dull *grammaticus*, a declaimer despised by the boys themselves, let alone the governments—what is he compared with Cicero, Varro, Caesar? Where is the Roman spirit in the alleged Roman language? *317/318*

I am glad that it is not my place to concern myself extensively or primarily with the times of *decay in the sciences*. What did the governments contribute to it? Their biggest contribution was that they *destroyed the freedom and the common-wealth*[16] *of individual republics* and wanted to put up an *edifice that collapsed upon itself*. What drove the Greek Alexander towards Asia? What was he looking for, what could he find there? Pain, labors, excess, death, dissolution of his forces and his empire. Of course Providence brings something good even when human beings are not paying

---

16. Herder's own term.

attention to it: Alexander's columns, which were spilling Greek blood as far away as the Indus, were also spreading the *Greek language* and *science* and here and there founded Greek cities and colonies. The empires of his successors brought forth *new seats of the sciences* in Syria, in Asia, especially in Egypt: the Museum, the Library, the Seven Poets,[17] the grammarians and philosophers of Alexandria are most famous, and it cannot be denied that they contributed their share to the preservation and expansion of the sciences in later times. Meanwhile it is also true that this late bloom under the Greek kings was no more than a beautiful autumn day: its blossoms had much color but little fragrance; the

318/319 spring and summer had passed. It is usually the fate of such monarchies *to gather magnificently what remains* when the harvest is over, seeking to replace by a wealth of books, by libraries and erudition, what science lacks in worth and power. But everything has its time. The grammarians at Alexandria, too, and the library there would have been a treasure owed entirely to monarchy, if it had survived until the day of the printing press rather than being destroyed by a harsher monarchy.[18]

As for the Roman monarchy, it is perhaps most deplorable that Caesar, its true founder, was not also able to structure it, to set the Senate and the military forces against one another in a mutual order, and to be properly Caesar, the first monarch. The thirty-two stabs by which he died exposed the Roman state to infinitely more wounds. Just as the weak Augustus did not know how to be anything but a private citizen, and therefore left everything in a state of suspension, so his influence on the sciences, too, could of course have been no more than that of a *private citizen*. He gave poets his friendship and access to his house; he was a poet himself, as were his Maecenas and his Agrippa. But this could be no more than a pleasant afternoon for the sciences—some pleasant hours followed by an evening of envy and a stormy night! When Tiberius had the man killed who exceeded him; when Gaius Caligula wanted to eradicate Homer, Virgil, Livy, and all legal learning; when Nero had his bad verses sung in all the streets and read in

17. Philitas of Cos, Theocritus, Callimachus, Hermesianax of Colophon, Zenodotus of Ephesus, Apollonius of Rhodes, and Euphorius of Chalcis. Herder likens them to the constellation of the Pleiades (*Siebengestirn*).

18. Herder may have believed the myth according to which the library at Alexandria was not destroyed until 641, by the Caliph Omar (Compare DKV 4:1162). If so, this might explain the tone of his remark at *Another Philosophy of History*, 86:23–24.

all the schools; when even Hadrian, a better man, was petty enough to belittle Cicero, Homer, and Virgil because he wished to be first in every way—then, indeed, the *Roman government* had a *bad* influence on the *sciences and arts.* And although even then the Roman government was not able to spoil everything, since the Roman Empire was so vast and the good examples and true souls of the Romans were still close at hand, and especially since there were also good rulers that made the world appear in a brighter light; nonetheless the Roman sciences were no longer what they had been at the time of the republic, for now they were—*without effect in the state.* The art of rhetoric remained silent or merely declaimed. History became embittered, lied, and produced flatteries or obscure puzzles. Poetry produced epigrams or satires; the language deteriorated with every new century. Gaius [Caligula] had instituted *competitions in eloquence;* Nero, *competitions in poetry*, which were renewed by Domitian; but this alone could not alter the nature of the matter, nor that of the state. Even the *better efforts* made by Vespasian, Titus, Trajan, Hadrian, Antonius, Marcus Aurelius, Severus, and others for the encouragement of science—the *schools, libraries,* and public *rewards* that were instituted on their orders—could not, however good and necessary they were for curbing a violently advancing barbarism and for at least preserving the memory of good example, bring back the world in which those examples had been active and alive. Only what is indispensable—what is useful and effective now—only that lives. And with the exception of a few extraordinary individuals, this applied at that time to none but the *crafts* and the *bread-and-butter sciences:* grammar, legal learning, astrology, sophistry, medicine. The higher sciences had vanished along with the Roman air.

319/320

Even less do I wish to concern myself with what was contributed to the *decay* of the sciences not by the rulers but rather by the *governments* as such and in general: namely, the *instability*, the *rule of the military*, the *weakness* of an empire no longer able to defend itself against the invading barbarians and instead drawing them towards itself; and, finally, the granting to all the world of the *right of citizenship*, whereby even the Roman language was debased, as were many other things besides. How could an empire that cannot defend itself protect the sciences, tender shoots of its bloom, from decay? A body corrupted in all its limbs—how could it be healthy in its head and vital fluids? Add a new, already very corrupted *religion* that introduced into the laws

and the manner of writing, into orders and the art of rhetoric an
Oriental element that was little suited to the Roman state. The
weakness of the emperor fostered the pursuit of heresies, miserable sophistries, and verbal acrobatics that served no purpose but
that of utter corruption. In short, where else could the dishar-
mony of such a weak, unstable, and self-contradictory government end but with barbarism and the death of all rational, useful
literature? Here, then, was no more Greece, no more Rome;
Europe was a dark tumult of roaming barbarians.

BIOGRAPHICAL REGISTER

Abbt, Thomas (1738–1766). German philosopher and author; ecclesiastical councilor at the court of the Count of Schaumburg-Lippe, where he was succeeded by Herder.

Aeschylus (525–456 BC). Greek dramatist whose works changed the nature of Greek tragedy and brought the genre to prominence. Author of *Oresteia, Prometheus Bound, Persians, Seven against Thebes,* and *Suppliants,* among other plays.

Agrippa, Marcus Vipsanius (63–12 BC). Roman general and statesman; Augustus' son-in-law, and builder of the Pantheon in Rome.

d'Alembert, Jean le Rond (1717–1783). Philosopher, mathematician, co-editor of the *Encyclopédie* and author of its *Discours préliminaire* (1751).

Alexander the Great (356–323 BC). King of Macedon; widely regarded as the greatest general of antiquity. Tutored by Aristotle as a young man, Alexander completed the conquest and subjugation of Greece begun by his father, Philip II. He defeated the Persian king Darius at Issus in 333 BC and crossed the Indus River in 326. When Alexander died in Babylon in 323 BC, his empire stretched from Epirus to India and from Egypt to Scythia.

Amor [or Cupid] (mythical). Roman god of love, the son of Mercury and Venus; the equivalent of the Greek god Eros.

Antonius, Marcus (143–87 BC). Roman orator, and consul in 99; a source of inspiration for Cicero and subject of his *De oratore.*

Apollo (mythical). Greek god of prophecy, music, and light; the son of Zeus and Leto, the brother of Artemis, and the protector of Delphi.

The Argonauts (mythical). The group of heroes that followed Jason, in the ship Argo, in the quest to bring back the Golden Fleece from Colchis, with which Jason could recover the throne of Iolcus from his uncle. The group included the mythical heroes Theseus and Hercules, as well as Castor and Pollux.

143

Ariosto, Ludovico (1474–1533).   Renaissance poet; author of *Orlando Furioso* (1516).

Aristides (c. 540–c.467 BC).   Athenian statesman and general famous for leading the battles at Marathon and Salamis.

Aristophanes (c. 455–c. 386 BC).   The greatest Athenian comic poet; author of *Acharnians, Knights, Clouds, Wasps, Birds, Lysistrata, Frogs,* and *Ecclesiazusae,* among other plays.

Aristotle (384–322 BC).   Greek philosopher and student of Plato, tutor to Alexander the Great, and founder of the Lyceum in Athens. Author of highly influential works on politics, ethics, metaphysics, rhetoric, physics, zoology, and psychology.

Aspasia (fifth century BC).   Mistress of the great Athenian statesman and general Pericles who was frequently derided and attacked for her alleged influence over his political activities.

Atticus (109–32 BC).   Roman writer; friend and correspondent of Cicero.

Augustus, Caesar (63 BC–AD 14).   Adoptive son of Julius Caesar and the first emperor of Rome after the demise of the republic.

Baco, Roger (1214–1294).   Franciscan monk and scholar; early proponent of the experimental method.

Bayle, Pierre (1647–1706).   French philosopher and early Enlightenment thinker; author of *Historical and Critical Dictionary* (1697).

la Beaumelle, Laurent Angliviel de (1726–1773).   French Enlightenment thinker; correspondent of Voltaire and friend of Montesquieu.

Blackwell, Thomas (1701–1757).   Scottish classical scholar; author of *An Enquiry into the Life and Writings of Homer* (1735).

Borgia, Cesare (1475–1507).   Also known as "Duke Valentino;" Italian ruler, and son of Pope Alexander VI, whose notorious cruelty and cunning are examined by Machiavelli in *The Prince* (especially Chapter VII).

Bossuet, Jacques Bénigne (1627–1704).   French preacher; author of *Discourse on Universal History, etc.* (1681).

Boulanger, Nicolas Antoine (1722–1759).   Author of *Inquiries into the Origin of Oriental Despotism* (published posthumously in 1761), which includes the author's observations on Montesquieu's *The Spirit of the Laws.*

Bourdaloue, Louis (1632–1704).   French Jesuit sometimes referred to as "the king of preachers and the preacher of kings."

Brutus, Marcus Junius (c.85–42 BC).   Roman politician who was favored and made praetor by Caesar but later joined a conspiracy against him and assassinated him.

Buffon, George Louis Leclerc Comte de (1707–1788). Prominent mathematician and natural historian of his day who published a *Natural History* in thirty-six volumes and laid some of the foundations for probability theory.

Caesar, Gaius Julius (100–44 BC). Roman general and statesman who served as governor in Spain, conquered Gaul, and sent expeditions to Britain and Germany. In 49 BC, he ignored the Senate's order to disband his army, crossed the Rubicon River, and initiated a civil war, which he won, and became dictator. He was murdered by Cassius and Brutus on 15 March 44 BC.

Caiaphas. Jewish high priest who prophesied that Jesus would die (John 11:49–53) and presided over the council that condemned Jesus to death (Matthew 26:57–68).

Caligula [Gaius Julius Caesar Germanicus] (AD 12–41). Roman emperor known for his extravagance and despotism.

Cato, Marcus Porcius (234–149 BC). Also known as "the Elder" or "the Censor;" Roman statesman and moralist known for the severity with which he served as censor, as well as for continuously trying to convince the Senate that "Carthage must be destroyed."

Cervantes Saavedra, Miguel de (1547–1616). Spanish poet and writer famous for his satirical masterpiece *Don Quixote* (in two volumes, 1605 and 1615).

Cicero, Marcus Tullius (106–43 BC). Roman philosopher and statesman, and the greatest of Rome's orators; author of *On Duties, On the Nature of the Gods,* and *Tusculan Disputations,* and numerous other works whose style exerted a wide influence on subsequent writers.

Clarendon, Edward Hyde, Earl of (1609–1674). English statesman and historian, adviser to Charles I and II, and author of *History of the Rebellion and Civil Wars in England, etc.* (published posthumously, 1702–1704).

Comines [Commynes], Philippe de (1447–1511). French statesman and historian; author of the *Mémoires* (1523).

Corneille, Pierre (1606–1684). French poet and dramatist credited with having given rise to French classical tragedy; author of *Le Cid* (1637), *Médée tragédie* (1639), and *Horace* (1641), among other works.

Cornelia (second century BC). Second daughter of Scipio Africanus and mother of Tiberius and Gaius Gracchus; famous for her devotion to her children.

Crassus, Lucius Licinius (140–91 BC). Roman orator; a model for Cicero, memorialized in his *De oratore.*

Crevier, Jean Baptiste Louis (1693–1765). French author and professor of rhetoric; editor of Livy's *History* and author of *Observations on the Book The Spirit of the Laws* (1764).

Crousaz, Jean-Pierre de (1663–1750). Swiss theologian and philosopher; author of *Treatise on Beauty* (1715).

Dante [Dante Alighieri] (1265–1321). Commonly considered the greatest Italian poet; most famous for his *Divine Comedy* in general and his depiction of the various circles of hell in particular.

Demosthenes (c.384–322 BC). Athenian orator known for his opposition to Philip II of Macedon.

Descartes, René (1596–1650). One of the founders of the modern, skeptical philosophy, who sought to reconfigure his knowledge from a point of perfect certainty and who thought that he had found such a point in his famous *cogito (ergo sum)* [I think, therefore I am], which Herder reformulated as "*Ich fühle mich! Ich bin!*" [I feel (myself)! I am!].

Diderot, Denis (1713–1784). French philosopher and chief editor of the *Encyclopédie*.

Diodorus Siculus (first century AD). Greek historian; author of an early world history, his *Historical Library*.

Domitian [Caesar Domitianus Augustus] (AD 51–96). Roman emperor from 81 until his assassination in 96; renowned for his ruthlessness and cruelty.

Egeria (mythical). A water nymph who, as Roman legend would have it, met Numa Pompilius at night to advise him on matters of statesmanship and religion.

Ennius, Quintus (239–169 BC). Roman poet and tragedian; author of a narrative poet on the history of the Roman people, the *(libri) Annales*, which influenced Cicero, Lucretius, Catullus, Virgil, Ovid, and Lucan, among others.

Epaminondas (d. 362 BC). Theban general famous for his victories at the battles of Leuctra and Mantinea. His tactics at Leuctra threw the Spartans into confusion and put an end to their domination of land warfare.

Epictetus (c.50–120). Stoic philosopher, freed slave; his lectures were attended by the historian Arrian, who later published his notes of them as well as a summary of Epictetus' philosophy known as *Encheiridion* (Manual), from which Herder quotes in the epigraph to *Another Philosophy of History*.

Fabius Maximus Aemilianus, Quintus (c.186–130 BC). Roman soldier and consul; fought alongside and under Scipio.

Fénelon, François de Salignac de la Mothe (1651–1715). French archbishop and theologian; tutor to the Duke of Burgundy, who before his untimely death was to succeed Louis XIV, and for whose education Fénelon wrote *The Adventures of Telemachus* (1699).

Ficino, Marcilio (1433–1499). Florentine physician and philosopher, translator of Plato, and president of the Platonic Academy in Florence.

Frederick II of Prussia (1712–1786). Also known as "Frederick the Great." King of Prussia under whose "enlightened despotism" Prussia rose to prominence among European states. Equally fond of lofty rhetoric and war, Frederick was especially tolerant in religious matters but ruled his people with an iron hand: "Reason as much as you will, but obey!"

Furius Antias, Aulus (first century BC). Roman epic poet whose *Annals* influenced Virgil.

Galileo [Galileo Galilei] (1564–1642). Italian astronomer, mathematician, and philosopher often taken for the model of "universal genius" on account of his boundless curiosity and his many groundbreaking contributions to the physical sciences. Galileo's observations of the heavens confirmed the Copernican heliocentric theory and led to his persecution by the Inquisition.

Goethe, Johann Wolfgang von (1749–1832). The most celebrated German poet, dramatist, and novelist; author of *The Sorrows of the Young Werther* (1774) and *Faust* (part I: 1808, part II: 1833).

Gracchus, Tiberius Sempronius and Gaius Sempronius (169–133 BC, 160–121 BC). Roman tribunes who enacted a series of agrarian reforms; the sons of Cornelia.

The Graces or Charites (mythical). Ancient Greek goddesses personifying charm, grace, and beauty; always depicted as beautiful maidens, often dancing, singing, or bathing.

Grotius, Hugo [Huigh de Groot] (1583–1645). Dutch jurist; author of *On the Law of War and Peace* (1625); considered one of the founders of international law.

Gustavus II Adolphus (1594–1632). King of Sweden who intervened in the Thirty Years' War and brought military momentum to the Protestant side before he was killed at the battle of Lützen in 1632.

Hadrian [Caesar Traianus Hadrianus Augustus] (76–138). Roman emperor from 117–138; great admirer of the civilization of Greece.

Haller, Albrecht von (1708–1777). Swiss anatomist, botanist, doctor, professor at the University of Göttingen, and author of the influential *Physiological Elements of the Human Body* (in eight volumes, 1757–1778).

Hamann, Johann Georg (1730–1787). German philosopher and mystic known as "The Magus of the North"; Herder's friend and mentor, and one of the main influences on Herder's thought.

Harder, Johann Jakob (1733–1775). Priest and dean of the Lyceum of Riga; translated Voltaire's *Philosophy of History* into German, in 1768.

Helvétius, Claude Adrien (1715–1771). French philosopher, contributor to the *Encyclopédie,* and author of *On the Mind* (1758).

Herodotus (c.485–c.425). Early Greek historian known as "the father of history" for his account of the war of the Greeks against the Persians.

Hippocrates (c.460–377 BC). The most famous physician of antiquity, called "the father of medicine" and celebrated for having saved several Greek cities from the ravages of plague; author of the oath that physicians still take upon entering their profession.

Hirtius, Aulus (90–43 BC). Roman soldier and writer; one of Caesar's officers in the Gallic wars, and most likely the author of the eighth book of his *Commentaries.*

Hobbes, Thomas (1588–1679). English philosopher and political theorist; author of *The Elements of Law* (1640), *De Cive* (1642), and *Leviathan* (1651); translator of Thucydides' *History of the Peloponnesian War* (1629).

Homer (c.700 BC). Greek poet to whom the epics *Iliad* and *Odyssey* are attributed.

Horace (65–8 BC). Major Roman poet known chiefly for his *Odes.*

Hortensius, Hortalus Quintus (114–50 BC). Roman orator and politician; Cicero's opponent in the trial of Gaius Verres.

Hume, David (1711–1776). Scottish philosopher, essayist, and historian; author of numerous influential works, especially *A Treatise of Human Nature* (1739–1740) and *The History of England, etc.* (1754–1762).

Hurd, Richard (1720–1808). English scholar and theologian, Bishop of Worcester, and author of *Letters on Chivalry and Romance* (1758) and *Dialogues on the Uses of Foreign Travels, etc.* (1764).

Ignatius of Loyola (1491–1556). Founder and first general of the Jesuits; canonized in 1622.

Iselin, Isaak (1728–1782). Swiss historian, philosopher, and pedagogue; author of *On the History of Mankind* (1768) and editor of *Ephemerides of Mankind, or Library of Ethics and Politics,* in which he published his translation of the complete text of the *Declaration of Independence,* the first in German, in October 1776.

Julian [Flavius Claudius Julianus] (331–363). Roman emperor from 361 to 363, who converted from Christianity to paganism in 361 and thereby acquired the appellation "the Apostate."

Kant, Immanuel (1724–1804). The most punctilious of German philosophers, who never left his home town of Königsberg. Famous for his teaching and for his groundbreaking philosophy formulated in the *Critique of Pure Reason* (1781), the *Critique of Practical Reason* (1788), and the *Critique of Judgment* (1790), Kant was an admirer of Frederick the Great as the model of the enlightened monarch, and a proponent of an ethic of categorical imperatives that speak with the indisputable authority of reason itself. He taught Herder during the latter's stay at Königsberg, when the two men became friends, but later criticized Herder's philosophy of history in unfavorable reviews of the *Ideas*.

Kircher, Athanasius (1602–1680). German Jesuit priest and scholar; author of various works on ancient Egypt.

Klopstock, Friedrich Gottlieb (1724–1803). German poet and author; one of the founders of German Irrationalism.

Laelius, Gaius (b. 186 BC). Roman soldier and orator, noted for his great learning; a character in Cicero's writings.

Leda (mythical). According to some legends, Leda gave birth to Castor and Pollux after Zeus, in the form of a swan, seduced her.

Leibniz, Gottfried Wilhelm (1646–1716). German mathematician, philosopher, legal scholar, and theologian who sought to reconcile Cartesian perspectives with religion and posited "monads" as the living, ultimate units of the universe.

Leonidas (d. 480 BC). Spartan king whose force of three hundred defended the pass at Thermopylae against the advancing Persian army until it was betrayed by Ephialtes.

Lessing, Gotthold Ephraim (1729–1781). Classic German playwright and social critic whose *Emilia Galotti* (1772) and *Nathan der Weise* (1779) Herder admired especially.

Lipsius, Justus (1547–1606). Neo-Stoic philosopher, editor of the works of Tacitus and Seneca, and author of *De Constantia* (1584).

Livy [Titus Livius] (59 BC–AD 17). Roman historian whose classic *History of Rome* is among the most influential works of its kind.

Louis XIV (1638–1715). Ruling France from 1643 to 1715, the "Sun King" surrounded himself with poets and artists, set the tone for his age, and embodied absolutism for later generations. He revoked the Edict of Nantes in 1685 and ruined the state finances with the costliness of his wars and the extravagance of his court. From a German perspective, the unprovoked seizure of Alsace and Lorraine under Louis' reign, as well as the brutal destruction of Heidelberg and Mannheim, were of especially lasting significance.

Lucilius, Gaius (180–103 BC). Roman poet credited with the invention of Roman satire.

Lucullus, Lucius Licinius (c.114–c.57 BC). Roman patrician and general, proverbial in German for his wealth and the opulence of his feasts.

Luther, Martin (1483–1546). German miner's son, Augustinian monk, and doctor of theology who is said to have nailed his "Ninety-Five Theses" to the church doors at Wittenberg, for many the symbolic beginning of the Protestant Reformation; sought to refocus Christianity on salvation by grace alone (*sola fide*) and on the overriding authority of Scripture; shaped modern German by his translation of the Bible.

Lycurgus (seventh century BC?). Legendary Spartan lawgiver.

Mably, Gabriel Bonnet, Abbé de (1709–1785). French author and priest who wrote his *Observations* on the Romans (1751) and on the history of France (1765).

Machaon (mythical). Son of Asclepius and himself a healer; fought on the Greek side in the Trojan War and cured Philoctetes.

Machiavelli, Niccolò (1469–1527). Florentine statesman, political theorist, and historian; author of *The Prince* and *Discourses on Livy* (both published posthumously, in 1532 and 1531, respectively).

Maecenas, Gaius Clinius (70–8 BC). Roman statesman, adviser to Augustus, and patron of Horace and Virgil.

Mandeville, Bernard (1670–1733). Dutch philosopher; author of the much-noted *Fable of the Bees; or, Private Vices, Public Benefits, etc.* (1714).

Marcus Aurelius [Caesar Marcus Aurelius Antoninus Augustus] (121–180). Roman emperor who came to symbolize Rome's golden age for succeeding ages; famous for his philosophical temperament in general and his *Meditations* in particular.

Medea (mythical). The daughter of King Aeëtes of Colchis, Medea helped Jason steal the Golden Fleece and became his wife; the subject of tragedies by Euripides and Seneca, she figures also in Ovid's *Heroides*.

Menander (c.342–292 BC). Greek poet and dramatist; author of *Dyscolus*.

Minerva [Greek: Athena] (mythical). Daughter of Zeus, warrior-goddess, and patron of wisdom; protectress of the city of Athens.

Montaigne, Michel de (1533–1592). French philosopher and skeptic, whose *Essays* (1588) introduced a new literary form.

Montecuculi [Montecuccoli, Raimondo] (1609–1680). Austrian general during the Thirty Years' War; defeated the Turks in 1664 and led the imperial army against the French in 1672.

Montesquieu, Charles-Louis de Secondat, Baron de La Brède et de (1689–1755). French philosopher; author of *Persian Letters* (1721), *Reflections on the Causes of the Grandeur and Declension of the Romans* (1734), and the highly influential *The Spirit of the Laws* (1750).

Moser, Friedrich Carl, Freiherr von, (1723–1798). German politician and jurist; author of *On the German National Spirit* (1765), as well as of several other political treatises.

The Muses (mythical). Greek and Roman goddesses; patrons of the arts and sciences, often invoked by poets. On Hesiod's account: Calliope, Clio, Erato, Euterpe, Melpomene, Polymnia, Terpsichore, Thalia, and Urania.

Nemesis (mythical). Greek goddess of punishment and personification of vengeance; more figuratively, the agent of just retribution.

Nepos, Cornelius (c.100–c.24 BC). Roman historian and biographer; author of *On the Great Generals of Foreign Nations.*

Nero [Nero Claudius Caesar Augustus] (37–68). Roman emperor (54–68) and persecutor of the Christians who was responsible for the murder of his mother and his wife, and who was blamed for the fire that destroyed much of Rome in 64. Following revolts in the provinces, he fled Rome and committed suicide in 68.

Newton, Sir Isaac (1643–1727). Preeminent English physicist and mathematician; discovered the infinitesimal calculus and formulated the law of universal gravitation; author of the highly influential *Philosophiae Naturalis Principia Mathematica* (Mathematical Principles of Natural Philosophy, 1687).

Numa Pompilius. According to legend, the second king of Rome, succeeding Romulus, and the founder of the Roman state religion.

d'Origny, Pierre-Adam (n.d.). Author of *Ancient Egypt, etc.* (1762).

Pandora (mythical). Fashioned from clay and adorned by the gods so that she might be irresistibly attractive to men, Pandora was received into Epimetheus' house as a gift from Zeus and became his wife. With her she brought a large jar ("Pandora's box") that no one was allowed to open. When, tempted by curiosity, Epimetheus opened the lid, out poured all the troubles that have been afflicting mankind ever since.

Penelope (mythical). The wife of Odysseus who, for twenty years, faithfully awaits her husband's return and manages by her cunning to resist a gaggle of suitors.

Pericles (c.495–429 BC). Athenian general, orator, and statesman who led Athens to the peak of its powers and thence into the Peloponnesian War.

Peter I (1672–1725). Also known as "Peter the Great;" czar whose radical program of modernizing, Westernizing reform is commonly credited with making Russia a major power. In relation to the symbolism of facial hair that Herder mentions at *APH* 71, it might be noteworthy that Peter taxed beards, for example, to promote a more Western, clean-shaven look.

Petrarch [Francesco Petrarca] (1304–1374). Italian poet and humanist, considered one of the greatest scholars of his age and a major force in the development of the Renaissance; especially famous for his poems addressed to Laura, an idealized beloved.

Phidias (b. c.500 BC). Said to be the greatest Greek sculptor; oversaw the construction of the Parthenon and the making of two particularly famous statues of Athena and Zeus, the latter of which is considered one of the seven wonders of the ancient world.

Philip II (c.382–336 BC). King of Macedon and father of Alexander the Great.

Philoctetes (mythical). One of the Greek commanders who set sail for Troy. He was bitten by a snake during a sacrificial ceremony along the way; his wound festered and gave off such a stench that he was left behind on the island of Lemnos (*Iliad* II.722–3).

Phocion (c.402–317 BC). Athenian general and statesman who sought to protect his city from the rising power of Philip II, but was nevertheless deposed, tried, and executed by Athens.

Pindar (c.518–c.438 BC). Said to be the greatest Greek lyricist; celebrated in particular for his Odes.

Plato (428–348 BC). Greek philosopher who expressed his ideas in the form of dialogues, many of which, such as *Republic, Meno, Crito,* and *Phaedo,* feature Socrates as the protagonist.

Pliny the Elder [Gaius Plinius Secundus] (23–79). Roman scholar and naturalist; author of the celebrated *Natural History.*

Polybius (c.200–c.118 BC). Renowned Greek historian; author of a universal history of which only parts are extant.

Pompey the Great [Gnaeus Pompeius Magnus] (106–48 BC). Roman military commander and statesman; joined with Caesar and Crassus in the first triumvirate in 60 BC but fell out with Caesar in 48 BC, was defeated in battle and killed on the run.

Proteus (mythical). Sea-dwelling Greek god possessing the power of changing his shape, representing the great changeability in the appearance of the sea.

Ptolemy (100–170). Greek astronomer and mathematician whose geocentric system of the universe was dominant until the 16th century, when it gave way to the Copernican, heliocentric system.

Pufendorf, Samuel, Freiherr von (1632–1694). German jurist, proponent of natural law, and author of *The Whole Duty of Man According to the Law of Nature* (1698); considered one of the founders of international law.

Pythagoras of Samos (c.580–c.500 BC). Greek philosopher and mathematician whose ideas influenced Plato and Aristotle.

Racine, Jean (1639–1699). French poet and dramatist; one of the foremost French tragedians, whose characters are known for their struggles for social recognition.

Rameau, Jean-Philippe (1683–1764). French composer and groundbreaking musical theorist initially admired by the *Encyclopédistes;* collaborated with Voltaire on musical projects in 1745.

Retz, Jean François Paul de Gondi, Cardinal de (1613–1679). French aristocrat who, during the minority of Louis XIV in 1648–1653, joined the Prince of Condé and the Parlement of Paris in leading the resistance ("the Fronde") to the growing authority of the crown exercised by Richelieu and Mazarin, a series of events that he recounts in his classic *Memoirs.*

Richelieu, Armand-Jean du Plessis, Cardinal (1585–1642). French statesman renowned for his role in establishing the absolute authority of the French crown by subduing the nobility and defeating the Huguenots.

Robertson, William (1721–1793). Scottish historian, clergyman, and principal of the University of Edinburgh; author of *The History of Scotland during the Reigns of Queen Mary and of King James VI, etc.* (1759) and *The History of the Reign of Emperor Charles the Fifth* (1769).

Rousseau, Jean-Jacques (1712–1778). Genevan philosopher and writer. Although initially associated with the *Encyclopédistes* and their project, Rousseau became a severe critic of the *philosophes* of the Enlightenment (most notably in his *Letter to M. d'Alembert on the Theater,* 1758). In addition to the prize-winning *Discourse on the Sciences and the Arts* (1750), Rousseau wrote such seminal works of political philosophy as the *Discourse on the Origin and Foundations of Inequality among Men* (1755) and *On the Social Contract* (1762); *Émile* (1762), his treatise on education; the highly successful novel *Julie: ou, la nouvelle Héloïse* (1761); as well as numerous works on music and constitutional projects for Poland and Corsica.

Sallust [Gaius Sallustius Crispus] (86–34 BC). Roman politician and influential historian; author of *The Conspiracy of Catiline* and *The War with Jugurtha.*

Scaevola, Quintus Mucius (d. c.115 BC).   Roman jurist; author of the first systematic treatise on civil law.

Scipio Africanus the Younger (185–129 BC).   Roman general; hero of the Third Punic War and destroyer of Carthage.

Scipio, Publius Cornelius (d.211). Roman general and proconsul during the Second Punic War.

Semiramis (ninth century BC; pseudo-mythical).   Assyrian queen whom Greek legend credits with great conquests and the building of Babylon, in particular its Hanging Gardens.

Sesostris I (20th century BC; pseudo-mythical).   Pharaoh, reformer, and conqueror, under whose rule Egypt thrived.

Severus, Septimius (146–211).   Roman emperor who reformed the government of the empire and its system of laws, gave increased prominence to the army, and conducted an extensive building program.

Shaftesbury, Anthony Ashley Cooper, Earl of (1671–1713).   English politician and philosopher; author of *Characteristicks of Men, Manners, Opinions, and Times* (1711). A Neoplatonist and Deist, Shaftesbury was the employer and friend of John Locke.

Shaw, Thomas (1694–1751).   English travel writer; author of *Travels, or Observations relating to Several Parts of Barbary and the Levant* (1738).

Socrates (469–399 BC).   Athenian philosopher and teacher of Plato; the subject of works by Aristophanes, Plato, and Xenophon.

Solon (c.640–c.560 BC).   Athenian statesman and poet, primarily known as Athens' lawgiver; one of the "Seven Wise Men."

Sophocles (c.495–406 BC).   Celebrated Athenian playwright; author of *Oedipus the King, Electra*, and *Ajax*, among other plays.

Sulla, Lucius Cornelius (138–78 BC).   Roman general and leader of the aristocratic party in the Civil War against Marius; was elected dictator and made great changes to the constitution in order to strengthen the Senate; notorious for his arrogance and cruelty.

Sully, Maximilien de Béthune, Duc de (1560–1641).   French statesman and reformer after the Wars of Religion (1562–1598).

Tacitus, Cornelius (c.56–c. 120).   Major Roman historian; author of *Agricola, Germania*, and *Annals of Imperial Rome*.

Temple, Sir William (1628–1699).   English statesman and diplomat; author of *An Essay upon the Original and Nature of Government* (1680).

Terence [Publius Terence Afer] (c.190–159 BC). Roman comic dramatist of North African origin; freed slave.

Thales of Miletus (624–546 BC). Legendary engineer, geometer, and astronomer; considered the first natural philosopher and cosmologist by Aristotle.

Theophrastus (c.370–286 BC). Greek philosopher, student of Aristotle, and author of *Characters;* became head of the Lyceum upon Aristotle's departure from Athens, in 323 BC.

Theseus (n.d.). Legendary king of Athens who, with the aid of King Minos' daughter Ariadne, entered the labyrinth and defeated the Minotaur; credited with having united the various communities of Attica into a single political unit.

Thuanus [Jacques-Auguste de Thou] (1553–1617). French statesman and historiographer; author of a *History of His Own Times* (1604–1608) about the French Wars of Religion of the 16th century.

Thucydides (c. 460–c. 400 BC). Athenian historian and general; author of the *History of the Peloponnesian War,* which records the war between Athens and Sparta that took place between 431 and 404 BC.

Tiberius (42 BC–AD 37). Adopted son of Augustus; Roman emperor from AD 14–37 whose rule has given rise to rather divergent opinions.

Titus [Flavius Vespasianus] (41–81 BC). Roman emperor, son of Vespasian, and general, under whose command Jerusalem was besieged and sacked in AD 70 and the Temple was destroyed.

Trajan [Marcus Ulpius Trajanus] (53–117). Roman emperor from 98–118, celebrated for his benevolence and justice; corresponded with Pliny.

Tubero, Quintus Aelius (first century BC). Roman legal expert and consul mentioned in passing by Livy and Suetonius.

Turenne, Henri de La Tour d'Auvergne, Vicomte de (1611–1675). French military commander who distinguished himself in the Thirty Years' War, sided with the rebels at the time of the Fronde, but was reconciled to the crown and fought as marshall of France under Louis XIV.

Tyrtaeus (seventh century BC). Spartan elegiac poet whose verses were recited to encourage the Spartan armies in the field.

Varro, Marcus Terentius (116–27 BC). Roman scholar of legendary learning who is said to have written seventy-four works in over six hundred volumes.

Venus [Greek: Aphrodite] (mythical). Roman goddess of love, mother of Cupid.

Vespasian [Titus Flavius Vespasianus] (9–79).   Roman emperor known for his successful economic reforms and extensive building program.

Virgil [Publius Vergilius Maro] (70–19 BC).   Roman poet famous for his *Aeneid*, an epic tale of the founding of Rome.

Voltaire, François-Marie Arouet de (1694–1778).   French philosopher, dramatist, essayist, and historian; contributor to the *Encyclopédie* and author of *Candide* (1758) as well as a *Philosophy of History* (1765), to which Herder's *Another Philosophy of History* is a response.

Warburton, William (1698–1779).   English literary critic and bishop of Gloucester; befriended by Alexander Pope for his 1740 defense of the latter's *Essay on Man* (1733–1734) from the criticism of de Crousaz.

Webb, Daniel (c.1718–1798).   Author of *Observations on the Correspondence between Poetry and Music* (1769), which was reviewed by Herder in the *General German Library* (1772).

Winckelmann, Johann Joachim (1717–1768).   German archaeologist and art historian whose writings revived interest in Greek and Roman art; author of *History of the Art of Classical Antiquity* (1764).

Wood, Robert (c.1717–1771).   Irish scholar, archeologist, and politician; member of Parliament, undersecretary to William Pitt, and author of various works on the ancient Middle East.

Xenophon (c.426–c.354 BC).   Athenian historian and soldier who fought in the Peloponnesian War and took part in the expedition of the Greek mercenary force of Cyrus, an experience that he describes in his famous *Anabasis;* a student of Socrates, about whom he wrote in his *Memorabilia, Symposium,* and *Apology.*

Zeno of Elea (c.495–c.430 BC).   Greek mathematician and philosopher known for his paradoxes.

INDEX

German terms are given in italics, in parentheses

157